COVENANT AND ELECTION IN THE REFORMED TRADITION

COVENANT
— and —
ELECTION
— in the —
REFORMED
TRADITION

DAVID J. ENGELSMA

Reformed Free Publishing Association
Jenison, Michigan

Reformed Free Publishing Association
1894 Georgetown Center Drive
Jenison, Michigan 49428–7137
Phone: 616-457-5970
Fax: 616-457-5980
www.rfpa.org
mail@rfpa.org

ISBN: 978–1–936054–02–2
LCCN: 2011936937

For my grandchildren:
children of the covenant

Now to Abraham and his seed
were the promises made.
He saith not, And to seeds, as of many;
but as of one,
And to thy seed, which is Christ.
—Galatians 3:16

CONTENTS

PREFACE

Although this book is not about the contemporary development of covenant theology that calls itself the federal vision, *Covenant and Election* was occasioned by the heresy.

As a thoroughly covenantal theology, the federal vision brings to a head in the Reformed churches an ages-old controversy over the covenant of grace. Fundamentally, the controversy centers on the issue of the relation of covenant and election.

Heresy has a divinely ordained purpose. This purpose is that the true church, orthodox theologians, and genuine believers reexamine the truth attacked and corrupted by the heresy, so that they purify their understanding of the truth, establish themselves more firmly in the truth, and even develop the knowledge of the truth. In this conviction, I reexamine the truth of the relation of covenant and election.

I conduct this examination mainly in the Dutch Reformed tradition. This is the understanding, transmission, and development of the truth of Holy Scripture by the Reformed churches in the Netherlands. This tradition expressed its faith concerning covenant and election importantly in the Reformed baptism form in the late sixteenth century; in the Canons of Dordt in the early seventeenth century; in the teaching of the fathers of the Secession in the early nineteenth century; and in the dogmatics of Herman Bavinck in the late nineteenth and early twentieth centuries. The Protestant Reformed Churches in America consciously hold this tradition today, esteeming it highly and counting themselves honored by the Holy Spirit to do so.

The Holy Spirit of the truth used the reformer John Calvin for the forming of the Dutch Reformed tradition at its beginning.

Therefore, I include Calvin's own doctrine of covenant and election in my examination of the issue.

I concentrate on the Reformed tradition that took form in and has come out of the Netherlands for several reasons. First, this is my tradition and the tradition of the churches of which I am a member. Second, the Dutch Reformed tradition has been a powerful, prominent force for good for the Reformed faith concerning the covenant worldwide. Third, it is my specific purpose with this book to expose as utterly fallacious the deliberately fostered and common notion that the doctrine of a close relation between election and covenant has no, or an insignificant, place in the Dutch Reformed tradition. I will demonstrate that the Reformed baptism form, the Canons of Dordt, and Herman Bavinck, among other Reformed writings and writers, not only relate covenant and election closely, but also affirm that election governs the covenant.

"Tradition" in the title may be off-putting. Reformed Christians are wary of authoritative traditions. It is right that they are, when the tradition is mere human decrees. But in the title of the book, "tradition" has the good sense of 2 Thessalonians 2:15: "hold the traditions." The Reformed tradition regarding covenant and election is the legitimate handing down, sound development, and official confession of the apostolic doctrine of Scripture.

The order of my treatment of covenant and election in the tradition is not chronological. The book is not a history of dogma. It is theological. Its order is logical. The long opening chapter establishes the crucial importance of the relation of covenant and election in light of the controversy over the covenant in the Reformed churches at the beginning of the twenty-first century. The chapters that immediately follow demonstrate that the Reformed churches in the Netherlands very early settled the issue of covenant and election in two authoritative creeds. The powerful influence on the Dutch churches was simply the Reformation's gospel of sovereign grace, especially as taught by John Calvin. The chapters on the gospel of the Reformation and on Calvin's doctrine of the covenant are next. Because the contemporary Presbyterian theologian Peter A. Lillback's erroneous presentation of Calvin's doctrine of covenant and election is extremely influential both in shaping the mind of Reformed and Presbyterian churches and ministers and in directing the decisions of church assemblies, a chapter is devoted to freeing Calvin from Lillback's bondage in his book. Out of the early twentieth century then comes the loud and clear witness to the tradition's orthodox view of covenant and election from the highly respected Herman Bavinck. The book concludes, in several chapters, with a fresh, comprehensive, exegetical survey of the relation of covenant and election in all phases of the biblical revelation of the covenant—the ultimate and decisive source and standard of the tradition.

The appendix is uniquely and intimately part of the subject of the book. The Declaration of Principles of the Protestant Reformed Churches is the document in which these churches, under the leadership of Herman Hoeksema, expressed their belief concerning the unconditional covenant. This is the covenant of grace governed by election. The Protestant Reformed Churches made this official declaration sixty years ago when they were threatened by the doctrine of the covenant now promoted and developed by the federal vision—the doctrine of a conditional covenant, a covenant cut loose from election. Thus the confession of the unconditional covenant by the Protestant Reformed Churches, in the heat of controversy, has become an important aspect of the Reformed tradition concerning covenant and election.

Chapter 1

THE COVENANT CRISIS

The doctrine of the covenant of grace is thrust to the foreground in Reformed and Presbyterian churches by the contemporary heresy of the federal vision. The name of the heresy, by which its proponents themselves call their teaching, clearly indicates that this teaching puts the doctrine of the covenant on the front burner of the Reformed churches, for "federal" means covenant. Although the heresy corrupts every aspect of the confessionally Reformed doctrine of salvation, from justification to perseverance, as well as the doctrine of the atonement of the cross, it is fundamentally a vision of the covenant.

Closely related to the new perspective on Paul (which especially in the theology of N. T. Wright is also a covenant doctrine[1]), the federal vision teaches that God in grace establishes his covenant with all the physical children of believers alike at and by their baptism. In baptism God unites all of them alike savingly to Jesus Christ. At baptism God graciously addresses the promise of the covenant to all of them alike: "I will be your God, and you shall be my son or daughter." By baptism God also begins graciously to bestow on all of them alike the spiritual gifts of salvation obtained for them all by the death of Jesus Christ. This by no means, however, assures the salvation of any

---

1. The influence of Wright on many of the advocates of the federal vision, as on many other evangelicals, is great. For Wright's distinctly covenantal presentation of the new perspective on Paul (which rejects the Reformation's understanding of Paul in its entirety, that is, the gospel of grace as recovered by the Reformation), see, among his many books, N. T. Wright's *The Climax of the Covenant: Christ and the Law in Pauline Theology* (Minneapolis: Fortress Press, 1991); *What Saint Paul Really Said: Was Paul of Tarsus the Real Founder of Christianity?* (Grand Rapids, MI: Eerdmans, 1997); and *Justification: God's Plan and Paul's Vision* (Downers Grove, IL: InterVarsity, 2009).

of the baptized children, for, according to the federal vision, the covenant of grace, the gracious covenant promise, the gracious covenant union with Christ, and the blessings of covenant salvation are *conditional*. That is, they depend for their continuation with the children and for their realization in the final salvation of the children upon works that the children must perform, namely, faith and obedience. The failure of a child to perform the conditions results in the retraction of the covenant promise, the breaking of the covenant union with Christ, and the loss of the benefits of the covenant.

From this doctrine of a conditional covenant it follows, according to the men of the federal vision (as indeed it does), that justification in the covenant is by faith and works.[2]

In the providence of God, who invariably uses heretics and heresies for the development of the truth, the federal vision brings to a head the controversy over the covenant within the Reformed churches from the time of the sixteenth-century Reformation of the church to the present day. Again and again, this controversy has flared up in serious conflict, often resulting in schism.

The federal vision is the avowed development of the covenant doctrine that teaches that the covenant is graciously made by

---

2. For the doctrine of the federal vision by the men of the federal vision themselves, see Norman Shepherd, *The Call of Grace: How the Covenant Illuminates Salvation and Evangelism* (Phillipsburg, NJ: P&R, 2000); John Barach, *Covenant!*, audio tapes of lectures by John Barach, Steve Wilkins, Steve Schlissel, and Douglas Wilson at the 2002 Pastors' Conference in Auburn Avenue Presbyterian Church, Monroe, LA (Brooklyn: Messiah's Ministries, 2002); Douglas Wilson, John Barach, Steve Wilkins, and others, *The Auburn Avenue Theology, Pros and Cons: Debating the Federal Vision*, ed. E. Calvin Beisner (Fort Lauderdale, FL: Knox Theological Seminary, 2004); and Steve Wilkins and Duane Garner, eds., *The Federal Vision*, (Monroe, LA: Athanasius Press, 2004). Contributing writers in the last volume include Steve Wilkins, John Barach, Rich Lusk, Peter J. Leithart, Steve Schlissel, and Douglas Wilson. For the only critique heretofore (after at least ten years of the open promotion of the heresy in the Reformed and Presbyterian churches, dating from Shepherd's publication of his *The Call of Grace* in 2000) of the federal vision *with regard to its doctrine of a conditional covenant*, the root of the heresy and the issue that the men of the federal vision themselves proclaim as fundamental to their vision, see David J. Engelsma, *The Covenant of God and the Children of Believers: Sovereign Grace in the Covenant* (Jenison, MI: Reformed Free Publishing Association, 2005).

God in Christ with all the physical offspring of believers alike, but is dependent for its continuance with a child and for its fulfillment in the salvation of a child upon the works of the child. This is the doctrine of a *conditional* covenant.

In diametrical opposition to the doctrine of a conditional covenant has stood, and still stands today, a doctrine of the covenant that holds that the covenant of grace, its gracious promise, its saving union with Christ, its blessings, its maintenance, and its fulfillment in everlasting salvation are dependent upon the will of God. The will of God, upon which the covenant depends, is his eternal decree of election in Christ. This is the doctrine of the *unconditional* covenant.

The fundamental issue in the controversy between these two doctrines of the covenant is whether the covenant of grace is governed by election. The doctrine of a conditional covenant, especially in its contemporary development in the federal vision, rejects, indeed abhors, the teaching that election governs the covenant. The doctrine of an unconditional covenant, in contrast, boldly and gladly confesses that God's eternal election, accompanied by eternal reprobation, governs the covenant.

The contemporary doctrine that calls itself the federal vision brings the ages-long controversy in the Reformed churches between the two covenant doctrines to a head because the federal vision makes plain, indeed *insists*, that the doctrine of a conditional covenant is the denial of justification by faith alone. With this fundamental truth of the gospel of grace are also denied the five points of Calvinism as confessed in the Canons of Dordt.

As AD 325 was the hour of crisis for the truth of the Godhead of Jesus, as the early sixteenth century was the hour of crisis for the truths of the bondage of the will and justification by faith alone, and as the early seventeenth century was the hour of crisis for the doctrine of predestination, so the present time is the hour of crisis for the truth of the covenant of grace.

At this crucial hour in the history of the progress of the truth of the gospel, Reformed churches are called to examine and reexamine the doctrine of the covenant. They are to conduct this examination in light of Scripture, particularly Galatians 3, where the apostle embeds justification by faith alone and the cross of Christ, which is the judicial basis of justification, in the covenant God established with Abraham and Abraham's "seed" and where the apostle identifies Abraham's seed as "Christ" (v. 16) and those who are Christ's (v. 29).

But in their examination of the doctrine of the covenant, the Reformed churches do well also to let John Calvin, in so many ways the doctrinal, ecclesiastical, and spiritual father of these churches, shed light on the truth of the covenant.

The men of the federal vision do not much appeal to Calvin, and with good reason. The federal vision is closely tied to the theology of the new perspective on Paul, especially as taught by N. T. Wright. The new perspective on Paul openly rejects the Reformation's (and thus Calvin's) understanding of justification, the cross, and all of Paul's teaching about salvation, especially as that teaching is found in Romans and Galatians. The federal vision itself rejects the doctrines of grace confessed in the Canons of Dordt, whose source in Calvin is correctly indicated by their popular name, the five points of Calvinism.

Nowhere has the doctrine of the covenant figured as prominently, or been so thoroughly developed, from the sixteenth-century Reformation of the church to the present, as in the Dutch Reformed tradition. For this the Christian church owes the Dutch Reformed tradition a huge debt of gratitude, inasmuch as the truth of the covenant is central to the Christian faith and life.

The contemporary controversy over the covenant ought to be the occasion especially for those churches and Christians who are heirs of this tradition to examine the Dutch Reformed tradition concerning covenant and election.

A fundamental truth of the covenant of grace was determined early in the history of the Reformed faith in the Netherlands. That God establishes the covenant with the elect only, particularly with the elect children of godly parents only; that God directs the promise of the covenant to the elect only; that God is gracious in the covenant to the elect only; and that God gives all the covenant blessings and the covenant salvation to the elect only, on the basis of the covenant death of Christ for the elect only, was authoritatively decided in the time of the spread of the Reformation into the Netherlands in its distinctively Reformed form. This was roughly the period from about the middle of the sixteenth century to the meeting of the Synod of Dordrecht in 1618–19. At this time, the very beginning of the Dutch Reformed tradition, the Spirit of truth led the Reformed churches in the Netherlands to decide that election governs the covenant.

What this means is that God's covenant grace is not wider than the eternal decree in Christ ordaining certain humans unto salvation, in distinction from others appointed to damnation. In arriving at this official decision, the Reformed churches in the Netherlands simply applied to the reality of the covenant the fundamental truth of the Reformation, namely, that salvation is by sovereign grace alone.

Covenant Doctrines in Conflict

Two considerations seem to belie the assertion that the Reformed churches in the Netherlands decided the doctrine of the covenant early, and that it confessed the covenant to be governed by election. The first consideration is that the earliest Dutch Reformed theologians, for example, Franciscus Gomarus, and the three forms of unity lacked a developed doctrine of the covenant. In fact, the covenant did not have a prominent place in the theology of the earliest Dutch Reformed theologians or in the three forms of unity.

The second consideration is that the development of the doctrine of the covenant in the Dutch Reformed tradition after Dordt has taken place by controversy. Two radically different and diametrically opposed doctrines of the covenant have existed in the Reformed churches since the time of the sixteenth-century Reformation. But they have not peacefully coexisted. On the contrary, they have fought vigorously, indeed violently, tearing at their mother's innards, as Jacob and Esau once contended over the covenant in the womb of Rebecca.

As C. Graafland has shown in his magisterial three-volume

study of the origin and development of the doctrine of the covenant in Reformed Protestantism,[3] the issue in the controversy over the covenant in the Dutch Reformed tradition, as in Reformed Protestantism generally, has always been the relation of the covenant and election. More particularly, the issue has always been the question whether election governs the covenant. Summing up his study, Graafland identifies the "main line" as "the relation which the doctrine of the covenant has (had) to the doctrine of election."[4]

Soon after the Reformation the humanists, Dirk Coornhert, Joannes Veluanus, Gellins Snecanus, and Cornelis Wiggertsz, and the heretics, James Arminius and Philippus van Limborch, taught a doctrine of the covenant that divorced the covenant from the eternal decree of election. Thus these foes of predestination extended the grace of God in Jesus Christ more widely than only to the elect and denied the sovereignty, that is, the irresistibility, of grace. These men employed the doctrine of the covenant to blunt the force of election and, in the end, to overthrow it.[5]

Gomarus, in contrast, like Jerome Zanchius and Theodore Beza, thought it of central importance "that participation in the new covenant of grace has been ordained only for the elect." The reprobate are merely in "the external covenant," or in the covenant "externally." For Gomarus the covenant was so dominated by election that it was "a part of election."[6]

Arminian Controversy

The two covenant doctrines were very much involved in the controversy of Reformed orthodoxy with the Arminian heresy in the Netherlands, and indeed in all of Europe, in the early seven-

---

3. C. Graafland, *Van Calvijn tot Comrie: Oorsprong en Ontwikkeling van de Leer van het Verbond in het Gereformeerd Protestantisme* [From Calvin to Comrie: Origin and development of the doctrine of the covenant in Reformed Protestantism], 3 vols. (Zoetermeer: Boekencentrum, 1992–96).

4. Ibid., 3:394. All quotations from Graafland's three-volume work are my translation of the Dutch. The work has not been translated.

5. Ibid., 3:88–278.

6. Ibid., 3:376.

teenth century. It is unfortunate that the important conflict of Reformed orthodoxy with the Remonstrants, or Arminians, in the late 1500s and early 1600s over the doctrine of the covenant is all but lost sight of as both defenders and opponents of the Canons of Dordt concentrate on the five points of Calvinism, which do not expressly include a doctrine of the covenant.

Canons 2, Article 8 and Canons 2, Rejection of Errors 2–4 demonstrate that an essential aspect of the Arminian heresy was (*and is*) the doctrine of a conditional covenant, necessarily implying justification by works. Against the Arminian doctrine that the cross of Christ merely acquired the right for God to establish a conditional covenant with all men, the Canons teach that the "blood of the cross," which "effectually redeem[ed] . . . all those, and those only, who were from eternity chosen to salvation," "*confirmed* the new covenant."[7] The Canons condemn that aspect of the Arminian heresy that consisted, and still today consists, of the teaching that "faith itself and the obedience of faith" are "conditions" of the new covenant of grace.[8]

It was the doctrine of Arminius that, after Adam's breaking of the first covenant (which Arminius regarded as a covenant of works), God made a new covenant in Christ with the entire human race, head for head. The source of the new covenant with every human is God's love for all. The possibility of the new covenant with every human without exception is Christ's death for all.

The love of God for all, which moves God to desire the salvation of all, and the death of Christ for all do not, however, assure the salvation of all, or indeed the salvation of any. For the new covenant of grace, in the thinking of Arminius, is conditional. The condition is faith. In the theology of Arminius, covenant salvation depends on one's believing. Believing—the performance of the condition—is possible only with the help

---

7. Canons of Dordt, 2.8, in Philip Schaff, ed., *Creeds of Christendom with a History and Critical Notes,* 6th ed., 3 vols. (New York: Harper and Row, 1931; repr., Grand Rapids, MI: Baker Books, 2007), 3:587; emphasis added.

8. Canons of Dordt, 2, Rejection of Errors 3–4, in *The Confessions and the Church Order of the Protestant Reformed Churches* (Grandville, MI: Protestant Reformed Churches in America, 2005), 164–65.

of grace. But grace is resistible. Whether one avails himself of the assisting grace (which is shown to and bestowed on all) and believes on the offered Christ, and then keeps on believing to the very end of his life, depends in the final analysis on his own will.

For Arminius, as for Arminian theology then and now, covenant salvation is conditional from beginning (conversion) to end (the perseverance of a believer unto eternal life). It is also necessarily highly uncertain. Salvation depends on the will and efforts of the sinner, helped, of course, but *only* helped, by grace.

The obvious truth about Arminian theology that is commonly overlooked or ignored is that *the entire theology—the entire gospel of salvation—of Arminius was and is a covenant theology—a covenant gospel.*[9]

When, therefore, the Synod of Dordt rejected Arminian theology in five points of sound doctrine, the synod was rejecting a theology of covenant, specifically, a theology of the new covenant of grace in Jesus Christ. Even though (unfortunately) the term *covenant* seldom appears in the Canons of Dordt, everything the Canons affirm, they affirm about *covenant* salvation and a *covenant* gospel. Everything they reject, they reject with regard to a heretical doctrine of the *covenant of grace in Jesus Christ.*

The entire first head of doctrine of the Canons of Dordt, regarding predestination, affirms that predestination is closely related to the covenant and covenant salvation. Such is the relation between election and the covenant that election is the source of the covenant and covenant salvation.

The entire second head of doctrine, regarding the particular, effectual death of Christ for elect sinners, and elect sinners only,

---

9. "The covenant, the way chosen by God to deal with people, takes a central place in Arminius' theology." "After nothing came of the Legal theology because of the fall, God chose to establish a new covenant with the human race in Adam. On different occasions Arminius pointed out that God excluded no one from this new covenant." "God's justice demands that the new covenant be no less conditional than the first." "Arminius admits that faith is not an effect of election, but a necessary condition foreseen by God in those who will be elected" (William den Boer, *God's Twofold Love: The Theology of Jacob Arminius (1559–1609)*, trans. Albert Gootjes [Gottingen: Vandenhoeck & Ruprecht, 2010], 66, 90, 126–27).

affirms that election determines the cross's confirmation of the covenant on behalf of certain guilty, totally depraved sinners, namely, the elect.

The third and fourth heads of doctrine, regarding the conversion of totally depraved sinners by irresistible grace (the almighty Spirit of Jesus Christ), affirm that election governs the establishment of the covenant with totally depraved sinners personally. Election determines who are united to Jesus Christ in the bond of the covenant, are made alive spiritually with covenant life, and receive the covenant gifts of faith and repentance. Election assures that everyone whom God loves and desires to save will infallibly receive covenant salvation, for election accomplishes it.

The fifth head, regarding God's preservation of regenerated and sanctified persons, affirms that election makes absolutely certain that every true believer will persevere in covenant salvation unto the perfection of covenant life, bliss, and glory in the new world.

Dordt condemned, and intended exactly to condemn, that doctrine of the covenant and covenant salvation that cuts the covenant loose from election, so that it may relate the covenant to the decisive will of the sinner. Dordt rejected the doctrine of a conditional covenant.

Rightly understood, Dordt authoritatively settled the covenant controversy for all churches and church members, including theologians and ministers, who bind themselves to, and are bound by, the Canons of Dordt.

Conflict in the Churches of the Secession

Nevertheless, the conflict between the two covenant doctrines raged in the Reformed churches of the Secession in the Netherlands in the nineteenth century.[10]

The leading men of that wonderful reformation of the church in the Netherlands proclaimed that election governs the covenant. Regarding the children of believers, they taught that God

---

10. The Dutch term for this reformation of the Reformed churches in the Netherlands, which began in 1834, is *Afscheiding*.

establishes his covenant with the *elect* children, and with them only. Hendrik de Cock, the father of the Secession, wrote that the covenant promise to Abraham of Genesis 17:7 "did not refer to all the children of Abraham's family, head for head, but to all the elect children, which God would later indicate." De Cock added:

> For a child that went lost circumcision could not be a sacrament sealing the promise to this child, because the promise was not made to that child, but to Abraham, not with respect to every child head for head, but with respect to the elect children, to whom that reprobate child did not belong (Rom. 9:7–8; Gen. 17:10).[11]

Writing in 1857, Simon van Velzen, the outstanding theologian of the Secession, taught that election not only governs covenant grace and salvation but also determines who the children of covenant promise are. At the same time van Velzen made plain how the fathers of the Secession understood the phrase "sanctified in Christ" in the Reformed baptism form.

> We know that everyone who is sanctified in Christ is infallibly saved, that the covenant, of which baptism is sign and seal, is called an eternal covenant of grace, so that they who are included in it cannot perish. How then must we understand it, when at baptism the little children are said to be "sanctified in Christ"? Must we conceive this of all children who are baptized, of all children head for head who have believing parents? Neither the one, nor the other! It is incontrovertible, I think, that the words in view cannot be understood definitely of every child who is baptized.
>
> Rather, they have reference to the seed of the promise, and here the elect are counted for the seed.[12]

---

11. Hendrik de Cock, "Korte Verklaring van den Kinderdoop" in Vragen en Antwoorden, in *Verzamelde Geschriften,* vol. 2 [A brief explanation of infant baptism in questions and answers, in collected writings], ed. D. Deddens and others (Houten: Den-Hertog, 1986), 494. The translation of the Dutch is mine. The work has not been translated.
12. Simon van Velzen, "Brief over de Heiliging van de Kinderen der Geloovigen in Christus" [Letter about the sanctifying of the children of believers in Christ], *De*

The Secession Synod of Utrecht (1837) officially pronounced on the relation of covenant and election. Quoting Romans 9:6 and 8, the authoritative declaration of the Secession churches was that God's eternal decree of election determines covenant grace, covenant promise, covenant salvation, and the covenant membership of the children of believers.

> The children of believers are included in the covenant of God and his congregation with their parents by virtue of the promises of God. Therefore, synod believes with Article 17 of Head 1 of the Canons of Dordt that godly parents must be admonished not to doubt the election and salvation of their children, whom God takes away in their infancy. Therefore, synod, with the baptism form, counts the children of believers to have to be regarded as members of the congregation of Christ, as heirs of the kingdom of God and of his covenant. Since, however, the word of God plainly teaches that not all are Israel who are of Israel, and the children of the promises are counted for the seed, therefore synod by no means regards all and every one head for head, whether children or adult confessors, as true objects of the grace of God or regenerated.[13]

The synod of the Dutch Reformed churches added that it denied "a falling away of saints or a falling out of the covenant of grace."[14]

E. Smilde was correct when he said that the "churches of the Secession lived in Romans 9 and held fast the connection of election and the covenant of grace without wavering."[15]

In 1861, two ministers of the Secession churches, K. J. Pieters and J. R. Kreulen, introduced a radically different doctrine of the covenant into the churches. In a book titled *De Kinderdoop*

Bazuin [The trumpet], August 14, 1857. *De Bazuin*, the magazine of the Secession churches, was not paginated. The translation of the Dutch is mine.

13. Quoted in de Cock, "Wederleggende beschouwing en Ontwikkeling van het Leestuk des H. Doops" [Opposing view and development of the dogma of holy baptism], in *Verzamelde Geschriften*, 530. All quotations from this work are my translation of the Dutch. The work has not been translated.

14. Quoted in ibid.

15. E. Smilde, *Een Eeuw van Strijd over Verbond en Doop* [A century of struggle regarding covenant and baptism] (Kampen: Kok, 1946), 27. All quotations from this work are my translation of the Dutch. The work has not been translated.

they taught a doctrine of the covenant, particularly regarding the infant children of believers, that severed the relation of covenant and election.[16]

According to the doctrine of Pieters and Kreulen, God establishes the covenant of grace with all the baptized children alike, so that all alike are in covenant communion with God. He extends his gracious covenant promise to all the children alike. All the children are heirs of the covenant blessings. All of the baptized children without exception are "heirs of the kingdom of God and his covenant in this sense that they possess this [kingdom and its riches] in the promise and one day would possess it in actuality, if they do not despise this promise by unthankfulness and thus disinherit themselves by unbelief."[17]

In the covenant theology of Pieters and Kreulen, God is gracious to all the physical offspring of godly parents, those who perish in unbelief as well as those who are saved. The Dutch ministers applied the phrase in the baptism form that states that our children are "again received unto grace in Christ" to all the infants without exception. In order to avoid the obvious charge that they taught a resistible, saving grace to the nonelect (which, indeed, they did), they concocted a distinction between "subjective grace" and "objective grace." Only elect infants receive "subjective grace," that is, the regenerating grace of the Spirit in their hearts. But all the infants are the beneficiaries of God's "objective grace." Presumably (for Pieters and Kreulen were careful never to define "objective grace"), "objective grace" is the favor of God toward all the children, a desire to save them all, and the bestowal of favor and blessings by virtue of the gracious promise to all the infants.

---

16. K. J. Pieters and J. R. Kreulen, *De Kinderdoop volgens de Beginselen der Gereformeerde Kerk in Hare Gronden, Toedieningen en Praktijk. Op Nieuw Onderzocht, Beoordeeld en van Vele Schijnbare Zwarigheden Ontheven* [Infant baptism according to the principles of the Reformed church in its grounds, administrations, and practice. Critiqued and delivered from many apparent difficulties, by a new examination] (Franeker: T. Telenga, 1861). All quotations from *De Kinderdoop* are my translation of the Dutch. The work has not been translated.

17. Ibid., 58–59.

All the children alike are truly in the covenant by virtue of the covenant grace of God to all without exception. But all can also fall out of the covenant, separate themselves from covenantal union with God in Christ, become objects of the dreadful curse of the covenant, forfeit the covenant blessings, and perish everlastingly in hell.

For the covenant is conditional. Conditionality is a fundamental characteristic of the covenant doctrine of Pieters and Kreulen. "The gracious promise given by God to Abraham's seed in his covenant did not absolutely and unconditionally guarantee participation in the blessings of the covenant."[18] Answering their own question why, in view of the universality of the gracious covenant promise, "does it then happen that the great promises that are signified and sealed by baptism remain unfulfilled in the majority of those who are baptized?" Pieters and Kreulen wrote:

> The cause why this is the case must absolutely not be sought in this, as if on God's part the promises were given to the one and not to the other. But the cause is found in this, that the divine promises are not given, signified, and sealed *unconditionally* in baptism.[19]

The condition upon which the promises depend is the demand of the child that he repent and believe. "Without this [the performance by the child of the demanded condition], God is not held to his promises, to fulfill them."[20]

The main feature of the covenant doctrine of Pieters and Kreulen was that it banished election. "Let us then regarding baptism forget about eternal election and establish that the promise of the covenant is bestowed and offered as the revealed counsel of God and refers to every baptized [child] in the visible church without any exception."[21]

The covenant doctrine of Pieters and Kreulen, novel to the

---

18. Ibid., 28, 30.
19. Ibid., 48; emphasis is theirs.
20. Ibid.
21. Ibid.

Secession churches, did not go unchallenged. Simon van Velzen charged that the doctrine of Pieters and Kreulen was "in conflict with all our godly fathers, in conflict with the confession of the church, and in conflict with the Holy Scripture."[22] Van Velzen inveighed against their covenant doctrine as a doctrine of a "common and powerless grace."[23]

Prophetically, van Velzen warned:

> It is easy to perceive that this opinion [the covenant doctrine of Pieters and Kreulen] must have great influence on the preaching and that by necessary logical consequence the idea of the covenant of redemption, election and reprobation, limited atonement, and such truths [the doctrines of grace as confessed in the three forms of unity] must undergo enormous change.[24]

Van Velzen's prophecy has been fulfilled, among others, in the Christian Reformed Church, in the Reformed Churches in the Netherlands (liberated), and in the churches where the theology of the federal vision holds sway. All have embraced the conditional covenant doctrine of Pieters and Kreulen.

Despite the objections and formal ecclesiastical protests of van Velzen and others against the covenant doctrine of Pieters and Kreulen, the Secession churches declined to condemn this doctrine, although they also refused to adopt it. Regarding the conflict between the two diametrically opposed doctrines of the covenant, the churches vacillated and attempted a compromise.

As is invariably the case with compromise, the decision satisfied neither party and opened up the Reformed churches to bitter struggle over the doctrine of the covenant in the future.[25]

---

22. Simon van Velzen, quoted in Smilde, *Een Eeuw van Strijd over Verbond en Doop,* 45.

23. Simon van Velzen, commenting on Pieters' article "Eenige Opmerkingen over de 69e vr. En antw. Van den Katechismus" [Some observations about the 69th question and answer of the catechism], *De Bazuin* (May 12, 1865). The magazine is not paginated. The translation of the Dutch in this and the following quotation is mine. Van Velzen's Dutch phrase is *"eene algemeene en krachtelooze genade."*

24. Simon van Velzen, commenting on "Eenige Opmerkingen," in *De Bazuin* (May 19, 1865).

25. For a fuller account of the controversy over the covenant in the Secession

Schism in the Reformed Churches in the Netherlands (RCN)

This struggle over the doctrine of the covenant erupted in the early 1940s in the denomination that was the continuation of the churches of the Secession, as well as of the churches formed by the later reformation led by Abraham Kuyper—the Reformed Churches in the Netherlands (RCN). Although other issues both doctrinal and personal were involved, the struggle mainly concerned the same question regarding the covenant that had disturbed the churches of the Secession some eighty years earlier. Is the covenant of grace, particularly regarding the baptized children of believers, governed by election and therefore unconditional? Or is the covenant conditional, inasmuch as it is cut loose from the eternal decree?

The denomination took binding decisions that election governs the covenant. The implication is that some children—the elect—are in the covenant as members of the covenant, whereas others—the reprobate—are only under the administration of the covenant. The synod distinguished between an internal and an external membership. The synod of the RCN expressed its doctrine concerning the relation of covenant and election in the Substitution Formula of Utrecht 1946.

> In this covenant [of grace] the Lord comes to us with the promise of salvation and, on the basis of this promise, with the demand to faith and repentance. Both of these, promise and demand, are related to each other in such a way that human responsibility is fully maintained and yet the Lord is not dependent in his covenant on the doing of man. In the promise, surely, he not only testifies that everyone who believes in the Son has eternal life, but he also promises the Holy Spirit, who works faith, by which he makes us partakers of Christ and all his benefits.
>
> Accordingly, he works in his elect that which he demands of all, fulfilling to them all the promises of the covenant,

---

churches, see David J. Engelsma, "The Covenant Doctrine of the Fathers of the Secession," in *Always Reforming: Continuation of the Sixteenth-Century Reformation,* ed. David J. Engelsma (Jenison, MI: Reformed Free Publishing Association, 2009), 100–136.

reckoning for the seed, not "the children of the flesh," but "the children of the promise" (Gen. 17:7; Gen. 18:19; John 3:36; Isa. 59:21; Jer. 31:31–34; Gal. 4:28–29; Heb. 8:10–11; Heid. Cat., Q&A 74; Canons of Dordt, 3–4.10; Rom. 9:6–8; Gal. 3:16).

According to the word of God, the children of believers are included in the covenant of God and in his church, as well as the adults, and are sanctified in Christ, so that they have part in the promise and are placed under the demand of the covenant.

At the same time, Scripture teaches us that they are not all Israel that are of Israel. Yet, because it is not given to her to judge the secret things, the church must make no distinction between members, but, building on the promise of God and in harmony with the teaching of Scripture, view and deal with the children as such as partake of the regenerating grace of the Holy Ghost, unless they reveal themselves as unbelievers (Gen. 17:7; Heid. Cat., Q&A 74; the first question of the baptism form; Rom. 9:6; Ps. 22:31; Isa. 44:3; Isa. 59:21; Mark 10:14; Acts 16:31, 34; Eph. 6:1).[26]

Against this doctrine, that election governs the covenant, a large group in the denomination, of whom Klaas Schilder, Benne Holwerda, and Cornelis Veenhof were the theological leaders, reacted strongly. The result of the struggle over the covenant was schism. The denomination formed around the covenant theology of Schilder, Holwerda, Veenhof, and their likeminded allies is the Reformed Churches in the Netherlands (liberated) (RCN [lib.]).

Schilder, Holwerda, Veenhof, and the other leaders of the "liberation" (as they described their separation from the RCN) deliberately adopted the covenant doctrine of Pieters and Kreulen. Veenhof, one of the architects of the covenant doctrine of the RCN (lib.), informs us that "[the covenant doctrine of the RCN (lib.)] was drawn up in conscious connection with that which was taught by men such as Pieters and Kreulen."[27] The

---

26. Quoted in E. Smilde, *Een Eeuw van Strijd over Verbond en Doop*, 359–60.
27. C. Veenhof, *Prediking en Uitverkiezing* [Preaching and election] (Kampen:

reading of the book *De Kinderdoop* indicates that "drawn up in conscious connection with" is understatement. The theologians of the RCN (lib.) virtually made the doctrine of Pieters and Kreulen their own.

According to the covenant doctrine of the RCN (lib.), God makes his gracious covenant promise to all the baptized children alike. This establishes the covenant of grace with all the children alike. In this establishment there is an "objective" bestowal of the benefits of salvation, including justification, upon all the children alike (one remembers the important distinction of Pieters and Kreulen between "subjective" and "objective" grace). But the covenant is conditional. The condition is the performance by the child of the demand of faith. The promise is a gracious gift. Faith, however, is a demand. Upon the performance by the infant of the demand, the covenant promise, the covenant, covenant blessings, and covenant salvation depend for their fulfillment, continuation, and perfection.

When criticized for teaching the Arminian doctrine of a conditional covenant, condemned by the Synod of Dordt, the theologians of the RCN (lib.) respond that God's grace enables some to perform the condition. Pieters and Kreulen taught the same. So did Arminius.

The theologians of the RCN (lib.) are vehement in their repudiation of the doctrine that election governs the covenant. Veenhof states that "very consciously what was taught [by the theologians of the RCN (lib.)] concerning covenant, covenant promise, and baptism was *not* placed under the domination of election."[28]

Kok, 1959), 299. All quotations from *Prediking* are my translation of the Dutch. The work is not translated.

28. Ibid. The emphasis is Veenhof's. The relation between election and covenant (rejected by Veenhof and his colleagues) is, typically, expressed in language calculated to put the relation in the worst light possible: "domination" (*beheersing*). As though the gracious will of God would brutally oppress his covenant! What Veenhof intends is the denial that election is the source of the covenant and that election governs the covenant. For an account of the controversy over the covenant in the RCN in the early 1940s from the viewpoint of the RCN (lib.), see Veenhof, *Prediking en Uitverkiezing*, 294–312. For an account of the controversy from the viewpoint of the RCN, see Smilde, *Een Eeuw van Strijd over*

Schism in the Protestant Reformed Churches in America

Within a few years after the split in the RCN, the divisive controversy concerning covenant and election brought schism into the Protestant Reformed Churches in America. In part through a personal visit to the Protestant Reformed Churches by Klaas Schilder in the late 1940s, a number of ministers in the Protestant Reformed Churches became enamored of the conditional covenant doctrine of Schilder and the RCN (lib.). In their pulpits and in public writings, they began advocating the doctrine of a conditional covenant.

The 1951 Synod of the Protestant Reformed Churches settled the controversy, which by this time was raging in the churches, by a decision that approved the doctrine of an unconditional covenant as creedal and biblical.[29] The decision declared that "election . . . is the sole cause and fountain of all our salvation"; that "all the covenant blessings are for the elect alone"; that "God's promise is unconditionally for them [the elect] only"; and that "faith is not a prerequisite or condition unto salvation, but a gift of God, and a God-given instrument whereby we appropriate the salvation in Christ."[30]

The synodical decision repudiated the covenant doctrine of Schilder and the RCN (lib.), and therefore also the covenant doctrine of Pieters and Kreulen. "We repudiate the teaching that the promise of the covenant is conditional and for all that are baptized . . . [and] the teaching that the promise of the covenant is an objective bequest on the part of God, giving to every baptized child the right to Christ and all the blessings of salvation."[31]

Verbond en Doop, especially pages 320–61. Veenhof and Smilde were on opposite sides of the conflict, but they agreed concerning the doctrine that was at issue: the relation of covenant and election.

29. The decision approving the doctrine of an unconditional covenant consisted of the adoption of the Declaration of Principles of the Protestant Reformed Churches. This document can be found in *Confessions and Church Order,* 409–431. It is also included as an appendix in *Covenant and Election.*

30. Declaration of Principles of the Protestant Reformed Churches, in *Confessions and Church Order,* 416, 418, 423.

31. Ibid., 424, 426. C. Veenhof took note of the controversy over the covenant in the Protestant Reformed Churches. Correctly, Veenhof observed that this

When a consistory disciplined a minister who persisted in preaching a conditional covenant, disregarding the decision of synod, a large number of ministers broke with the Protestant Reformed Churches, taking many members with them. Within a few years, the group returned to the Christian Reformed Church, whence the Protestant Reformed Churches had come some thirty-five years earlier.[32]

From the very beginning of their history as a denomination of churches, the Protestant Reformed Churches were committed to the doctrine of an unconditional covenant, governed by election. Already in 1927, Herman Hoeksema, founder and leading theologian of the denomination, had written a series of articles in the *Standard Bearer* that set forth and defended the doctrine that God establishes his covenant unconditionally with the elect children of believers, and with them only.[33] The articles subject-

controversy was "over the same questions" as those at the heart of the struggles in the churches of the Secession and in the RCN, namely, questions concerning covenant and election (Veenhof, *Prediking en Uitverkiezing*, 311).

32. For an understanding of the covenant controversy in the Protestant Reformed Churches, the editorials of Herman Hoeksema in the *Standard Bearer* in the late 1940s and early 1950s are of paramount importance. The editorials are especially important for their clear delineation of the two contrasting and opposing covenant conceptions and for their distinct indication of the implications of the two covenant doctrines for the gospel of grace. Two series of editorials are noteworthy. One is the series "The Liberated Churches in the Netherlands [with regard to their doctrine of the covenant]," in volume 22 of the *Standard Bearer* (1945–46). Included in this series is significant reflection on the controversy over the covenant in the RCN in the early 1940s. Hoeksema concluded this series with the declaration that the Protestant Reformed Churches do not "agree with the stand of the Liberated Churches on the covenant. In following Heyns they leave the track of Reformed truth" (Herman Hoeksema, "The Liberated Churches in the Netherlands," *Standard Bearer* 22, no. 18 [June 15, 1946]: 414). The other series is titled "As to Conditions." It ran in volume 26 of the *Standard Bearer* (1949–50). As the title expressed, this series examined the two opposing doctrines of the covenant with regard to the issue of the conditionality or unconditionality of the covenant.

33. These articles were almost at once published as a booklet in the Dutch language under the title *De Geloovigen en Hun Zaad* (*Believers and Their Seed*). The booklet was reissued in 1946 in the Dutch language. The occasion of the reprinting of the booklet was the controversy then going on in the Netherlands in the RCN. In a foreword to the second printing of the booklet, Hoeksema reminded the reader that the issues regarding the covenant that were dividing the Dutch churches were the same issues that he treated in the booklet, already in 1927.

ed the doctrine of a conditional covenant with all the children alike—basically the doctrine of Pieters and Kreulen—to searing criticism. Hoeksema charged that the doctrine of a conditional covenant, which is not governed by election, was "Arminianism injected into the covenant."[34]

For some twenty-five years all the ministers in the Protestant Reformed Churches preached and taught the unconditional covenant.

In fact, the origin of the Protestant Reformed Churches lay in Hoeksema's and others' repudiation of the doctrine of a conditional covenant. The doctrinal issue that occasioned the expulsion of Hoeksema from the Christian Reformed Church was that church's adoption of the teaching of a common grace of God, especially the teaching of a (saving) grace of God for all who hear the gospel. Hoeksema defended the doctrine that the grace of God in the preaching of the gospel is particular, that is, governed by election.

But, as Hoeksema observed in the series of articles that was later published as *Believers and their Seed,* the readiness of the Christian Reformed ministers in 1924 to adopt the doctrine of a conditional grace of God for all in the preaching of the gospel was due to their embrace of the doctrine of a grace of God to all baptized children in a conditional covenant.

The Christian Reformed seminary professor who taught generations of Christian Reformed ministers the doctrine of a conditional covenant with all the baptized children, and thus largely formed the covenant thinking of the Christian Reformed Church, was William Heyns. He taught that the covenant is a conditional "contract" established by God by gracious promise to all the baptized children. He also taught that God gives every child a certain "subjective," covenant grace, so that every child has the spiritual ability to perform the condition of believing, upon which the covenant promise and the covenant itself depend.

In his *Handboek voor de Catechetiek* Heyns inquired after

The booklet was published in English translation in 1971. An edition appeared in 1997 as *Believers and Their Seed: Children in the Covenant,* rev. ed. (Grandville, MI: Reformed Free Publishing Association). Quotations of the work are from this revised edition.

34. Ibid., 14.

"the subjective significance of inclusion in the covenant for the catechumens" [that is, for Heyns, all the little, baptized children being taught the word of God in the church's catechism classes]. With appeal to Isaiah 5:4, John 15:2, and other passages of Scripture, Heyns asserted that God gives to all the children of believers without exception an "inner capability" to produce the fruit of good works that God demands of them.

> Scripture teaches us the gift of a subjective grace to each child of the covenant, that is, to each child of believers, sufficient to bring forth good fruits. To *each* child of the covenant, not to the elect only, for it is abundantly plain that a grace that cannot be lost is not meant, a grace that flows out of election . . . Therefore, a subjective grace, which a) is sufficient in connection with spiritual operation by the means of grace for the producing of good fruits of faith and obedience . . . [and] b) does not exclude the possibility that the child of the covenant remains unfruitful, even in spite of the most outstanding operations by the means of grace.[35]

In light of this subjective, covenant grace in all the children without exception, the catechism teacher views all the children, not only as being put in possession of the benefits of the covenant objectively, by virtue of the gracious promise to all, but also as "a seed upon which God has performed covenant work and to which God has given capability for [spiritual] impressions. And that [subjective, covenant] grace [which God has given to every child], he must cherish and cultivate, so that they 'may increase and grow up in the Lord Christ,' in the way of a Christian and godly rearing."[36]

Since this subjective, covenant grace, which can be lost, gradually develops into mature Christian faith and life, it is undeniably evident that Heyns taught a saving grace of God that is resistible, and often resisted. This is the inescapable implication of a doctrine of the covenant that cuts the covenant loose from

---

35. W. Heyns, *Handboek voor de Catechetiek* [Manual for catechetics] (Grand Rapids: Eerdmans-Sevensma, n.d.), 141, 144–45. The emphasis is his. All quotations from this work are my translation of the Dutch. The work has not been translated.

36. Ibid., 146.

election, regardless that many of the defenders of a conditional covenant are not as open about it as was Heyns.

To make the picture complete, it should be noted that, in support of his teaching of a covenant grace to and within all the children without exception, Heyns promptly appealed to the "common grace" that God supposedly shows to all humans in the covenant with Noah.[37]

Hoeksema condemned Heyns' doctrine of the covenant as "nothing but Pelagianism applied to the historical sphere of the covenant."[38]

Fundamental Issue in the Ages-Long Covenant Controversy

The fundamental issue between the two doctrines of the covenant that have struggled for acceptance in the Reformed churches is whether the covenant of grace is governed by God's eternal, unconditional decree of election. That is, is God's purpose with the covenant the realization of the decree of election in the saving of the elect, and the elect only? Does election determine who will be, and who will not be, saved in the covenant? Does election determine who they are to whom God makes the promise of the covenant, with whom he establishes the covenant, to whom he gives the covenant blessings, and with whom the covenant is kept unto everlasting life?

Those who view the covenant as a conditional contract made by God with all the baptized children alike deny that the covenant is governed by election. Indeed, denial that election governs the covenant is inherent in the conception of a conditional covenant. The covenant, its promise, and the establishment of the covenant with all the baptized children are gracious—gracious with the grace of the redeeming blood of Jesus Christ,

---

37. Ibid., 145. In support of "*subjectieve genade*"—the saving, covenant grace in all the children—Heyns appealed to the "*gemeene gratie*" of the covenant with Noah. So it always goes in the Reformed churches as they abandon particular, sovereign grace, having its source and therefore its determination in election: first, a common grace to all in the gifts of providence; then, a resistible, saving grace to all in the covenant and in the preaching; finally, a universal, saving grace that saves all.

38. Hoeksema, *Believers and Their Seed*, 18.

in which the covenant is rooted, and gracious with the grace of the saving will of God, which is the source of the "blood of the cross" that confirmed the covenant, according to Canons 2, Article 8. If, now (as the defenders of a conditional covenant hold), God graciously promises the covenant to every baptized child, Esau as well as Jacob; if in grace God actually establishes the covenant with every baptized child alike; and if God even graciously begins to give every baptized child some of the blessings of the covenant, covenant grace is wider than election, and resistible. In this case, covenant salvation does not depend on divine election. Nor is covenant grace effectual simply by virtue of election. The covenant falls outside the control of election.

That on the view of those who teach a conditional covenant God's election does not govern the covenant is all the more evident when one considers that, according to Scripture and the Canons of Dordt, election—*biblical* election—is always accompanied by reprobation. For the teaching that God, "out of his sovereign, most just, irreprehensible and unchangeable good pleasure,"[39] has eternally rejected certain baptized children of believers and that his purpose with them, from their infancy, is their spiritual hardening and damnation, the doctrine of a conditional covenant has no place whatever. The proponents of a conditional covenant of grace established with all the children of believers alike reject the apostle's teaching in Romans 9:6–24 that God sovereignly reprobated Esau (grandson of Abraham and child of godly parents) unto eternal damnation, in hatred of him, before Esau was born or had "done any good or evil," including the evil of despising the covenant, its Christ, and its grace. The doctrine that affirms a conditional covenant, while denying that the covenant is governed by election, is, by virtue of this fact, a doctrine of conditional predestination. It is a covenant doctrine that is opposed to the first head of doctrine of the Canons and therefore to all the doctrines of sovereign grace.

The truth of this judgment concerning the doctrine of a conditional covenant is evident in the history of the Reformed Churches in the Netherlands (liberated), the churches associ-

---

39. Canons of Dordt, 2.15, in Schaff, *Creeds of Christendom*, 3:584.

ated with the name of Klaas Schilder and the churches whose covenant doctrine is now being developed by the men of the federal vision. Schilder himself attempted to hold on to a relation between covenant and election. But the relation, as Schilder sketched it, was so tenuous, and his description of the relation so tortuous, as to leave his theology of covenant open to understanding and development that view predestination as conditional. Having defined the covenant as an agreement between two parties, Schilder declared that the covenant is "determined" by God's "speaking, through his word (promise and demand). And by this speaking he executes his counsel (of election)." Schilder added, "As well as that of his reprobation (inasmuch as it is a predestination unto punishment specifically regarding a despising of the administration of the covenant of grace.)"[40]

Development of this covenant doctrine that views predestination as conditional was promoted, if not required, by the fact that, as theologian C. Veenhof of the RCN (lib.) tells us, Schilder and his colleagues, including Veenhof, deliberately formulated their distinctive, "liberated" doctrine of the covenant in such a way that "concerning covenant, covenant promise, and Baptism very consciously this was *not* placed under the control of election."[41] When Schilder wrote that the covenant is "determined" by God's speaking, he intended emphatically to deny that the covenant is "determined," that is, governed, by election.

In a recent, important essay, theologian Erik de Boer of the RCN (lib.) demonstrates that Schilder's conditional covenant doctrine has resulted in criticism by theologians in the RCN (lib.) and in other denominations of the doctrine of predestination confessed in the first head of the Canons.[42]

---

40. Schilder, *Looze Kalk: Een Wederwoord over de (Zedelijke) Crisis in de "Gereformeerde Kerken in Nederland"* [Untempered mortar: A response concerning the (moral) crisis in the Reformed churches in the Netherlands] (Groningen: Erven A. de Jager, 1946), 66. All quotations from *Looze Kalk* are my translation of the Dutch. The work has not been translated.

41. Veenhof, *Prediking en Uitverkiezing,* 299. The emphasis is Veenhof's.

42. Erik de Boer, "Unfinished Homework: Charting the Influence of B. Holwerda with Respect to the Doctrine of Election," trans. Nelson D. Kloosterman, *Mid-America Journal of Theology* 18 (2007): 107–36. The importance of de Boer's essay is not only the candid acknowledgment by a contemporary "liberated"

This criticism of predestination in the Canons of Dordt began immediately upon the "liberation" in the early 1940s with the teaching of Holwerda that virtually every mention of election in the Bible, *including Ephesians 1:4,* refers to a *historical* choice on God's part.[43] Construing election as historical, which is the ultimate form of conditionality, effectively nullifies the biblical basis of the first head of the Canons and, thus, the Reformed doctrine of predestination.

The criticism has continued down the years to the present day. In 1992, H. Venema wrote, "Clearly the notion must be abandoned that God already in eternity has fixed who will be elect and who will be reprobate and this without considering human acts of commission or omission."[44]

---

theologian that the "liberated" doctrine of the covenant, deliberately framed to be *free* of God's predestination, found itself at once in conflict with the Reformed doctrine of predestination as confessed in the first head of doctrine of the Canons of Dordt. But its importance is also the disclosure that Schilder was fully aware of the conflict caused by his covenant doctrine. De Boer relates that seminary students made Schilder aware of his colleague, Holwerda's, nullification of the Reformed doctrine of predestination—and the first head of the Canons of Dordt— in one fell swoop, by declaring that election in the Bible, *including Ephesians 1:4,* is a historical decision of God. And Schilder permitted it. In de Boer's words, "Schilder . . . gave his junior colleague some elbow room" (113). The importance of the essay is also its exposure of the falsity, if not the duplicity, of the schismatic faction in the Protestant Reformed Churches in the early 1950s, as well as of the Reformed community that looked on (including Schilder, Holwerda, and the other theologians of the RCN [lib.]), when they loudly and persistently denied that anything Reformed was at stake in Hoeksema's and the Protestant Reformed Churches' lonely battle against the teaching of a conditional covenant that is not governed by election. *Everything* was at stake! At stake was the Reformed doctrine of predestination as set forth in the first head of doctrine of the Canons of Dordt and, with this doctrine, the whole of the gospel of grace, including, as the federal vision makes undeniably evident today, justification by faith alone. For the rejection of the gospel of (particular, sovereign) grace, there was no "elbow room" in the Protestant Reformed Churches.

43. Ibid., 109–11.

44. Cited in ibid., 123. Liberated theologian H. Venema assailed the doctrine of election confessed by the Canons of Dordt in his book *Uitverkiezing? Jazeker! Maar hoe?* [Election? Certainly! But how?] (Kampen: Van den Berg, 1992). Venema charged that Calvin's doctrine of predestination has "heavily oppressed" many church members (12). He expressed his indebtedness in viewing predestination as a conditional, historical decision of God, determined by the fulfillment or nonfulfillment of the conditions of the covenant, to Professor Holwerda, one of the founding fathers of the RCN (lib.): "I am indeed indebted to him [B. Holwerda]" (8; the translations of the Dutch are mine).

In 2003, B. Kamphuis, professor of dogmatics at the liberated seminary, declared that the "Canons of Dort . . . cannot be the church's last word about divine election." By "last" word, Kamphuis meant "authoritative" word. The reason, said Kamphuis, is that "back then the discussion about the relationship between covenant and election still had to occur."[45] He meant that theologians had not yet attempted to impose the liberated doctrine of the covenant on biblical predestination. Kamphuis was mistaken. The fathers at Dordt were well aware of the conditional covenant doctrine of James Arminius, Simon Episcopius, and their disciples, and rejected it.

De Boer makes clear that the criticism of the Canons is ongoing among liberated theologians. One ominous item on the agenda is "fresh reflection on the doctrine of reprobation" that will do away with "*gemina praedestinatio,*" that is, double predestination.[46]

This criticism of the Canons, arising out of the liberated doctrine of a covenant that is cut loose from election and conditional, comes to full fruition today in the covenant theology of the federal vision.

Graafland, who proposes Schilder's covenant doctrine as the solution to the ages-long controversy over the covenant in the Reformed tradition, freely acknowledges that in his doctrine of the covenant "K. Schilder pursued the track [of Saumur!]," that is, Amyraldism.[47]

Amyraldism was essentially a doctrine of the covenant. It taught a gracious covenant of God in Christ with all humans alike, dependent, however, upon the condition of faith for the realization of God's universal, gracious, saving will motivating this covenant. Added to this universal, gracious covenant, which is not governed by election but rather opposed to it, is another covenant with the elect. The universal, conditional covenant of grace is primary.

45. Cited in de Boer, "Unfinished Homework," 132.
46. Ibid., 133–34.
47. Graafland, *Van Calvijn tot Comrie,* 3:403.

Amyraldism was a deliberate attack on Dordt, a subtle form of Arminianism (the essence of which is the doctrine of universal, conditional, and therefore resistible grace), and, once approved, the opening up of Reformed churches to blatant Arminianism.[48]

The doctrine of an unconditional covenant, in contrast, affirms that the grace, promise, blessing, and salvation of the covenant flow from and depend upon the sovereign good pleasure of the electing God. It denies that the (saving) grace of the covenant is wider than election. It denies that the (saving) grace of the covenant is resistible. It denies that the (saving) grace of the covenant is dependent upon the willing or working of the baptized child.

Confessing that the covenant was confirmed in the blood of Christ, concerning which "it was the will of God" that that blood "effectually redeem ... all those, and those only, who were from eternity chosen to salvation," the Canons of Dordt not only obviously bring the covenant into the closest relationship with election but also teach that election governs the covenant.[49]

The Protestant Reformed Churches have officially declared "that all the covenant blessings are for the elect alone" and "that God's promise is unconditionally for them only: for God cannot promise what was not objectively merited by Christ."[50] In the course of the controversy over the covenant in the Protestant Reformed Churches in the early 1950s, Herman Hoeksema wrote, "The relation between election and the covenant ... [is] at the very heart of the Protestant Reformed truth."[51]

---

48. On the Amyraldian doctrine of Moyse Amyraut of Saumur, France, in the middle 1600s, see A. G. Honig, "Amyraut (Moyse)," in *Christelijke Encyclopaedie voor het Nederlandsche Volk* [Christian encyclopedia for Dutch people], ed. F. W. Grosheide, J. H. Landwehr, C. Lindeboom, and J. C. Rullmann, vol. 1 (Kampen: Kok, 1925), 111. Honig notes that "Amyraldianism has prepared the way for the falling away again into Arminianism." The translation of the Dutch is mine.

49. *Canons of Dordt*, 2.8, in Schaff, *Creeds of Christendom*, 3:587.

50. Declaration of Principles, in *Confessions and Church Order*, 418.

51. Herman Hoeksema, "The Declaration [of Principles,] Not a Mistake," *Standard Bearer* 27, no. 7 (January 1, 1951): 152.

Culmination of the Covenant Controversy

The ages-long controversy between these two doctrines of the covenant in the Reformed tradition is brought to a head today by the theology of the federal vision. For the federal vision is the logical, necessary, full development of the doctrine of a conditional covenant with all the baptized children alike. That is, the federal vision is the development of the doctrine of the covenant that denies that election governs the covenant. Norman Shepherd has written that the federal vision is essentially the doctrine of a gracious covenant with all the physical children of Abraham and all the physical children of believers alike, which covenant, however, is conditioned by the faith and obedience of the children. "The Abrahamic covenant was not unconditional."[52] "Faith, repentance, obedience, and perseverance . . . are conditions" upon which "the new covenant" in Jesus Christ depends for its realization in the salvation of any child.[53] Shepherd and the federal vision theology of which he is a leading proponent emphatically do *not* "view the covenant from the perspective of election."[54]

The reputedly conservative Reformed and Presbyterian theological world is well aware that the federal vision is rooted in the doctrine of a conditional covenant, particularly the covenant doctrine of the RCN (lib.) and of the Canadian Reformed Churches. At the meeting of leading advocates of the federal vision and its mild critics at Knox Seminary in 2003 (a meeting from which real critics of the federal vision were excluded), Carl D. Robbins responded to John Barach's bold promotion and defense of the covenant theology of the men of the federal vision. Barach had taught a conditional covenant of grace with all the physical children of Abraham and with all the physical children of believing parents alike. From this covenant doctrine, Barach drew the implications that all the physical children of Abraham and of believers alike are "genuinely" united to Christ in the sense of Galatians 3:27; were died for by Christ; and are elect in

---

52. Shepherd, *Call of Grace*, 22.
53. Ibid., 50.
54. Ibid., 83.

the sense of Ephesians 1:4 and 2 Thessalonians 2:13. Nevertheless, according to Barach, many of these fall away and perish eternally, since they fail to perform the prerequisite conditions.

Responding to this open rejection of the five points of Calvinism as set forth in the Canons of Dordt and the Westminster standards, before all the worthies assembled at Knox Seminary, Carl Robbins declared:

> I've finally grasped that he [John Barach] is simply re-stating *the* distinctive of the "Liberated" Reformed Churches. Therefore, it must be fairly pointed out that Pastor Barach cannot be charged with "theological novelty," for his views were first propounded by Klaas Schilder in the 1940's and (before him) Calvin Seminary Professor William W. Heyns from the early 1900's. In fact, Pastor Barach has simply and faithfully re-stated those covenantal understandings—even to the extent of using Schilderian phraseology such as "head for head" and other catch-phrases popularized in the Dutch covenantal debates.[55]

Robbins accurately traces the more recent history of the covenant doctrine now fully developed by the federal vision: Heyns/Schilder/federal vision. However, Robbins omits the two earliest sources of the doctrine: Pelagius and Arminius. By Robbins' own judgment ("Pastor Barach has simply and faithfully restated those covenantal understandings"), Robbins must condemn the "covenantal understandings" of Heyns and Schilder as the Arminian heresy in principle. The alternative is his approval of Barach's and the federal vision's covenant doctrine, which teaches justification by faith and works; conditional, inefficacious election; universal atonement, at least regarding all baptized children; resistible grace in the sphere of the covenant; and the falling away of covenant saints, as Barach and the other men of the federal vision confessed at the Knox meeting. As Robbins and all of those assembled at Knox Seminary understood perfectly well, the doctrine of John Barach and the federal vision

---

55. Carl D. Robbins, "A Response to 'Covenant and Election,'" in *The Auburn Avenue Theology,* 157.

is not "theological novelty." It is essentially the old doctrine of a conditional covenant taught by Schilder and Heyns. It is the covenant doctrine held by the (mild) critics of the federal vision themselves, as by the churches to which most of them belong. This is the reason, with the rarest exception, that the reputedly conservative Reformed and Presbyterian churches will not, indeed cannot, discipline the men of the federal vision and why the Reformed and Presbyterian theologians who express some unhappiness with the federal vision (the denial of justification by faith alone!) are determined not to take hold of the heresy at its root, that is, its covenant doctrine.

Making explicit what is implicit in the doctrine of a conditional covenant, the federal vision denies justification by faith alone in the covenant and, with this doctrine (the heart of the gospel of grace), all the doctrines of grace as confessed by the Canons of Dordt. The men of the federal vision boldly announce to the Reformed churches what the earlier advocates of a conditional covenant did not like to acknowledge: If the *covenant of grace* is conditional, *all of salvation* is conditional, beginning with *justification*; and if *God's* will—*election*—does not govern the covenant, the only alternative is that the will of the *sinner* governs the covenant, specifically the *will of the sinful child*.[56]

The Reformed and Presbyterian churches are now put to the test, not so much by the men of the federal vision as by God himself, who uses heresies not only to confirm and develop the truth, but also to expose the lie. The question is not whether the churches will produce nonbinding study papers about justification. The question is not even whether the churches will uphold justification by faith alone (which some have already ignominiously and fatally failed to do—*at their major assemblies*).[57]

---

56. For the demonstration of the federal vision's denial of justification by faith alone and, with this cardinal doctrine, all of the five points of Calvinism, see Engelsma, *The Covenant of God and the Children of Believers,* 135–232.

57. On the failure, indeed, willful, scandalous refusal, of the Orthodox Presbyterian Church and Westminster Seminary (Philadelphia) to defend the doctrine of justification by faith alone in the hour of crisis, thus approving and promoting justification by faith and works, see O. Palmer Robertson, *The Current Justification Controversy* (Unicoi, TN: Trinity Foundation, 2003); A.

But the question is: Will the churches now condemn the doctrine of a conditional covenant, which has produced the heresy of the federal vision, particularly the denial of justification by faith alone? And the question is: Will the churches now embrace, wholeheartedly and openly, the doctrine of the covenant that has election governing the covenant, which doctrine is the only theological soil in which the truth of justification by faith alone and the five points of Calvinism flourish? Will the churches confess the doctrine of the unconditional covenant? Will they preach it? Will they teach it to the children in catechism?

Fundamental Issue Decided Early

If there was little development of the doctrine of the covenant in the early Dutch Reformed theologians and in the Reformed creeds, and if the subsequent history of the dogma in the churches in the Netherlands and in churches whose roots are in the Netherlands has been almost continual controversy between those who affirmed and those who denied that election governs the covenant, how can it be said (as was said at the beginning of this chapter) that the doctrine of the covenant was established early in the history of the Reformed churches in the Netherlands?

The answer to this question lies in two documents that were drawn up and adopted by the Reformed churches in the Netherlands very early in her history. Both have creedal status and

---

Donald MacLeod, "A Painful Parting, 1977–1983: Justifying Justification," in *W. Stanford Reid: An Evangelical Calvinist in the Academy* (Montreal: McGill-Queen's University Press, 2004), 257–79; Paul M. Elliott, *Christianity and Neo-Liberalism: The Spiritual Crisis in the Orthodox Presbyterian Church and Beyond* (Unicoi, TN: Trinity Foundation, 2005); and W. Robert Godfrey, "Westminster Seminary, the Doctrine of Justification, and the Reformed Confessions," in *The Pattern of Sound Doctrine: Systematic Theology at the Westminster Seminaries,* ed. David van Drunen (Phillipsburg, NJ: P&R, 2004), 127–48. Godfrey states that a "majority of the faculty" at Westminster Seminary in Philadelphia "supported ... as orthodox" a professor—Norman Shepherd—who was known to be teaching that "justification was both definitive and progressive, and ... that there were two instruments of justification: faith and works." Godfrey identifies himself as a member of the Westminster faculty during the time of the controversy over justification, and as a "critic" of Shepherd's doctrine of justification (*Pattern of Sound Doctrine,* 136–37).

are therefore of binding authority. One is the baptism form. The other is the Canons of the Synod of Dordt.

Chapter 2

THE REFORMED BAPTISM FORM: "RECEIVED UNTO GRACE IN CHRIST"

The Reformed baptism form is a very early document in the Dutch Reformed tradition. It dates from before 1574. In 1574, the Dutch provincial synod of Dordrecht approved the form for use in the Dutch churches. This form, as slightly revised by the Synod of Dordt, is the baptism form used by the Protestant Reformed Churches in common with most, if not all, the Reformed churches in the tradition of the Reformation in the Netherlands.[1]

This form establishes that election governs the covenant with respect to something that is crucially important both to the covenant itself, and to the controversy concerning the covenant within the Reformed churches. Election determines the salvation of the children of believing parents. Indeed, election determines who the covenant children of believers are. The salvation of the children of believers is obviously an important aspect of God's covenant. Always the covenant promise is that God will be the God of believers and their children. And the controversy within the Reformed churches over the relation of covenant and election has always centered on the question of whether God's covenant grace is for all the children without exception or for the elect children only.

Elect Infants "Received unto Grace in Christ"

The Reformed baptism form teaches that election governs the covenant with regard to the covenant children and their salva-

---

1. The original Dutch text of the form can be found in B. Wielenga's helpful commentary on the baptism form, *Ons Doopsformulier* [Our baptism form], 2nd rev. ed. (Kampen: Kok, 1920), 17–24. Here and throughout the book I quote the form as it appears in the Form for the Administration of Baptism, in *Confessions and Church Order*, 258–60.

tion when, in the doctrinal part, it states: "Although our young children do not understand these things, we may not therefore exclude them from baptism, for as they are without their knowledge, partakers of the condemnation in Adam, so are they again received unto grace in Christ."[2]

According to this part of the baptism form, infant baptism is based on, and signifies, the work of God in the covenant of receiving our young children again unto grace in Christ. Their reception unto grace in Christ is the salvation of our infants. To be received unto grace in Christ is salvation. As is implied by the contrast with their natural state of being "partakers of the condemnation in Adam," their being again received unto grace in Christ is our infants' justification. It is also their sanctification, that is, the regenerating work of the Spirit of Christ in their infant hearts, just as their natural condemnation in Adam also involves their total depravity. No one is ever received unto grace in Christ by being freed only from the guilt of sin, without also being cleansed from sin's pollution.

The Reformed baptism form affirms that God bestows this salvation upon our infants *in their infancy*. The thought of the form is unquestionably this: As our infants at the baptism font are "without their knowledge" partakers of the condemnation in Adam, so are these infants at the baptism font "without their knowledge" again "received unto grace in Christ." Just as they are, in their tenderest infancy, naturally exposed to the wrath of God by virtue of their connection with Adam, so are they, in their tenderest infancy, the objects of the saving grace of God by virtue of their relation to Jesus Christ in the new covenant.

Thus the form makes plain that election governs the covenant with regard to the salvation of the children of believers. For one thing, the salvation of infants can be ascribed to nothing else but God's gracious election. Infants are not only incapable of performing any act upon which their salvation might depend (they are completely oblivious to what is happening in the administration of the holy sacrament), but are also by nature

---

2. Form for the Administration of Baptism, in *Confessions and Church Order*, 259.

guilty and totally depraved. God saves our infants according to his covenant promise, which is founded exclusively upon his eternal election.

Election governs the covenant in this important respect, that election determines and accomplishes God's reception of the infant children of believers unto grace in Christ, that is, the salvation of these infant children, in their infancy.

It is certainly nothing in the children themselves that determines their salvation in the covenant, for they are "partakers of the condemnation in Adam."

It is certainly no condition performed by the children that determines their salvation in the covenant, for when they are received by God again into grace in Christ, they are *infants*. The oldest edition of the baptism form had the words "*onze kinderkens*" (our infants).[3] This is the meaning of the translation "young children" in the form. Our infant children are objects of the saving grace of God in Christ, "without their knowledge," at an age when they are not even capable of performing a work or fulfilling a condition.

Election Determines Covenant Children

There is another indication in these words of the baptism form that election governs the covenant regarding the salvation of the covenant children. Election determines who "our young children" are, that is, who the children of believers are to whom God makes, and then fulfills, the covenant promise "I will be the God of you and of *your children*" (see Gen. 17:7 and Acts 2:39). Natural birth does not make covenant children. But election produces covenant children from the physical offspring of believers.

The baptism form speaks of "our young children."[4] As is evident from the quotations of Genesis 17:7 and Acts 2:39 that immediately follow, the form refers to the "seed," or "children," who are the objects of God's covenant promise. "Our young

---

3. Wielenga, *Ons Doopsformulier,* 19.
4. Form for the Administration of Baptism, in *Confessions and Church Order,* 259.

children," in the baptism form, are those children of believing parents whom God had in mind when he said to Abraham, "I will establish my covenant between me and thee and thy seed after thee in their generations" (Gen. 17:7), and whom the apostle Peter had in mind when he declared, "For the promise is unto you, and to your children, and to all that are afar off, even as many as the Lord our God shall call" (Acts 2:39).

The form identifies these young children as all those, but only those, who are "again received unto grace in Christ": "our young children . . . are . . . again received unto grace in Christ." "Our young children," with whom God establishes his covenant according to Genesis 17:7, and unto whom is the covenant promise of salvation according to Acts 2:39, are not all our physical offspring, for all our physical children are not "received unto grace in Christ." Only some of the physical offspring of believers are "received unto grace in Christ." They are the true, spiritual children of believers. The others, who, upon growing up, wickedly refuse to believe in Christ and who transgress the covenant by impenitent unholiness of life, are illegitimate children, even as there are spiritual "bastards" within the visible family of God, the church (Heb. 12:8). Election determines which of the physical children of believing parents are "our young children" whom God again receives unto grace in Christ.

The simple truth underlying these words of the baptism form is that the Reformed faith in its earliest period understood the covenant promise to refer to the elect children of believing parents. Election governs the covenant with regard to the important matter of the salvation of the children of believers. Indeed, election determines who the children of believers are, just as election determines who the believers are. Already in 1574, the Reformed churches in the Netherlands incorporated this understanding of the covenant promise and this view of the relation between election and the covenant into their baptism form. Inasmuch as the baptism form is an authoritative document, a minor creed, to say nothing of its prominence in the life of the Reformed churches, its understanding of the covenant promise and its view of the relation between election and covenant are binding upon Reformed churches and theologians.

Doctrinal Objections

All objections to this plain teaching of the baptism form are doctrinal in nature. They are not due to a right reading of the clear language of the form, but to a doctrine of the covenant that differs from that of the form. They are not explanations of the form, but contrary views foisted on the form.

One such view holds that the form merely teaches that all the physical children of believers are formally and outwardly set apart from the world at baptism. Election, therefore, does not enter in. This is supposed to be the explanation of the statement that the infants are "again received unto grace in Christ."

That reception unto grace in Christ is salvation does not need to be *proved* to any student of Scripture, but only *declared*. Besides, if the reception of our infants unto grace in Christ is merely outward and formal, having nothing to do with salvation, so also, according to the contrast in the baptism form, is their condemnation in Adam merely outward and formal, having nothing to do with being lost.

To be condemned in Adam is real lostness!

To be "received unto grace in Christ" is real salvation!

Another view likes to read the form as though it said, "so *shall* they again *be* received unto grace in Christ, if they fulfill a condition, or if they have a conversion experience, or if they believe." But the form does not say this. It is not speaking of a possible future salvation of the baptized infants when they are no longer infants, but grown men and women. Rather, the form teaches an actual, present salvation of the infants, *in their infancy*: "so *are* [emphasis added] they again received unto grace in Christ." It speaks of an actual, present salvation of the infants "without their knowledge." Therefore, to introduce the notion of conditions, or conversion experiences, into the form is absurdity.

Yet another view explains the form as teaching that all the physical children of believers without exception are in some way "received unto grace in Christ." Infant baptism signifies and seals covenant grace toward all without exception, or a gracious covenant promise to all without exception, or even a gracious work of God within all. According to those who hold this view, "our young children" in the baptism form, like the seed of Abraham in Genesis 17:7 and the children of the promise in Acts 2:39, are all the physical offspring of believers without exception. All the physical children of godly parents without exception, therefore, are "again received unto grace in Christ."

This popular view is the destruction of the Reformed faith at its very heart. It is the denial of the sovereignty and efficacy of the grace of God in Christ. Inasmuch as some of the physical offspring of believers perish, this view teaches the possibility of resisting, losing, and falling away from God's grace in Christ. Once the child was received by God unto grace in Christ; later the same child was cast away by God from his grace in Christ. It makes absolutely no difference whether this reception unto grace is conceived as God's favorable attitude toward the child, or as a spiritual power working within the child. In either case, there is a falling away from the grace of God in Christ. The grace of God in Christ fails to save some who once received this grace.

Implied also is the failure of the cross of Christ. As the first part of the baptism form teaches, reception unto grace in Christ in the covenant is based on the death of Christ. "When we are baptized in the name of the Son, the Son sealeth unto us that he doth wash us in his blood from all our sins."[5] If all the physical offspring of believers are alike received unto grace in Christ, and if this is the significance of infant baptism, Christ must have died for all the physical offspring of believers without exception. Inasmuch as some of them perish in unbelief, the death of Christ did not actually atone for their sins and secure their everlasting salvation.

This raises the question: According to those who teach that all the physical offspring of believers without exception are received unto grace in Christ, what does determine the salvation of children in the covenant? It cannot be the grace of God, for all are the objects of this grace. It can only be the performance or nonperformance of certain conditions by the children them-

5. Ibid., 258.

selves. And this is the teaching of those who contend that all
the children alike are objects of God's covenant grace. All the
children alike are received unto grace in Christ at baptism, but
whether any will finally be saved depends upon their performance of certain works, their fulfilling of prescribed conditions of
covenant salvation.

Determined to separate the covenant and its grace, promise,
and salvation from God's election, this view subjects the covenant and its salvation to the will and works of the covenant
child. Not the will of God, but the will of the children governs
the covenant.

If this were the doctrine of the Reformed churches in 1574,
when the baptism form was adopted by the provincial synod of
Dordt, and in 1618–19, when the form was adopted by the national Synod of Dordt, the Reformed churches would never have
condemned the Arminian heresy.

Biblical Basis of the Doctrine of the Form

The baptism form is right in its conviction that election governs
the covenant, particularly regarding the children to whom God
makes his covenant promise. In support of its declaration that
"our young children . . . are . . . again received unto grace in
Christ," the baptism form appeals to two passages of Scripture.
The first is Genesis 17:7, the covenant promise to Abraham: "I
will establish my covenant between me and thee and thy seed
after thee in their generations for an everlasting covenant, to be
a God unto thee, and to thy seed after thee." In Galatians 3:16,
the apostle identifies the "seed" of Abraham as Christ: "Now
to Abraham and his seed were the promises made. He saith not,
And to seeds, as of many; but as of one, and to thy seed, which
is Christ." In Galatians 3:29, the apostle adds that the Christ
who is the covenant seed of Abraham is not only Christ himself
individually, but also all those humans who are Christ's people:
"And if ye be Christ's, then are ye Abraham's seed, and heirs
according to the promise."

The children of Abraham in the Old Testament to whom God
extended the covenant promise were not all the physical off-

spring of the patriarch. They were Christ and those who belonged to Christ by eternal election. The apostle himself applies this truth to the New Testament church: On the one hand, because you New Testament believers and genuine children of believers are Christ's, you are "Abraham's seed," and "heirs according to the promise." On the other hand, no hypocrite in the visible church or reprobate child of godly parents is Abraham's seed, or heir according to the promise, regardless that he is baptized, inasmuch as he is not Christ's.

The second text is similarly clear in identifying the covenant children, to whom God makes the promise of the covenant, as the elect children of believers. The form quotes Acts 2:39, Peter's reaffirmation of the promise of the covenant on Pentecost to the New Testament Israel: "For the promise is unto you, and to your children, and to all that are afar off, even as many as the Lord our God shall call." As little under the new covenant as under the old is the promise to all the children of believers. Those children of believers in the new dispensation, to whom and for whom is the promise of the covenant, are all those, and only those, whom God calls: "even as many as the Lord our God shall call." Romans 8:30 teaches that God calls those whom he has predestinated: "Moreover whom he did predestinate, them he also called." The promise of the covenant in the New Testament is to our children, that is, to as many of our physical offspring as God calls according to his eternal decree of election.

Chapter 3

THE REFORMED BAPTISM FORM: "SANCTIFIED IN CHRIST"

The preceding chapter began a demonstration of the relation of election and the covenant in the Reformed baptism form. It examined the important line in the doctrinal section of the form, "And although our young children do not understand these things, we may not therefore exclude them from baptism, for as they are without their knowledge partakers of the condemnation in Adam, so are they again received unto grace in Christ."

This chapter continues the examination of the baptism form, considering the controversial phrase that describes the infants who are to be baptized as "sanctified in Christ."

Infants "Sanctified in Christ"

That the Reformed baptism form views the covenant children of godly parents as the elect among their offspring, and therefore sees the covenant as governed by election, is evident from the first question in that section of the form that is an admonition to the parents: "Whether you acknowledge that although our children are conceived and born in sin, and therefore are subject to all miseries, yea to condemnation itself, yet that they are sanctified in Christ, and therefore, as members of his church, ought to be baptized?"[1]

Regardless of the age-old controversy that has raged over the phrase "sanctified in Christ," the meaning of the baptism form is clear. "Our children" are cleansed from the pollution of sin by their union with Christ through his sanctifying Spirit in them. By this sanctifying work of the Spirit of Christ, they are living members of the church, the body of Christ made up

---

1. Form for the Administration of Baptism, in *Confessions and Church Order*, 260.

of all the elect who are gathered out of the world by the Son of God.[2] This internal cleansing is based on Christ's shedding his blood for them on the cross. And this cleansing of "our children," which unites them to Christ's body, the church, is a reality already before they are baptized, since it is the reason they ought to be baptized: "and therefore, as members of his church ought to be baptized."[3]

Obviously, it is not true that all of the physical offspring of believing parents are "sanctified in Christ." The experience of godly parents teaches otherwise. Scripture also teaches otherwise, both in its history and in its doctrine. There are Cains, Esaus, Absaloms, and Manassehs. There are those young people who, having been baptized, having been reared in the truth, and having made public confession of faith, tread the Son of God under their feet, count the blood of the covenant with which they were sanctified an unholy thing, and insult the Spirit of grace (Heb. 10:29). It is evident, therefore, that the form refers to the elect infants of believing parents, and that the form considers the elect infants to be the children of believers.

It is also the plain teaching of the form that the Spirit of Christ as a rule regenerates the elect children of believers in their infancy, already before their baptism. They ought to be baptized, not because someday they will be sanctified, but because they already are sanctified.

Since the form, including the admonition to the parents, was adopted by the Reformed churches in the Netherlands as early as 1574, this was the doctrinal position of the Reformed churches from the beginning of their history.

Inasmuch as the baptism form is an official document of those Reformed churches that stand in the Dutch Reformed tradition, the form binds all these churches to this doctrinal position concerning the covenant and the baptized children of believers.

Nevertheless, many of these churches repudiate the doctrine of covenant children clearly taught by the first question to par-

---

2. Heidelberg Catechism, A 54, in Schaff, *Creeds of Christendom*, 3:324–25.
3. Form for the Administration of Baptism, in *Confessions and Church Order*, 260.

ents in their own baptism form. In every case the reasons for this repudiation are doctrinal in nature. These churches reject the doctrine taught by the first question. They are determined to hold a doctrine of covenant children that differs from that taught by the first question. The reason for their repudiation of the doctrine taught by the first question is not that the language of the first question is unclear or that the language permits the contrary doctrine held by these churches.

There are two main objections to the doctrine taught by the first question among churches in the Dutch Reformed tradition. Both offer a different explanation of the language of the first question from that given above, an explanation that legitimizes their doctrine of the covenant, of covenant children, of the salvation of covenant children, and of the significance of infant baptism. Although these two objections differ from each other, they have this in common: both insist that the children of believers referred to in the phrase "they are sanctified in Christ" are all the physical offspring of believers without exception. Both objections deny that the reference is to the elect infants.

All Merely Set Apart Outwardly

One objection is raised by those churches maintaining the doctrinal position that infants of believers are merely outwardly and formally set apart from children of unbelievers. Because the infants of believers have this privileged position in a Christian home and in a Christian church, some of them are more likely to be converted when they grow up than are other children. This is all that "sanctified in Christ" means. This is all that the covenant promise to the children of believers means. This is all that infant baptism means. "Sanctified in Christ" in the first question of the baptism form has nothing whatever to do with any inward, spiritual cleansing of the infants from sin, and nothing to do with any union of the infants with Jesus Christ by the work of the Spirit of Christ in their hearts.

In fact, according to this position, all the infants of believers, with the exception of the elect among them who may die in infancy, are and remain spiritually dead, spiritually separated from Christ, and spiritually in Adam, until some of them may be converted in later life. Their spiritual condition is and remains the same as that of the children of unbelievers.

Not only does this essentially Baptist doctrine govern the interpretation of the phrase "sanctified in Christ" in the baptism form, but it also governs the view that the churches who hold this doctrine take of the covenant itself and of the covenant promise. God's covenant promise to be the God of the children of believers does not mean that he will be the God of our infant children *when they are infants*. But it merely means that he will be the God of our children *when they grow up, become teenagers or even young adults, and are converted*. That is, God will be the God of our children when they are no longer children.

Likewise, the covenant of God with believers and their infant children does not mean that infant children are actually included in the covenant as small friends of God, or in the kingdom as little subjects of Christ the king. All of them are, in spiritual reality, strangers from the covenant of promise and foreigners regarding the kingdom. That is, they are all outside of Christ.

Infant baptism does not signify infant salvation, that is, the translation of the infants of believers from the kingdom of darkness into the kingdom of God's dear Son, by the regenerating work of the Spirit uniting the infants to Christ. Not at all! It merely signifies that the infants of believers, who are and remain outside of Christ, are set apart outwardly for evangelistic work by church and parents in the hope that some of them someday may be converted as adults.

This is the doctrine, and corresponding explanation of the phrase "sanctified in Christ," of the Netherlands Reformed Congregations, the Heritage Reformed Congregations, the Free Reformed Churches in North America and, as the book *The Case for Covenantal Infant Baptism* shows, many other Reformed and Presbyterian churches as well.[4]

G. H. Kersten gives the view of baptized infants, and therefore of the significance of infant baptism, of the Netherlands

---

4. Gregg Strawbridge, *The Case for Covenantal Infant Baptism* (Phillipsburg, NJ: P&R, 2003).

Reformed Congregations and of the Heritage Reformed Congregations. "In a certain sense they [baptized infants] are holy because they are separated and distinct from the children of unbelievers, and because they are granted many benefits that are not allotted to the children of heathens. They . . . live *in the possibility of salvation.*" Commenting on the phrase "sanctified in Christ" in the Reformed baptism form, with specific reference to elect infants, Kersten denies that the phrase refers to "the subjective sanctification," that is, the regeneration of the infant in union with Christ.[5]

Joel R. Beeke and James W. Beeke, prominent spokesmen for the Heritage Reformed Congregations, explain that "our baptized children are outwardly separated by God from the heathen to be brought up under his word." The baptized infants are merely "in the outward sphere of the covenant." They are "as yet unregenerated." God may regenerate them later "through Spirit-worked application of his precious, inerrant word." Therefore, the Heritage Reformed Congregations do "not view our children as saved before they reveal biblical evidences of salvation."[6]

The view of baptized infants and therefore the understanding of the administration of baptism to the children of believers of both the Netherlands Reformed Congregations and the Heritage Reformed Congregations are set forth in the Statement of Purpose [and] Constitution of Plymouth Christian Elementary School. This is the school in Grand Rapids, Michigan, that is owned by the First Netherlands Reformed Congregation of Grand Rapids and used by the members of both denominations. In this school

> the education of children should proceed on the principle [*sic*] that they are in an unregenerate state, until evidence of saving grace clearly appear[s] . . . But though the religious education of children should proceed on the ground that

---

5. G. H. Kersten, *Reformed Dogmatics*, trans. J. R. Beeke and J. C. Weststrate (Grand Rapids, MI: Eerdmans, 1983), 2:515; emphasis added.

6. Joel R. Beeke and James W. Beeke, "The Netherlands Reformed Objection Stated," in Engelsma, *Covenant of God*, 56–57.

they are destitute of grace, it ought ever to be used as a means of grace.

This Statement of Purpose goes on to locate the root of this educational philosophy in the "core belief" of the churches that operate and use the school, namely, that infant baptism merely "places us under the privileges of an external (non-saving) covenant relationship with God."[7]

That many Reformed and Presbyterian theologians and churches share this view of infant baptism—merely the formal setting apart of the children for possible, future salvation—is evident in the book *The Case for Covenantal Infant Baptism.* The majority of contributors, who are supposed to be defending the Reformed doctrine and practice of infant baptism against the Baptist objection, present the baptism of infants as nothing more than merely the setting of unregenerated, unsanctified, unsaved infants apart for possible future salvation, when at a later date the young people (no longer infants!) will perform certain conditions. Defending infant baptism as a covenant seal, against the charge that the infants do not yet possess the covenant blessings, one writer explains that

> the seal of circumcision could be applied long before recipients of promised and signified blessings met the conditions of the covenant. The seal was simply *the visible pledge of God that when the conditions of his covenant were met, the blessings he promised would apply.*[8]

This, of course, is supposed to explain the seal of baptism applied to the infant children of believers.

Observing that the Bible speaks of "certain people as consecrated or sanctified to God by their close associations with the people of God and with the activities of true believers," another writer defends infant baptism as signifying merely

---

7. Statement of Purpose [and] Constitution of Plymouth Christian Elementary School (Grand Rapids, MI: 1988, photocopy), 8, 5. This Statement is quoted and commented on in Engelsma, *Covenant of God,* 76.

8. Strawbridge, *Case for Covenantal Infant Baptism,* 15; emphasis is his.

the consecration of the children "by their involvement in the more external aspects of life in the new covenant." The writer does not even consider the possibility that God's inclusion of infants in his covenant might exactly mean the "internalization promised in the new covenant," that is, Christ's uniting them to himself by his Spirit.[9]

Another writer responds to Baptist Paul K. Jewett's argument that infants are not regenerated. Evidently, it never entered the mind of the Presbyterian to challenge this false assumption. Apparently, he has never read Calvin in the *Institutes* on infant baptism with regard to the very same Baptist argument against Reformed infant baptism. Rather, in one of the most atrocious defenses of infant baptism ever written, he contends that the Bible teaches that "there are people *set apart* in the new covenant ... who indeed fall away ... There are unregenerate members of the new covenant." His defense of infant baptism is simply that there are always unregenerate persons in the covenant. Defying belief, he concludes by putting baptized infants in the same category with Simon the sorcerer and Judas Iscariot.[10]

With friends like this, infant baptism needs no enemies.

Merely Outward Holiness in Light of the Form

It is not my purpose to criticize this essentially Baptist doctrine. I have done this in my book *The Covenant of God and the Children of Believers: Sovereign Grace in the Covenant.*[11] My purpose here is to demonstrate that the explanation this doctrinal position gives of the phrase "sanctified in Christ" in the Reformed baptism form is false.

First, to explain "sanctified in Christ" as a mere outward and formal setting apart of the infants unto Christ does not harmonize with the description of the infants in the first part of the first question of the baptism form. In the first part parents are asked to acknowledge that "our children are conceived and born in sin, and therefore are subject to all miseries, yea to

---

9. Ibid., 172.
10. Ibid., 280–81, 283.
11. Engelsma, *Covenant of God*, 10–86.

condemnation itself."[12] Only then follow the words, "yet that they are sanctified in Christ." The natural condition of our infants as conceived and born in sin and subject to all miseries, including condemnation, is not merely outward and formal. It is real, actual depravity and guilt. It is real, spiritual union with Adam. So, likewise, is their sanctification in Christ, which is contrasted with their depravity and guilt, a real, actual spiritual cleansing of them by virtue of their new union with Christ.

If their sanctification in Christ is merely outward and formal, their corruption and guilt are, likewise, merely outward and formal.

Second, the first question significantly describes the sanctification of the infants of believers as a sanctifying of them *"in Christ* [emphasis added]." This is decisive for the issue of whether the sanctifying of them is an inner, saving work of the Spirit or merely a certain formal act by the church. Those who insist that the phrase in the first question merely refers to an outward and formal setting apart of the children, and not to a saving work of the Spirit in infants, find the biblical source of the phrase in 1 Corinthians 7:14, where the apostle assures believers married to unbelievers that "your children . . . are . . . holy." The defenders of a merely external and formal holiness then argue that the holiness of the children in 1 Corinthians 7:14 must be a merely formal, "positional" holiness, since the passage teaches that also the unbelieving husband or wife is "sanctified" by the believer.

Even if it be granted that the holiness of the children of a believer married to an unbeliever spoken of in 1 Corinthians 7:14 is merely an outward position, rather than inward cleansing (which is not the case), nothing has been decided concerning the phrase "sanctified in Christ" in the baptism form. For the phrase in the baptism form adds two words that are not found in 1 Corinthians 7:14: *"in Christ."* The source of the phrase "sanctified in Christ" is not 1 Corinthians 7:14, at least, not 1 Corinthians 7:14 exclusively. This is why it was a mistake in the

---

12. Form for the Administration of Baptism, in *Confessions and Church Order,* 260.

1988 edition of *The Psalter,* used by the Protestant Reformed Churches, that someone inserted a footnote giving 1 Corinthians 7:14 as the biblical basis of the phrase "sanctified in Christ."

The source of the teaching of a holiness "in Christ" is such passages as 1 Corinthians 1:2: "Unto the church of God which is at Corinth, to them that are sanctified in Christ Jesus, called to be saints." Regarding the sanctifying of the children of believers, the source is such passages as Ephesians 6:1: "Children, obey your parents in the Lord [Jesus Christ]."

"In Christ" describes the sanctifying of the infants as taking place in the union the infants have with Christ. This is a real, spiritual union. This is the living communion of covenant fellowship with Christ. Although the infants of believers are by nature in Adam, by virtue of God's gracious covenant promise to them, they are in Christ. In that covenantal union with Christ, they are sanctified—really, inwardly, spiritually cleansed from sin and delivered from condemnation. It is only by virtue of this spiritual union with Christ the Lord, as Ephesians 6:1 teaches, that they can and do obey their parents from their earliest childhood. For children who are merely outwardly set apart unto Christ, obedience to the fifth commandment is an utter impossibility.

A third evidence that the explanation of the phrase "sanctified in Christ" as meaning merely outward and formal holiness is false, is the fact that every other mention of holiness, or sanctifying, in the baptism form refers to inner, spiritual cleansing from sin. That sanctification in the baptism form refers to actual, inner cleansing from sin by virtue of living union with Jesus Christ is established at the outset.

> When we are baptized in the name of the Holy Ghost, the Holy Ghost assures us, by this holy sacrament, that he will dwell in us and sanctify us to be members of Christ, applying unto us that which we have in Christ, namely, the washing away of our sins and the daily renewing of our lives, till we shall finally be presented without spot or wrinkle among the assembly of the elect in life eternal.[13]

---

13. Ibid., 258.

Fourth, explaining "sanctified in Christ" as merely outward and formal runs stuck on the important words that immediately follow in the first question. The first question does not only say about the infants of believers that they are sanctified in Christ, but it also says that they are "members of his church." They are members of his church before they are baptized, for membership in his church is the reason they ought to be baptized. And they are members of his church by virtue of being sanctified in Christ.

The baptism form cannot mean that the infants are members of the instituted church. They become members of an instituted church by virtue of their baptism. But the form says that they are members of Christ's church already before they are baptized. The form teaches that the infants are living members of the universal body of Christ, made up of all the elect. They were gathered into the body of Christ when they were "sanctified in Christ." Sanctification in Christ, which alone baptizes one into the body of Christ (1 Cor. 12:13), is the inner, regenerating work of the Spirit in these infants. It is the work in our children that the baptism form joyfully announced in its opening line: "The principal parts of the doctrine of holy baptism are these three: First. That we with our children are conceived and born in sin, and therefore are children of wrath, in so much that we cannot enter into the kingdom of God *except we are born again.*"[14]

The language of the baptism form is clear and conclusive: "sanctified in Christ" is the saving work of the Spirit of Christ in the hearts of the infants of believers, already in their infancy, in accordance with the covenant promise that God will be the God of our infants, and in accordance with the obvious significance of *infant* baptism. But this is true only of the elect children of believers. The form regards the elect children of believers as the true (spiritual) children of the covenant.

All the Children Sanctified Conditionally

There is another objection to the interpretation of "sanctified in Christ" in the Reformed baptism form that explains the phrase

---

14. Ibid.; emphasis added.

as describing God's regeneration of the elect children of believers in their infancy. This objection too arises from a distinct doctrinal position regarding the covenant promise to the children of believers and regarding the covenant itself. This doctrinal position abominates the truth that God governs his covenant by his eternal decree of election. Particularly, it rejects the truth that God's covenant promise to be the God of the children of believers refers to the elect children.

This covenant doctrine vehemently denies that "sanctified in Christ" in the Reformed baptism form describes the elect infants of believers. Rather, the phrase refers to all the children without exception. But the explanation of the phrase by this covenant doctrine differs from that of those who refuse to see anything more in the phrase "sanctified in Christ" than an outward and formal holiness. This covenant doctrine recognizes that the first question of the baptism form speaks of a saving work of God in Christ with regard to infants who are, after all, the objects of the promise of the covenant. The covenant promise has the cross of Christ as its basis, the Spirit of Christ as its power, the spiritual blessings of salvation as its content, and eternal life as its goal. Its sign and seal is infant baptism—the sacrament of the atoning blood of Christ applied to the infant children of believers.

Accordingly, this covenant doctrine teaches that "sanctified in Christ" refers to a gracious covenantal attitude of God toward the infants and to a gracious covenantal work of God with regard to them. This attitude and work are saving in nature, even as the covenant has to do with salvation. This covenant doctrine does not like to speak of an inward, subjective, saving work of the Spirit in the infants. Infant regeneration is anathema to it, in spite of the fact that the opening lines of the baptism form teach that our infant children are "born again." But this doctrine of the covenant prefers to speak of an objective covenantal act of God with regard to the children of believers: He justifies all the offspring of believers and adopts them as his children.

In keeping with its determined opposition to the truth that election governs the covenant, this covenant doctrine applies its understanding of "sanctified in Christ" to all the children without exception. The first question of the baptism form is explained as teaching that all the children without exception are sanctified in Christ in the sense that all alike are covenantally justified and covenantally adopted by God. All alike are covenantally "in Christ."

But all are alike "sanctified in Christ" *conditionally.*

The covenant with the children is *conditional.* Whether the children remain in the covenant and are saved depends upon a work the children must perform, namely, faith. If a child refuses to believe, as many children of believers do, he perishes outside of Christ, regardless that once he was "in Christ." He is condemned, regardless that once God justified him. He becomes a child of the devil, regardless that once God adopted him.

This is the covenant doctrine and corresponding explanation of the phrase "sanctified in Christ" of the RCN (lib.) and of the Canadian and American Reformed churches.

Klaas Schilder, foremost theologian of the RCN (lib.), described the covenant of grace as a "legal relationship" in the form of an agreement between two parties, God and his people. In the covenant "two . . . parties . . . bind each other in an agreement."[15] Because "man is a responsible creature who has to act according to independent thought and as an independent being, . . . the covenant becomes, because of the nature of man, a two way street." The "two way street" is "the promise and the demand."[16] The covenant of grace is God's promise to and demand upon every baptized child.

The promise comes to every baptized child of godly parents alike. With the promise comes to every baptized child the right to Christ and salvation. "What is promised and demanded you may consider as something that you have coming to you, as a right, and that gives certainty."[17]

The promise to every child gives (covenant) grace to every

---

15. Klaas Schilder, "The Main Points of the Doctrine of the Covenant: A Speech Given by Professor Dr. K. Schilder in the Waalsche Kerk in Delft, the Netherlands on August 31, 1944," trans. T. van Laar (Canada: n.p., 1992), 3, 5.

16. Ibid., 9, 11.

17. Ibid., 12.

child. "A baptized child has that grace and that demand which he is allowed to have, which have been promised."[18] "Through the promise of the washing through the blood of Christ they [all the baptized children without exception] have the right to righteousness, and now the Spirit wishes to continuously sanctify them."[19]

Schilder fiercely inveighed against the doctrine that the covenant promise of grace has its source in, and is as particular as, God's eternal election.

> Some are saying that God has chosen His covenant children from eternity. God promises them His grace, and only there where He pours out His grace is man actually in the covenant . . . They say the covenant contains from the Lord's side, as a complete gift in election, eternal salvation: that is the covenant. No, say we, that we will never accept! Those people who describe the promise in this way so that it is stripped of the demand are gutting the covenant of its significance![20]

In the promise God on his part is gracious to every baptized child, but the actual reception of grace depends on the child's obeying the demand. The demand is, in fact, a condition, upon which the realization and fulfillment of the promise in the child's salvation depend. "We must speak of conditions: I will not receive it [the covenant salvation that is promised] if I do not comply with the demand—faith is the first demand."[21] "The goods [lie] in the promise; if you accept the promise then it is for you."[22]

Performance of the condition by a child is "from Him."[23]

In the covenant theology of Schilder and the RCN (lib.), the covenant promise of grace to all the baptized children without exception is grace to all the children, including the loving desire of God to save all the children. It is a *conditional* grace to all the

18. Ibid., 13.
19. Ibid., 14.
20. Ibid., 9–10.
21. Ibid., 13.
22. Ibid., 14.
23. Ibid.

children, but it is *grace* to all the children—the covenant grace of God in the mediator of the covenant, Jesus Christ.

What Schilder expressed cautiously, another architect of the covenant theology of the RCN (lib.), C. Veenhof, expressed boldly. Explaining that (infant) baptism is a seal "on the promise of God," Veenhof wrote,

> It has seemed good to the Lord in his wonderful love to give his *promise* to *all* the children of believers. Or, to say it differently, it has pleased him to make a *glorious promise* to those children. That is, he says to all those children, head for head, day in and day out, seriously and sincerely: *I am the Lord thy God*. I establish my covenant with you. I wash you from all sins in the blood of our Lord Jesus Christ. My Holy Spirit will dwell in you. In sum, I promise you the complete forgiveness of sins and eternal life: all the treasures and riches that I will and can give to men.

Veenhof added that this gracious promise comes to all the children with a demand. But "this demand does not make the promise poorer or weaker."[24]

Not only is every baptized child, "head for head," object of the (covenant) grace of God, but every baptized child is also the recipient of (covenant) salvation by virtue of his or her baptism, according to Veenhof.

> The Lord gives His promise to all children. In that promise, He solemnly pledges the whole of salvation to them. That salvation is, so to say, "wrapped up" in those promises. And

---

24. C. Veenhof, "De zaak waar het om gaat" [The real issue (in the controversy over the covenant in the Reformed churches in the Netherlands, resulting in the formation of the RCN, liberated)], in *Appel!* [Appeal!], 5–6. The emphasis is Veenhof's. This booklet has no publishing data. Internal evidence indicates that it was published in or soon after 1948. One thing the date of the booklet makes plain is that those ministers who brought about schism in the Protestant Reformed Churches in 1953 over the issue of the relation of covenant and election knew full well, or could have known and should have known, what Schilder's covenant theology (for which they opted) really was and that that covenant doctrine differed radically from the covenant doctrine that the Protestant Reformed Churches had been confessing from the beginning of their history. The translation of the Dutch in this and the following quotation from the booklet is mine.

now baptism is the seal upon that promise, in which complete salvation is "contained." Therefore, when God baptizes a child [Veenhof referred to the administration of the
sacrament to every child], that child thus receives, in that
baptism, in that sealed promise, the entire salvation that
God wills to bestow upon sinners.[25]

Whether the gracious promise, which is theirs, and the "whole
of salvation," which all receive in the promise at baptism, do
them any good and continue with them depend, of course, upon
the children's performing the condition.

This covenant doctrine, too, I have examined and criticized in
my book *The Covenant of God and the Children of Believers,*[26]
so that I can be brief here. This explanation does as little justice
to the phrase "sanctified in Christ" as does the explanation of
an outward and formal holiness. As I have already demonstrated, "sanctified in Christ" describes a work of the Spirit within
infants who are united to Christ by the bond of a true faith.
This work makes them living members of the one, holy, catholic, apostolic church of Christ.

It is impossible that an infant (or anyone else) who has been
sanctified in Christ and made a member of the body of Christ
shall ever perish. The mighty grace of God that began the work
of salvation in the infant will maintain and perfect the work.
"God is faithful, who having conferred grace, mercifully confirms and powerfully preserves them [all those whom he has
regenerated] therein, even to the end."[27] The Canons explicitly
deny that anyone can lose his adoption and justification, something the covenant doctrine I am presently examining affirms by
its explanation of the phrase "sanctified in Christ." According
to this covenant doctrine, all the children of believers without
exception are justified and adopted by God. This is supposed to
be the meaning of "sanctified in Christ." However, since these
covenant works of God are conditional, many of the children
eventually lose this justification and adoption. But the Canons

---

25. Ibid., 11–12. The emphasis is Veenhof's.
26. Engelsma, *Covenant of God,* 14–20, 87–132.
27. Canons of Dordt, 5.3, in Schaff, *Creeds of Christendom,* 3:593.

deny that God ever permits any of his people "to lose the grace of adoption and forfeit the state of justification."[28]

The explanation of "sanctified in Christ" that applies the phrase to all the offspring of believers alike, while acknowledging that the phrase refers to a work of God's grace in the covenant, is a denial of the sovereignty of grace and therefore of the gospel of grace itself. Regardless that God's gracious work in the covenant is described as objective, taking form in a justification and adoption of the children, rather than in a subjective regeneration of the children, the covenant work of God that consists of sanctifying children in Christ is not effectual. It does not assure the salvation of any. It is resisted by many, who then perish forever outside of Christ.

Denial of the sovereignty of grace is always, necessarily, the affirmation of the dependency of grace on the work of the sinner. God's covenant work of sanctifying all the offspring of believers, according to the explanation of "sanctified in Christ" by the RCN (lib.), fails in the case of many children, because his covenant work is conditional. It depends on the work of the children. The clear and necessary implication is that the reason some continue in the covenant and are finally saved is their performing the condition.

It is this conditional covenant doctrine regarding baptized children that the men of the federal vision are now developing into a bold attack on every one of the doctrines of grace confessed in the Canons of Dordt.

At bottom, the heresy of the federal vision, like the conditional covenant doctrine it is developing, is opposition to the truth that election governs the covenant.

"Sanctified in Christ" in Light of the Prayer of Thanksgiving

The prayer of thanksgiving immediately following the baptism of the infants makes it indisputably plain that by "sanctified in Christ" the baptism form means the actual saving work of God upon and within the elect infants of believers. Just moments earlier, the Reformed church had asked the believing parents

---

28. Canons of Dordt, 5.6, in ibid., 3:593.

whether they acknowledge that their children are "sanctified in Christ and, therefore, as members of his church ought to be baptized." Then the baptism of the infants took place. At once, with the words "sanctified in Christ" still ringing in the ears of the congregation, and with the visible word of the sprinkling of the infants with the water of baptism vivid in their minds, the church thanks the God of the covenant in prayer:

> "Almighty God and merciful Father, we thank and praise thee, that thou hast forgiven us and our children all our sins through the blood of thy beloved Son Jesus Christ, and received us through thy Holy Spirit as members of thine only begotten Son, and adopted us to be thy children, and sealed and confirmed the same unto us by holy baptism."[29]

The Reformed church thanks God for the actual salvation of the children of believing parents; the forgiveness of their sins through the blood of Christ; the shedding of Christ's blood for them on the cross; and the uniting of them by the Holy Spirit to Christ by the mystical union of the bond of faith and regeneration, so that they are living members of Christ as adopted children of God.

This actual salvation of the children consists of the (objective) work of Christ *for* them on the cross: "through the blood of thy beloved Son Jesus Christ." It consists as well of the (subjective) work of Christ *in* them by his Spirit: "received us through thy Holy Spirit as members of thine only begotten Son."

The Reformed church thanks God for this actual salvation of the children of believing parents *in the infancy of the children,* indeed, already at the time of the baptism of the infants. With regard to the infants who have just been baptized, the prayer thanks God that he *has* forgiven them on the basis of Christ's death for them and that he *has* received them by his Holy Spirit as members of Christ.

The prayer of thanksgiving makes plain beyond any shadow of doubt what the Reformed form meant by the words "sanctified in Christ and . . . members of his [Christ's] church" a few

---

29. Form for the Administration of Baptism, in *Confessions and Church Order,* 260.

minutes earlier in the service. "Sanctified in Christ and . . . members of his church" meant, and means, that God has forgiven the infants all their sins through the blood of his beloved Son Jesus Christ and that God has received the infants through his Holy Spirit as members of his only begotten Son as adopted children.

And this is the meaning of infant baptism, for it is this actual salvation by the blood and Spirit of Christ that is "sealed and confirmed" to believing parents and their children by holy baptism.

As the meaning of infant baptism based on the covenant promise, "I will be the God of your children," this is also the meaning of the covenant promise. God promises to save the infant children of believers.

By no means does the prayer of thanksgiving after infant baptism describe, or intend to describe, a saving work of God upon and in all the offspring of believers without exception. The prayer refers to the elect infants of believers, because with the entire form it understands the elect children to be the true, spiritual seed of Abraham and of believing parents.

If the prayer refers to all the offspring of believers without exception, Esaus as well as Jacobs, it teaches universal, conditional election; a universal, inefficacious atonement; revocable justification; losable adoption; resistible grace; and the falling away of saints, in the sphere of the covenant, regarding the children of believers. Sanctified in Christ by the covenant grace of God, so that one enjoys all the blessings of salvation, today! Outside of Christ, devoid of the blessings of salvation, and under God's damning wrath, tomorrow! In this case, James Arminius was right, and the men of the federal vision can appeal in support of their grievous heresy to one of the foundational, most prominent, and most precious documents of Reformed Protestantism.

That the Reformed churches in the Netherlands did not teach this heresy, and could not have taught this heresy, in their baptism form is evident, first, from the fact that they adopted the form in 1574, when they stood firm in the truth of sovereign grace (against which James Arminius would soon remonstrate), and again in 1618–19 at the Synod of Dordt, where they would condemn the teaching of a universal, ineffectual grace.

Second, the prayer of thanksgiving itself shows that it speaks of the saving work of God in Christ with regard to elect infants, not of a saving work of God regarding all the offspring of believers without exception. The rest of the prayer, in which the church beseeches God on behalf of the children, affirms that all of the children who are the objects of the "fatherly goodness and mercy" of God will certainly persevere in righteousness "to the end that they may eternally praise and magnify" God.[30] This is true only of the elect children.

Nowhere in the prayer of thanksgiving is there any mention of a condition that the children must perform in order either to enter the covenant or to remain in the covenant. Every notion of a conditional covenant promise to the children, of a conditional covenant with the children, of a conditional covenant salvation of the children, and of a condition for abiding in the covenant and being saved is decisively ruled out. For the prayer thanks God for the salvation of our children *in their infancy*, when they are utterly incapable of fulfilling any condition. It thanks God for saving them with a salvation that cannot be lost: the forgiveness of their sins through the blood of Jesus Christ and incorporation into Christ by the Holy Spirit. It finds in their baptism a seal and confirmation of this salvation, that is, the divinely appointed ceremony that assures that our children are saved and that this salvation is everlasting. On the basis of this sure salvation of the infants, sealed by baptism, the prayer has the church confidently ask God for the continuing, developing, and perfecting of the salvation of the children.

Thus the prayer of thanksgiving exposes as erroneous the covenant doctrine, and corresponding explanation of "sanctified in Christ," that views all the offspring of believers alike as objects of a certain covenantal grace and as taken into covenant union with Christ ("sanctified *in Christ*"), but as under the demand to perform a condition upon which depends their abiding in the covenant and their eternal salvation.

---

30. Ibid.

The prayer of thanksgiving also exposes as false the covenant doctrine that explains "sanctified in Christ" as merely a formal and outward holiness of the children of believers. Every time the officiating minister and congregation that hold this barren covenant doctrine use the Reformed baptism form, the prayer of thanksgiving rises up to condemn them and their doctrine:

> Almighty God and merciful Father, we thank and praise thee that thou *hast* forgiven [not *will* forgive the infant children, if someday they have the conversion experience] us *and our children* [already in their infancy] all our sins through the blood of thy beloved Son Jesus Christ, and *received* us [past tense, with reference to believing parents and their infant children] through thy Holy Spirit as members of thine only begotten Son [so that we and our infants are living saints in Christ, not dead sinners], and adopted us [believing parents and infant children] to be thy children [so that it is monstrous to view the infants as little vipers], and sealed and confirmed the same unto us by holy baptism.[31]

The latter part of the prayer is no less conclusive in exposing the notion of a mere formal, external holiness of covenant children as erroneous. Those who hold this view of the baptized children make the duty of parents, church, and even Christian school toward the children the evangelizing of them, so that they may be converted. What this means is that the children are regarded as unregenerated, spiritually dead, and outside of Christ. The evangelizing of them is a work of getting these dead sinners saved, long after their infancy, if God pleases.

But the concluding part of the prayer of thanksgiving does not beseech the "merciful Father" of believers and their children that he will be pleased to govern these baptized children by the external supervision of parents, church, and Christian school, so that they may be zealously evangelized as spiritually dead sinners in Adam and one day perhaps have a conversion experience, which saves them.

---

31. Ibid.; emphasis added.

"Increase and Grow Up"

On the contrary, the prayer beseeches God to "govern these baptized children by thy Holy Spirit" (which is a work of the Spirit
indwelling the just-baptized infants), "that they may be piously
and religiously educated" (which is not the evangelizing of unregenerated children, but the instruction of little children who
are born again and alive in Christ, with the gospel, so that they
can and will repent, believe, and obey from their earliest years),
"increase and grow up in the Lord Jesus Christ" (which is not a
dramatic conversion from death to life in youth or old age, but a
gradual maturing in Christ of those who are alive in Christ from
infancy), and then "acknowledge thy fatherly goodness and mercy, which thou hast shown to them" (from their infancy). The
children will prove the work of covenant grace in themselves,
both to themselves and to others when they come to years, not
by experiencing a dramatic, mystical conversion but by living
"in all righteousness under [their] only Teacher, King, and High
Priest, Jesus Christ." They will also "manfully fight against and
overcome sin, the devil, and his whole dominion."[32]

Conclusion

There are two ways to evade this doctrine of the baptism form,
and both are pursued by Reformed churches and theologians.
One is to extend the grace of the covenant to all the physical offspring of believers alike. This involves making covenant
grace and salvation conditional, that is, dependent upon the
work of the child. This is the denial of the gospel of salvation
by sovereign grace, as the men of the federal vision are now
demonstrating to the entire community of Reformed and Presbyterian churches.

The other way reduces the covenant work of God with the
infants of believers to nothing more than the church's formally
and externally setting the infants and small children apart from
the children of unbelievers in the hope of the conversion of some
of the children in later life. This evasion also denies that in the

---

32. Ibid.

baptism form election determines the covenant children of believers. Specifically, it denies that election determines the infants of believers who are "sanctified in Christ."

Neither of the evasions does justice to the language of the form.

Inasmuch as the Reformed baptism form is a very early, official document of the Reformed churches in the Netherlands—a minor creed—these churches early established the truth that election governs the covenant as binding doctrine. For hundreds of years after 1574 and 1618–19, Reformed theologians and even denominations of churches in the Dutch Reformed tradition opposed this doctrine, arguing strenuously that the covenant is divorced from election, especially regarding the inclusion of children in the covenant and their salvation. Today, the overwhelming majority of theologians and churches that stand in the Dutch Reformed tradition and that have and use the Reformed baptism form take the position that the covenant is and ought to be divorced from election.

But they have no right to take this position.

In all the history of the Reformed churches in the Netherlands, or the history of Reformed churches standing in that tradition, no one ever had a right to take that position.

The Reformed Form for the Administration of Baptism ruled out that position from the very beginning, at least as early as 1574, binding upon all theologians and churches that have the form as their official document that election governs the covenant.

In 1618–19, the Canons of the Synod of Dordt did the same.

COVENANT AND ELECTION
IN THE CANONS

Contrary to the accepted wisdom in the Reformed churches, the Canons of Dordt do not leave it an open question whether election governs the covenant. It is not an open question, therefore, about which Reformed theologians and churches may debate until the world ends, whether God graciously establishes his covenant with all the children of believers alike, *conditionally,* or whether he establishes the covenant of grace *unconditionally* with the elect children.

Although they mention the covenant only rarely, and although the doctrine of the covenant is certainly not a major theme in the creed, the Canons of Dordt are conclusive: God's eternal decree of election governs the covenant of grace with believers and their children.

The Canons of Dordt is the second authoritative document, with the Form for the Administration of Baptism, that has bound upon the Reformed churches from their earliest beginnings a doctrine of the covenant that has the covenant governed by, and serving, election.

Election and Covenant Grace

The Canons teach that election governs the covenant inasmuch as they confess that election is the sole fountain of God's (saving) grace and the only determiner of those who are the objects of this grace.

Canons 1, Article 9 teaches that election is the source of God's grace in Jesus Christ and of all his saving works: "Therefore election is the fountain of every saving good; from which proceed faith, holiness, and the other gifts of salvation, and finally eternal life itself, as its fruits and effects."[1]

---

1. Canons of Dordt, 1.9, in Schaff, *Creeds of Christendom,* 3:583.

The covenant is a covenant *of grace;* the work of God in the covenant is a work of gracious salvation. The very establishment of the covenant with someone is gracious on God's part. But this grace and saving work, according to the Canons, have their fountain in God's election. It is true that the Canons do not specify that election is the fountain of God's grace and saving work *in the covenant.* Why should they? Wherever God's grace in Jesus Christ is directed toward men, wherever God's grace is communicated to men, and wherever God's saving work is found in men, whether on the mission field or in the family of believers, the fountain is election.

Are we to suppose that, whereas God's grace and saving work on the mission field are due to and governed by election, in the covenant there is a different source? Do the enemies of the truth that election governs the covenant really suppose, and want us to suppose, that the Canons' clear, emphatic teaching that election is the fountain of God's grace and saving work in Christ *excludes God's grace and saving work in the covenant?*

And if it is indeed the case that God's eternal decree is not the fountain of the grace and saving work of God in the covenant, among the physical offspring of godly parents, what is the source of grace and salvation in the covenant?

According to the Canons of Dordt, binding document for the churches in the Dutch Reformed tradition (the glorious tradition that has made more of the covenant of grace than any other), covenant and election are tightly linked. Election governs the covenant.

"Out of the Common Mass" of the Offspring of Believers

In closest connection with the teaching of the Canons that the grace and saving work of God, in the covenant as on the mission field, are due to election, Canons 1, Article 10 makes election the determiner of the objects of the grace and saving work of God: "Gracious election . . . doth . . . consist herein . . . that he [God] was pleased out of the common mass of sinners to adopt some certain persons as a peculiar people to himself."[2]

---

2. Canons of Dordt, 1.10, in ibid., 3:583.

In proof and demonstration of this assertion, the article immediately quotes Romans 9:11–13: "'For the children being not yet born, neither having done any good or evil, . . . it was said [namely to Rebecca] the elder shall serve the younger; as it is written, Jacob have I loved, but Esau have I hated.'"[3] This passage proves that election determines the objects of the grace of God *in the sphere of the covenant,* for Jacob and Esau were not heathens on the mission field, but twin sons of godly parents. In determining which of the two (as yet unborn) sons of Isaac and Rebecca would be the object of God's grace and saving work—Jacob—election determined the object of God's *covenant* grace and *covenant* salvation. As a discriminating decree, the same decree—reprobation—determined which of the physical offspring of Isaac and Rebecca—Esau—would not be the object of God's covenant grace and saving work, but the object of his covenant wrath and curse.

According to Article 10 of Canons 1, God is not gracious to "the common mass of sinners" born to godly parents. God is not pleased to adopt all of the children born to godly parents. Not all the physical children alike are "a peculiar people to himself," even though all are baptized. Which of the children of godly parents are the objects of God's covenant grace, are adopted as his children, and become his peculiar people is determined by election.

According to the Canons of Dordt, the eternal decree of election is so closely related to the covenant that election determines who are and who are not the covenant children of God.

It is the clear, forceful testimony of the Canons everywhere that the mediator, his death, the regenerating Spirit, the promise of the gospel, grace, blessings, and salvation have their origin in and are governed by God's eternal election of grace. This testimony applies to the covenant with believers and their children, inasmuch as the covenant has everything to do with the mediator, his death, the regenerating Spirit, the promise of the gospel, grace, blessings, and salvation. In addition, there are two specific statements in the Canons

---

3. Canons of Dordt, 1.10, in ibid., 3:583

that relate covenant and election in such a way that election governs the covenant.

Election and Salvation of Covenant Infants

The first statement is Article 17 of Canons 1: "Since we are to judge of the will of God from his Word, which testifies that the children of believers are holy, not by nature, but in virtue of the covenant of grace, in which they together with the parents are comprehended, godly parents have no reason to doubt of the election and salvation of their children whom it pleaseth God to call out of this life in their infancy."[4]

With explicit reference to the covenant of grace, to the infant children of believers, and to the salvation of these infant children of believers in the covenant of grace, the Canons explicitly declare that the covenant of grace is related to election: "election and [covenant] salvation." The Canons also explicitly teach that the relation between election and covenant salvation is that election governs the covenant: the salvation of infant children of believers is due to the election of these infant children. Believing parents "have no reason to doubt of the *election* and salvation [emphasis added]" of these children, that is, the parents may believe the salvation of these infant children because of God's election of these children.

In light of Article 17 of Canons 1, it is nothing less than astounding that Reformed churches and theologians, who have the Canons as their creed, deny that election governs the covenant, insist that this denial is in harmony with the Reformed confessions, and condemn those churches that teach the relation of election and covenant as being outside the stream of the Reformed tradition.

I note in passing that the election that governs the grace and saving work of God in the covenant, according to Article 17 of Canons 1, is not a conditional, changeable decision of God in history as taught by the RCN (lib.) theologian Benne Holwerda and by the men of the federal vision. But it is the eternal, unconditional, and unchangeable decision of Article 7 of Canons 1:

---

4. Canons of Dordt, 1.17, in ibid., 3:585.

"Election is the unchangeable purpose of God, whereby, before the foundation of the world, he hath, out of mere grace, according to the sovereign good pleasure of his own will, chosen," etc.[5]

It is true that Canons 1, Article 17 refers specifically to those children of believing parents who die in infancy. The fact remains that concerning these children election governs the grace and salvation of God in the covenant. Those Reformed theologians and churches that deny the relation of covenant and election oppose the teaching of Canons 1, Article 17.

And the teaching of this article regarding the salvation of a certain category of covenant children, namely, those who die in infancy, implies that God's salvation of the other covenant children, namely, all those who grow up to believe in Christ and walk in God's ways, is likewise governed by and due to election.[6]

Confirming the Covenant by Limited Atonement

The second statement in the Canons that explicitly relates covenant and election is Canons 2, Article 8:

> For this was the sovereign counsel and most gracious will and purpose of God the Father, that the quickening and saving efficacy of the most precious death of his Son should extend to all the elect, for bestowing upon them alone the gift of justifying faith, thereby to bring them infallibly to salvation: that is, it was the will of God, that Christ by the blood of the cross, *whereby he confirmed the new covenant,* should effectually redeem out of every people, tribe, nation, and language, all those, and those only, who were from eternity chosen to salvation, and given to him by the Father; that he should confer upon them faith, which, together with all the other saving gifts of the Holy Spirit, he purchased for them by his death; should purge them from all sin, both original and actual, whether committed before or after believing; and having faithfully preserved them

---

5. Canons of Dordt, 1.7, in ibid, 3:582.

6. For a thorough explanation of Canons 1.17 and its teaching of the confidence of godly parents concerning the salvation of their children who die in infancy, see Engelsma, "No Reason to Doubt," in *Covenant of God,* 27–40.

even to the end, should at last bring them free from every spot and blemish to the enjoyment of glory in his own presence forever.[7]

The line "whereby he confirmed the new covenant" appears in the fundamental article of the second head of the Canons on the death of Christ. It appears in the article in which the Canons affirm that the death of Christ was for those "who were from eternity chosen to salvation" and for "those only." This is the article that confesses limited atonement.

In this article, immediately following the reference to the electing will of God and immediately preceding the statement that the blood of the cross effectually redeemed the elect, and the elect only, occurs the line "whereby [that is, by the cross, which was designed by the will of God only for the elect and which effectually redeemed only the elect] he confirmed the new covenant."

The importance of this line regarding the controversy in the Reformed churches, whether election and covenant are related, specifically whether election governs the covenant, cannot be emphasized too strongly. Regardless that Reformed theologians from Martin Bullinger in the sixteenth century to Klaas Schilder and Norman Shepherd in recent times have denied that election governs the covenant, and regardless that the overwhelming majority of Reformed theologians and churches today insist on cutting the covenant loose from election, this short line in its context of Canons 2, Article 8 is decisive for the truth that the covenant is governed by election. This line in the Canons establishes the relation of covenant and election as the official, binding doctrine of all churches that subscribe to the Canons of Dordt.

First, generally, Article 8 of Canons 2 teaches that the death of Christ for sinners, which was due to and controlled by eternal election, "confirmed the new covenant." The same "will of God," that is, election, that determined the death of Christ de-

---

7. Canons of Dordt, 2.8, in Schaff, *Creeds of Christendom*, 3:587; emphasis added.

termined the confirmation of the new covenant by the cross. Regardless how theologians explain the confirmation of the new covenant, all must acknowledge the close relation between election and the covenant. The confirmation of the covenant of grace with believers and their children is due to and depends upon God's eternal election. For the blood of the cross that confirmed the new covenant has its origin in and is determined by "the sovereign counsel and most gracious will and purpose of God the Father, that the quickening and saving efficacy of the most precious death of his Son should extend to all the elect."[8]

Those who rail against relating covenant and election, usually by the ridiculous and misleading charge that a church or theologian identifies covenant and election, are in fact railing against Article 8 of Canons 2.

Second, specifically, this article teaches that the cross of Christ made the covenant of God firm and sure with all and every one of the covenant people of Christ and that it did this according to election. The blood of the cross confirmed the covenant in the way described in Article 8. The cross effectually redeemed all and every one of the covenant people of Christ; purchased for all and every one of them faith, as well as all the other saving gifts of the Holy Spirit; assured that Christ would purge all and every one of them from all sin; and made certain that Christ would preserve all and every one of them to the end, so that all and every one of them will enjoy glory in the presence of Christ forever.

This confirmation of the covenant with Christ's covenant people was due to and determined by election: "It was the will of God['s election], that Christ by the blood of the cross, whereby he confirmed the new covenant, should effectually redeem . . . all those, and those only, who were from eternity chosen to salvation."[9] The deliberate, explicit relating of covenant and election by Article 8 of Canons 2 establishes that God's covenant of grace is based on the death of Christ, so that the covenant and its blessings are as limited, or particular, as the death

---

8. Ibid.
9. Ibid.

of Christ itself; that the covenant of grace is made, maintained, and perfected with the elect in Christ alone; that membership in the covenant is determined by election; that the blessings of the covenant (which are certainly not different from the blessings mentioned in the article), as they were earned for the elect alone, are bestowed upon the elect alone; and that the salvation one begins to enjoy in the covenant cannot be lost.

Those Reformed theologians and churches that extend the gracious covenant promise, the grace of membership in the covenant, and the gracious covenant blessings more widely than election, if they take Canons 2, Article 8 at all seriously, are forced to give a radically different interpretation of the phrase "whereby he confirmed the new covenant." All that the cross of Christ accomplished was to obtain for God the right to make a new covenant with sinners. God makes this new covenant with all men alike, at least with all men alike who join the visible church by confession of faith and baptism and with all children alike who are born to believing parents.

This new covenant is highly uncertain. Membership in it does not at all assure that one will enjoy glory in the presence of Christ forever. Indeed, enjoyment of the beginning of covenant salvation and covenant blessings does not assure everlasting life and glory. For, according to the Reformed theologians and churches that will not have election govern the covenant, the new covenant is conditional. It depends not upon God's election, or even upon Christ's death, but upon the faith and obedience of the baptized member of the visible church and upon the faith and obedience of the children of believing parents. One can be object of the gracious covenant promise for a while, but later become object of the covenant curse. One can be member of the covenant, but fall out and perish. One can begin to enjoy covenant grace, blessings, and salvation, but lose them and go lost forever.

That Christ confirmed the new covenant means nothing more than that his death assures that all those who fulfill the conditions, and fulfill them to the very end of their lives, will be saved.

Some confirmation of the covenant!

It was exactly this heretical doctrine of the covenant that Dordt intended to contradict by the line "whereby he confirmed the new covenant":

> The true doctrine [of the relation of election, cross, and covenant] having been explained, the Synod *rejects* the errors of those . . .

> Who teach . . . that it was not the purpose of the death of Christ that he should confirm the new covenant of grace through his blood, but only that he should acquire for the Father the mere right to establish with man such a covenant as he might please, whether of grace or of works . . .

> Who teach that Christ, by his satisfaction, merited neither salvation itself for anyone, nor faith, whereby this satisfaction of Christ unto salvation is effectually appropriated; but that he merited for the Father only the authority or the perfect will to deal again with man, and to prescribe new conditions as he might desire, obedience to which, however, depended on the free will of man, so that it therefore might have come to pass that either none or all should fulfill these conditions.[10]

In light of Canons 2, Article 8, how can Reformed churches and theologians deny that covenant and election are related, so closely related, in fact, that election governs the covenant? Election purposed the cross "whereby he confirmed the new covenant."

In light of Canons 2, Article 8, how can Reformed churches and theologians extend the grace of the covenant more widely than to the elect? Did a limited atonement, purposed and designed by the decree of election, confirm a covenant with many more than those for whom Christ died and for many more than those whom God had chosen? Is a death of Christ for the elect alone the ground of a covenant of grace with all?

In light of Canons 2, Article 8, how can Reformed churches and theologians make faith and obedience *conditions* of a covenant supposedly established in grace with many more than the

---

10. Canons of Dordt, 2, Rejection of Errors 2–3, in *Confessions and Church Order,* 164–65.

elect children of believers? Faith and obedience were *purchased* by the blood of the cross for the elect. Christ *confers* faith and obedience, as *gifts,* upon those for whom he died.

In light of Canons 2, Article 8, how can Reformed churches and theologians teach that the new covenant is uncertain in the case of every one with whom it is established, inasmuch as the covenant depends on conditions? The new covenant was "confirmed" by the precious, effectual blood of the Son of God. The new covenant depends on "the sovereign counsel and most gracious will and purpose of God the Father."

Conclusion

At the very beginning of the history of the Reformed faith in the Netherlands, the Reformed churches embraced with all their heart, confessed, and made binding a fundamental truth concerning the covenant of grace with believers and their children. The covenant is governed by election. The necessary implication of this truth is that the covenant is unconditional, that is, a covenant *of grace.* The Reformed churches confessed this relation of covenant and election in two early, official documents: the Reformed Form for the Administration of Baptism and the Canons of the Synod of Dordt.

Reformed officebearers and Reformed churches, therefore, are not at liberty, and never have been at liberty, to teach a doctrine of the covenant that liberates the covenant from election.

A denomination of Reformed churches that confesses that election governs the covenant is not outside the mainstream of the Dutch Reformed tradition. On the contrary, it is the contemporary representative of the tradition—the *confessional* tradition.

APPLYING THE GOSPEL
OF THE REFORMATION

When they confessed that election governs the covenant, the Reformed churches in the Netherlands were simply applying the gospel recovered by the sixteenth-century Reformation to the covenant. The gospel of the Reformation was the message of salvation by grace alone, apart from the works of the sinner. With one voice the Reformation proclaimed that grace originates from, is directed by, and depends upon the eternal decree of election. The Reformation denied that either election or salvation is conditioned by any work of the sinner, including his faith. Therefore, the Reformation confessed that the sinner's justification is by faith alone, altogether apart from any work.

It belonged to the Reformation gospel that grace is effectual, or irresistible. Grace is as almighty as the divine will of which it is the expression. The grace that has its source in election always accomplishes the salvation of every human toward whom it is directed and in whom it begins to work. Grace is sovereign.

To apply the gospel of the Reformation to the covenant is to confess that election is the fountain of covenant grace, covenant blessings, and covenant salvation. It is, therefore, to confess a covenant of sovereign grace.

Surely, it is right to apply the gospel of the Reformation to the covenant!

Regardless how one conceives the covenant, whether as a cold contract, or as a vague arrangement, or as a living, lively bond of fellowship in love, the covenant is a gracious provision of God. It is a gracious provision of God in Jesus Christ, for Christ is head, mediator, and surety of the covenant (Rom. 5:12–21; Heb. 8:6; Heb. 7:22). The covenant is established and confirmed in the blood of the cross (Dan. 9:24–27; Luke 22:20;

Heb. 9:11–28). In and by the covenant, God intends to give, and does give, the blessings of salvation that Christ earned by his death. The resurrection of the body and life everlasting in the new creation is the goal of the covenant—its perfection in the day of Christ. The covenant is the new covenant of *grace*. It is the new covenant of grace *in Christ*.

Does not the gospel of the Reformation apply to *covenant* grace, *covenant* blessings, *covenant* salvation, and the *covenant* Christ?

Are the *covenant* Christ, *covenant* grace, and *covenant* salvation liberated from the eternal decree?

And if so, what does account for the *covenant* Christ, *covenant* grace, and *covenant* salvation? Whence do they originate? Upon what do they depend? By what are they governed?

There is only one answer: the will and work of the member of the covenant. The will of the sinner is preferred to the will of God.

This is the answer of all those Reformed churches and theologians today who deny that election governs the covenant, thus refusing to apply the gospel of the Reformation to the covenant. Instead, they apply the "gospel" of the Roman Catholic Church, rejected by the sixteenth-century Reformation, and the "gospel" of Arminianism, rejected by all Reformed children at the Synod of Dordt, to the covenant. That this is indeed the case becomes evident in the crass teaching of justification by works by the theologians of the federal vision, whose fundamental fault is their determination to cut the covenant loose from election.

Covenant and Election in Romans 9

The Reformed churches of the Netherlands, in the glorious days now long past, when in their youth they went after God in the "love of [their] espousals" (Jer. 2:2), applied the gospel of the Reformation to the covenant. They applied the gospel of the Reformation to the covenant, because (to speak anachronistically) Scripture does. Scripture teaches that election governs the covenant. Scripture teaches that election governs the covenant in Romans 9, which is not so much the *inspired* chapter on predestination as it is the chapter on the close relation of covenant and election. The relation is this: Election governs the covenant. Election governs the covenant promise. Election governs covenant grace. Election governs the covenant children. Election governs covenant salvation.

Romans 9 is the answer—the *inspired* answer—to the covenant problem: In light of God's covenant promise to Abraham, that he would be the God of Abraham's seed, how is it to be explained that so many of Abraham's physical offspring perished in unbelief? This is a problem that grieves godly parents and vexes Reformed theologians to this day: In light of God's covenant promise to believing parents, that he will be the God of their children, how is it to be explained that some of the children perish in unbelief?

Having acknowledged in verses 1–5 the perishing of many Israelites, the apostle is constrained to deny in verse 6 that "the word of God hath taken none effect." The "word of God" in verse 6 is the word of covenant promise to father Abraham, "I will . . . be a God unto . . . thy seed after thee" (Gen. 17:7).

The explanation of the perishing of many physical descendants of Abraham, throughout the Old Testament and in the apostle's own day, is not that God's covenant promise "hath taken none effect" (Rom. 9:6), that is, that the promise failed. But this certainly would be the explanation if God's covenant promise was the salvation of every one of Abraham's physical offspring. In this case, God made his promise to every physical child of Abraham without exception. He promised Christ, the blessings of salvation, and eternal life to all of them alike. In making the promise to all, God had a gracious attitude toward all of them alike. He sincerely desired their covenant salvation. At their circumcision he actually established the covenant of grace with them all. The subsequent unbelief, wickedness of life, and everlasting damnation of many of them would then represent the failure of the covenant promise. In the language of the Authorized Version, the word of God has "taken none effect" with regard to many children of Abraham. Specifically, it took none effect with regard to Abraham's profane grandson Esau.

It makes absolutely no difference that one objects that the reason the promise, made to all alike, has failed is that it was a conditional promise, depending for its efficacy and realization upon the works of the children. Then the promise failed because of the failure of the children to perform the condition. But the fact remains that the promise failed. It did not give what it said it would give. It did not do what it said it would do. Quite literally, the covenant promise of God took no effect. In the rough but understandable talk of everyday life, the promise did not deliver the goods. God had said to and about these particular children who perish, specifically Esau, "I will be your God, and you will be my people." But to all eternity, he is not their God, and they are not his people. His promise was empty words. It was worse. It was false.

Indeed, recourse to the conditionality of the promise to explain the perishing of many who were once the objects of the gracious covenant promise—as much the objects of the gracious covenant promise as those who are finally saved, according to the defenders of the universal, gracious, but conditional covenant promise—exposes the promise as impotent, utterly impotent. The promise has no power in itself whatever to realize what it promises. It is merely as strong as the children upon whom the promise depends for its efficacy and realization. Whatever power the promise may have is, in fact, that of the children upon whom the promise depends.

No wonder that the word of God's covenant promise has failed in multitudes of instances!

No wonder that the word of God's covenant promise failed specifically in the case of Esau!

The marvel is that this conditional, inherently powerless promise saves anyone.

The conditionality of the covenant promise, and therefore the inherent weakness of the covenant promise, is not the solution to the covenant problem that the apostle gives in Romans 9. This is the solution offered today by the majority of Reformed and Presbyterian churches and theologians. This is the solution offered with a vengeance by the proponents of the covenant doctrine known as the federal vision. In their covenant doctrine, they revise Romans 9:6. Reflecting on the unbelief and damnation of some baptized children of godly parents, the men of the federal vision explain: "The word of God has taken none effect in all these children, for the word of God's covenant promise is conditional."[1]

The solution given by Paul in inspired Romans 9 is radically different: "Not as though the word of God hath taken none effect" (v. 6). Not as though the covenant promise, "I will . . . be a God unto . . . thy seed after thee," has failed. Not as though the covenant promise has failed with regard to even one child included in the seed to whom and about whom God made the promise. Not as though the covenant promise has failed specifically in the case of Esau. Not as though a gracious promise to all the children without exception has failed in the case of many because they did not perform the condition upon which the gracious promise depended.

Two Kinds of Children

The apostle's solution to the covenant problem—a pressing problem because the truth of the word of God is at stake and with it the veracity of the promising God—is a clear, sharp distinction between physical offspring of father Abraham who are truly "Israel" and physical offspring of Abraham who are only "of Israel": "For they are not all Israel, which are of Israel" (v. 6).

There are offspring of Abraham who are mere physical progeny of the patriarch, for example, Esau. They are the "seed of Abraham" in the sense that they are of his body begotten, sharing his blood. But this does not make them those children of Abraham to whom God referred when he promised Abraham, "I will . . . be a God unto . . . thy seed after thee." "Neither, because they are the seed of Abraham, are they all children" (v. 7). "They which are the children of the flesh, these are not the children of God" (v. 8).

---

1. For statements by the men of the federal vision that the covenant promise fails to save many covenant children because it is conditional, see Engelsma, *Covenant of God*, 227–32.

In distinction from those offspring of Abraham who are only descended from him by physical generation, there is another, distinct group of people descended from Abraham. The apostle calls them the "children of the promise" (v. 8). To them, in distinction from the others, the covenant promise, "I will . . . be a God unto . . . thy seed after thee," referred. To them, in distinction from the others, God gave the covenant promise, "I will be your God." In them, in distinction from the others, the covenant promise worked (for the covenant promise is not empty words, but spiritual power and reality), making them God's covenant people by the gift of faith.

Only these "children of the promise are counted for the seed" (v. 8). When God promised, in Genesis 17:7, to be the God and savior of Abraham and Abraham's seed, God counted, or reckoned, only some of Abraham's offspring as the seed. He never regarded all of Abraham's physical descendants as the seed concerning whom and to whom he made his covenant promise. God had in mind only some of Abraham's physical offspring, "the children of the promise." Therefore, only these are the (true, spiritual) children of Abraham and the children of God. Those whom God counts for the seed are the seed. The others, those who are merely "the children of the flesh," are not counted by God for the covenant seed of Abraham.

Accordingly, the covenant promise to believing parents, "I will be the God of you and of your children (and grandchildren) after you," does not count all the physical descendants of this couple as their true, spiritual, and therefore real children. But the covenant promise makes distinction among the physical offspring. The promise refers, not to all the physical offspring without exception, but to some only. Only these children of the promise are counted by God as the believers' seed.

Discriminating Promise

From several clear examples in the Old Testament, the apostle proves that the covenant promise makes distinction among the physical descendants of believing parents and that the promise makes a child a covenant child. Whereas Abraham had a number of physical offspring (Ishmael and the children of Keturah) in addition to Isaac, God made plain to Abraham, "In Isaac shall thy seed be called" (Rom. 9:7). The covenant promise referred not to all Abraham's physical offspring without exception, but to Isaac. Not all the physical offspring of Abraham, but Isaac was the seed of Genesis 17:7 (not, of course, apart from Christ, who is *the* seed of Abraham, according to Galatians 3:16). The child produced by the power of the promise was Abraham's seed, and he only: "This is the word of promise, At this time will I come, and Sarah shall have a son" (Rom. 9:9).

Likewise, God's word of promise distinguished Jacob as the covenant child of Isaac and Rebecca, rather than his twin brother Esau: "The elder shall serve the younger. As it is written, Jacob have I loved, but Esau have I hated" (vv. 12–13).

It was the company of these children of the promise among Abraham's descendants who were God's "Israel" throughout the time of the Old Testament, no matter that they were usually the minority of Israelites, indeed the "very small remnant" (Isa. 1:9). The rest, although the large majority, were merely "of Israel" (Rom. 9:6). "Israel" was God's covenant people; those who were merely "of Israel" were in the sphere of the covenant. Or, to use the distinction often made in the Reformed tradition, God made his covenant with "Israel"; those who were merely "of Israel" were under the administration of the covenant.

God's covenant promise, the "word of God" of verse 6, did not fail, even though multitudes of Abraham's physical descendants perished in unbelief and disobedience. For the promising God never had all the physical offspring of Abraham in mind. The promise was discriminating: "In Isaac shall thy seed be called," and "the elder shall serve the younger." God counted the covenant seed, exclusive object of the promise, as those who are Christ's (Gal. 3:29). God's covenant promise took effect in every one of those on behalf of whom and to whom God made the promise: They believed, were justified, obeyed, repented when they sinned, persevered to the end, and inherited eternal life.

"Jacob have I loved."

The great question then is, who or what accounts for the distinction between being "Israel" and being merely "of Israel," between being "children of the flesh" and "children of the promise"? That is, who or what governs the covenant—its gracious promise, its gracious basis in the death of Christ, its gracious blessings, and its gracious salvation?

To *this* question concerning the source and governing of the *covenant* promise and *covenant* salvation, the answer of the apostle in *inspired* Romans 9 is election, not the performance or nonperformance of a condition by the children. The answer of the apostle is election as eternal, unchangeable decree, not some fickle decision of God in time, according as he sees children doing good or evil. God made the covenant promise to Jacob, in distinction from Esau, because he loved Jacob, in distinction from Esau, before the children were born or had done any good or evil (vv. 10–13). Some of Abraham's offspring were children of the promise, in distinction from the others, because "I will have mercy on whom I will have mercy" (v. 15).

Indeed, the others, who were also physical offspring of Abraham, were excluded from the covenant of grace and its gracious salvation on the basis of the death of Christ by God's eternal decree of reprobation: "and whom he will he hardeneth" (v. 18).

That the apostle is indeed teaching that election governs the covenant is proved by the objection to his doctrine: "Why doth he yet find fault? For who hath resisted his will?" (v. 19). To a doctrine of the covenant that teaches that all the children alike are the objects of God's gracious promise, that all alike are in the covenant by divine grace, but that continuing in the covenant and being saved depend upon the works of the children, no one ever objects with the words, "Why doth he yet find fault?"

To this objection, the apostle does not reply as do the defenders of the conditional covenant (which is to say, most of Reformed Christendom in our day) and especially the men of the federal vision, "My dear objector, you completely misunderstand my teaching. God does not determine which of the children of believers are included among his covenant people and which are not. God's gracious promise does not discriminate, certainly not among children of believers. The covenant of grace is not closely related to election; much less is it governed by election. Everything depends on the child, don't you see? If he fulfills the condition, he stays in the covenant and is saved. If he refuses to fulfill the condition, he falls out of the covenant and perishes. Your objection concerning the covenant 'Why doth he yet find fault?' makes no sense."

This is a popular reply in Reformed and Presbyterian circles to the indignant objection to the apostle's covenant doctrine in Romans 9. It sends the objector away pacified. It also sends him away believing that the word of God has indeed taken none effect in the case of many children of believing parents, and that covenant salvation is indeed of him who wills and runs (see v. 16).

What is the response of the apostle?

"Nay but, O man, who art thou that repliest against God? Shall the thing formed say to him that formed it, Why hast thou made me thus? Hath not the potter power over the clay, of the same lump to make one vessel unto honour, and another unto dishonour" (vv. 20–21)?

Scripture teaches that the gospel of salvation by grace alone applies to the covenant. In the covenant, salvation is of God who shows *sovereign, discriminating* mercy (v. 16).

The gospel of Holy Scripture proclaims that election governs the covenant.

For this reason the Reformed churches in the Netherlands, early on, established in their official, binding documents, particularly the Form for the Administration of Baptism and the Canons of Dordt, that election governs the covenant.

Chapter 6

CALVIN'S DOCTRINE OF THE COVENANT: UNION WITH CHRIST

In confessing that election governs the covenant, as they did at the very beginning of their history, particularly in the Reformed Form for the Administration of Baptism and in the Canons of Dordt, the Reformed churches in the Netherlands were guided by the reformer John Calvin. The basis of this doctrine for the Reformed churches certainly was Holy Scripture, but the Spirit used that mighty instrument, Calvin, to lead the Reformed churches in the Netherlands to the knowledge of this fundamental truth of the covenant.

It was not so much Calvin's explicit teaching about the covenant that influenced the Reformed churches in the Netherlands to view the covenant as governed by election, although there was such explicit teaching scattered throughout Calvin's writings.

But Calvin taught that the eternal decree of election is the source of the grace of God in Jesus Christ; that election determines the objects of his grace; and that election makes the grace of God in Jesus Christ effectual in the everlasting salvation of every one toward whom this grace is directed and in whom this grace begins to work. Thus Calvin taught that all the saving work of God in Jesus Christ originates from, depends upon, and is governed by God's election.

Calvin taught this clearly. Calvin taught this prominently. Calvin taught this from the beginning of his ministry to the end, and more zealously at the end than at the beginning. Calvin taught this everywhere in his writings. Calvin taught this emphatically. Calvin taught this as the very foundation of the Reformation gospel of salvation by grace alone. Therefore, he vigorously defended the truth of election as the sole source and determiner of grace and salvation against all those who opposed it.

The Reformed churches in the Netherlands (and elsewhere) understood that Calvin's doctrine of election as the fountain of grace and salvation applies to *covenant* grace and *covenant* salvation.

Prominence of the Covenant

It must freely be acknowledged that John Calvin did not systematically, thoroughly, and therefore perfectly clearly and consistently develop the biblical and Reformed doctrine of the covenant. Calvin wrote no monograph on the covenant of grace. He commented on the covenant wherever it happened to come up in his treatment of the Christian faith in the *Institutes* and in his explanation of Scripture in his lectures and commentaries. Therefore, one can find inconsistencies in his analysis of the covenant, especially in the commentaries.

This is nothing strange.

There is development of doctrine in the history of the postapostolic church as the Spirit of truth guides the church into deeper, clearer, purer, fuller understanding of the biblical revelation. Invariably, the Spirit has used heretics and heresies in this process, as today he uses the men of the federal vision. The Reformation, and Calvin in particular, *restored* the gospel of grace; they did not *perfect the church's understanding* of the gospel. The Spirit leaves something for us to do.

Although Calvin did not systematically and thoroughly develop the doctrine of the covenant, he taught it, and he taught it with regard to its fundamental aspects. So prominent is the covenant in Scripture that a biblical theologian, such as Calvin surely was, *had* to reckon with and explain the covenant. Such is the relation in Scripture between covenant, on the one hand, and the truth of salvation by grace alone, having its source in God's eternal election, on the other hand, that Calvin, wholly committed as he was to proclaiming sovereign grace, *had* to present the covenant not as contradicting sovereign grace, not as in some mysterious "tension" with sovereign grace, and not as independent of sovereign grace. But Calvin had to present the covenant as being in harmony with sovereign grace, indeed magnifying sovereign grace as its very goal.

Besides, Calvin was forced to pay close attention to the covenant in his defense of the Reformed faith against his Anabaptist adversaries. The basic error of the Anabaptists, Calvin contended, was their false doctrine of the covenant, just as the fundamental ground of infant baptism for Calvin was the right doctrine of the covenant. Against the erroneous covenant doctrine of the Anabaptists, Calvin taught the unity of the old and new covenants, the inclusion in the covenant of the infant children of believers, and covenant salvation by sovereign grace. Concerning this last, the basic issue in the controversy of Reformed orthodoxy with the federal vision, to a man the Anabaptists of Calvin's day proclaimed the false gospel of salvation by the free will of the sinner.[1] They denied that the grace of salvation is governed by divine election.

Fundamental Importance of the Covenant

Not only is the doctrine of the covenant prominent in Calvin's theology, but it is also of fundamental importance. I deliberately refrain from using the word *central*—of central importance—because I am not making a case for regarding the covenant as the "central-dogma" for Calvin in the sense in which some in the past regarded predestination as the "central-dogma" in Calvin's theology.[2]

What I am affirming is that Calvin clearly recognized the prominence of the reality of the covenant in Scripture, running as it does throughout the Bible from Genesis to Revelation and looming large in both the Old Testament and the New Testa-

---

1. John Calvin, *Institutes of the Christian Religion,* ed. John T. McNeill, trans. Ford Lewis Battles (Philadelphia: Westminster Press, 1960). The main places in the *Institutes* where Calvin engages in controversy with the Anabaptists are 2.10–11, 1:428–63, where the subject is the unity of the Old and New Testaments, and 4.16, 2:1324–59, where Calvin defends infant baptism.

2. On predestination as the proposed "central-dogma" in the theology of Calvin, see François Wendel, *Calvin: The Origins and Development of His Religious Thought,* trans. Philip Mairet (London: William Collins Sons, 1963), 263–65.

ment. And Calvin regarded the prominent doctrine of the covenant as a fundamental truth. It bears decisively on the other doctrines of Scripture. It is an integral element of the gospel of salvation by the grace of God in Jesus Christ. To ignore the covenant would make impossible the right understanding of the Bible. To go wrong on the covenant would be to corrupt the entire message of the Bible.

In its emphasis on the covenant, therefore, and in its relating all the other truths of the Bible, including the truth of the Trinity and the truth of the person and work of Jesus Christ, to the doctrine of the covenant, the Reformed church after Calvin has faithfully followed the guidance of the Holy Spirit through John Calvin.

Calvin expressed the fundamental importance of the covenant. Commenting on Zacharias' prophecy in Luke 1:67–79 concerning the birth of Jesus Christ, particularly the words "As he spake by the mouth of his holy prophets . . . to perform the mercy promised to our fathers, and to remember his holy covenant; the oath which he sware to our father Abraham," Calvin wrote, "[The prophets] all uniformly make the hope of the people, that God would be gracious to them, to rest entirely on that covenant between God and them which was founded on Christ." Calvin added, "Our chief attention is due to the signature of the divine covenant; for he that neglects this will never understand any thing in the prophets." He went on to declare, "The fountain from which redemption flowed [is] the *mercy* and gracious *covenant* of God."[3]

Calvin was teaching that Jesus Christ and all his salvation come to God's people in, and because of, the covenant of God with them. Jesus Christ is the covenant Christ. His salvation is covenant salvation. To be known rightly, Jesus must be known as the mediator of the covenant. His saving work is the establishment of the covenant. Every blessing that a regenerated and believing sinner enjoys in Christ Jesus is a covenant blessing.

---

3. John Calvin, *Commentary on a Harmony of the Evangelists, Matthew, Mark, and Luke*, trans. William Pringle (Grand Rapids, MI: Eerdmans, 1949), 1:70–71; the emphasis is the translator's.

Calvin emphasized that the blessings of salvation in Jesus Christ belong strictly to the covenant of grace. Continuing his commentary on Luke 1:67–79, Calvin called attention to "this order" of God's saving work in Jesus Christ:

> *First,* God was moved by pure mercy to make a covenant with the fathers. *Secondly,* he has linked the salvation of men with his own word. *Thirdly,* he has exhibited in Christ every blessing, so as to ratify all his promises . . . Forgiveness of sins is promised in the covenant, but it is in the blood of Christ.[4]

Commenting on Hebrews 9, the passage teaching the new covenant as fulfillment of the prophecy of Jeremiah 31:31–34, Calvin declared that like the forgiveness of sins, so also eternal life is the blessing of the covenant:

> The object of the divine covenant is that, having been adopted as children, we may at length be made heirs of eternal life. The Apostle teaches us that we obtain this by Christ. It is hence evident, that in him is the fulfillment of the covenant.[5]

In keeping with his understanding of the blessings of salvation as benefits of the covenant, in the prayer that concluded his lecture on Jeremiah 31:33, Calvin besought the enjoyment of salvation for himself and his auditors by asking God for the experience of the *covenant:* "Grant, Almighty God, that as thou hast favored us with so singular a benefit as to make through thy Son a covenant which has been ratified for our salvation,— O grant, that we may become partakers of it."[6]

Reformed pastors and believers might test their own regard for the covenant by asking themselves how often they implore God that they, their congregation, and their families may be partakers of the covenant.

---

4. Ibid., 71–72.

5. John Calvin, *Commentaries on the Epistle to the Hebrews,* trans. John Owen (Grand Rapids, MI: Eerdmans, 1949), 207.

6. John Calvin, *Commentaries on the Book of the Prophet Jeremiah and the Lamentations,* trans. John Owen (Grand Rapids, MI: Eerdmans, 1950), 4:134.

Calvin indicated his regard for the covenant as fundamental, if not central, by setting his entire doctrine of Christ, in the *Institutes,* in the context of the covenant of grace. Calvin began his exposition of the person and work of Jesus Christ in chapter 12 of book 2. Immediately preceding this exposition of the truth of Christ is Calvin's treatment, in chapters 10 and 11, of the unity and differences of the old and new covenants. Significantly, the opening line of Calvin's doctrine of Christ is "He who was to be our Mediator [must] be both true God and true man."[7] "Mediator" signals the reality of the covenant.

Unity of the Covenant

An essential aspect of the importance of the covenant for Calvin was the truth that the covenant with Old Testament Israel and the covenant with the New Testament church are one and the same covenant. They are two "forms," or "administrations," of the one covenant of grace established in one and the same Jesus Christ with one and the same people, bestowing one and the same salvation from sin. This truth, Calvin demonstrated and defended in his controversy with the Anabaptists.

Calvin located the heart of the Protestant and Reformed controversy with the Anabaptists in their rejection of infant baptism. The rejection of infant baptism implied that Old Testament circumcision and the covenant it signified and sealed were essentially different from New Testament baptism and the covenant of which it is sign and seal. Calvin correctly contended that rejection of infant baptism is inherently dispensational: denial of the unity of the covenant and therefore denial of the unity of the saving purpose and work of God in history. And this is to minimize, if not to lose sight altogether of, the fundamental importance of the (New Testament) covenant of grace.[8]

---

7. Calvin, *Institutes of the Christian Religion,* 2.12.1, 1:464.

8. Ibid., 2.10–11, 4.16; 1:428–64, 2:1324–59. The evidence of Calvin's contention that dispensational theology, intimately bound up with, if not rooted in, the rejection of infant baptism, reduces the covenant of grace with the New Testament church to an incidental, if not an afterthought of God, is contemporary dispensationalism's bold teaching that the church is merely a "parenthesis" in God's main text of saving national Israel and dispensationalism's equally bold

It is not the purpose of this chapter to explore this crucially important aspect of Calvin's doctrine of the covenant in detail. But let us appreciate Calvin's insistence on the unity of the covenant and our indebtedness to Calvin for this insistence. By that insistence we Reformed Christians have the entire Bible, specifically the Old Testament, as the word of God *to us*—with all its glorious promises, all its heartwarming and humbling history, and all its righteous laws. By that insistence, we have our children and our grandchildren in the communion of Christ and the fellowship of his church, the covenant family. And by that insistence, we are delivered from bizarre premillennial dispensationalism, particularly the pretribulation rapture, which is the logical development of the Anabaptist error.

Let us recognize how serious an error dispensationalism is, that is, the denial of the unity of the covenant and thus of the oneness of God's saving work in both Old and New Testaments. This error is inherent in the rejection of infant baptism. As Calvin warned, the Anabaptist doctrine tears Christ in pieces; makes the Jews of the Old Testament a "herd of swine" [9] (since the covenant with them was merely earthly, giving merely earthly goods); and diminishes the grace of God in Christ in the new covenant in comparison with his grace in the old covenant, inasmuch as in the old covenant his grace extended to the children of the godly, whereas in the new covenant it does not.

And let us hear at least a few brief statements by the reformer concerning the oneness of the covenant and the seriousness of denying this oneness: "[These] two [covenants] are actually one

---

teaching that the "blessed hope" of the church is the rapture, which gets the church out of the way so that God can fulfill his really important covenant with the Jews. It has always seemed to me that the ardent desire of dispensational, Baptist churches for their rapture, so that Christ may finally turn his attention to the Jews, is like the intense longing of a woman to be banished to a far country, so that her husband may make love to his other wife—a longing as ridiculous as it is inexplicable. And what is Christ doing with two wives?

9. "Certain madmen of the Anabaptist sect . . . regard the Israelites as nothing but a herd of swine . . . for they babble of the Israelites as fattened by the Lord on this earth without any hope of heavenly immortality" (Ibid., 2.10.1, 1:429).

and the same"; "[This truth] is very important"; "[The denial of this truth by the Anabaptists is] this pestilential error."[10]

Application of the Fundamental Importance of the Covenant

The Reformed churches must teach, and the members must know, God as the covenant God; Christ as the Christ of the covenant; salvation as the realization of the covenant with a covenant people; and the Christian life and experience as the practice and enjoyment of the covenant of grace.

How unbecoming, how ominous, is the silence concerning the covenant in many Reformed and Presbyterian churches today. The silence betrays lack of esteem for the covenant, if not total ignorance of it. It is as though a married woman would always be talking about the good things she gets from a certain man, while dismissing or ignoring the marriage to that man who is the source of the good things she receives. I use this figure advisedly. Scripture represents the covenant as God's marriage in Christ to the church and its members.[11]

One particularly glaring manifestation of sheer disregard for, if not total ignorance of, the covenant is that young people born to believers and baptized in infancy make a "decision for Christ" (as they say) in their teenage years (often under the pressure of a high-powered, Arminian evangelist) and then rejoice in the "personal relation" with God they have thus established. They should be rejoicing in *God's* covenant decision for them, already in their infancy, as expressed by baptism, and in the very personal relation of friendship that God's covenant decision has brought about between God and them by his Spirit.

It is the characteristic Baptist and dispensational minimizing of the covenant that renders the Baptist John Piper ineffectual against N. T. Wright, the influential advocate of the new perspective on Paul. Piper valiantly defends justification by faith alone against Wright's and the new perspective's denial of this cardinal doctrine. But as a Baptist, Piper does not, indeed cannot, grasp that Wright's doctrine of justification has its source

---

10. Ibid., 2.10.1–2, 1:428–29.
11. Ezekiel 16 and Ephesians 5:22–33.

in his doctrine of the covenant, as indeed Paul's doctrine of justification has its source in his doctrine of the covenant. Wright's response to Piper's attempt to defend the Reformation's doctrine of justification—an admirable attempt—is simply devastating.

> Paul's doctrine of justification is . . . about what we . . . call *the covenant*—the covenant God made with Abraham, the covenant whose purpose was from the beginning the saving call of a worldwide family through whom God's saving purposes for the world were to be realized. For Piper, and many like him, the very idea of . . . covenant . . . remains strangely foreign and alien. [12]

> *Recognize its* [the one covenant of grace established with Abraham] *existence* for Paul . . . and for any construction of his theology which wants to claim that it is faithful to his intention. For whenever you ignore it . . . you are cutting off the branch on which Paul's argument is resting. To highlight this element, which Reformed theology ought to welcome in its historic stress on the single plan of God (as opposed to having God change his mind in midstream [as is the teaching of dispensational Baptists such as John Piper]), is to insist on the wholeness of his train of thought.[13]

Wright demonstrates that justification by faith in Galatians 2 and 3, as also in the book of Romans, is a blessing of the covenant and cannot be understood if divorced from the covenant. Piper cannot get at the root of Wright's heresy, because that root is an erroneous doctrine of the covenant, and the very idea of covenant remains "strangely foreign and alien" to dispensational Piper.

Covenant was not "strangely foreign and alien" to John Calvin. On the contrary, it was fundamental. In the theology of Calvin, the doctrine of the covenant was fundamental simply because, as a perceptive, faithful interpreter of the word of God, Calvin did justice to the importance of the covenant of grace in Scripture.

---

12. Wright, *Justification,* 12.
13. Ibid., 94.

How important the reality of the covenant was to Calvin is seen even more clearly and convincingly when one considers the importance in Calvin of the union of the church and of believers and their children with Christ.

Nature of the Covenant

Calvin taught that the very essence of salvation is union with Jesus Christ and thus with the triune God. This is how Calvin opened his doctrine of salvation—soteriology in theological terms—in his *Institutes:*

> As long as Christ remains outside of us, and we are separated from him, all that he has suffered and done for the salvation of the human race remains useless and of no value for us. Therefore, to share with us what he has received from the Father, he had to become ours and to dwell within us ... We also ... are said to be "engrafted into him" [Rom. 11:17] ... for ... all that he possesses is nothing to us until we grow into one body with him.[14]

Calvin immediately added, "The Holy Spirit is the bond by which Christ effectually unites us to himself."[15]

A little later, treating of faith, Calvin wrote, "Not only does [Christ] cleave to us by an indivisible bond of fellowship, but with a wonderful communion, day by day, he grows more and more into one body with us, until he becomes completely one with us."[16]

In his defense of justification by faith alone, against the charge by Rome that the doctrine imperils a life of good works, Calvin replied that this is impossible. The impossibility resides in a saving work of the Spirit that precedes both justification and sanctification. This work always gives both the righteousness of justification and the consecration to God that is sanctification. It is the saving work of union with Christ.

> Although we may distinguish them [justification and sanc-

---

14. Calvin, *Institutes of the Christian Religion*, 3.1.1, 1:537.
15. Ibid.
16. Ibid., 3.2.24, 1:570–71.

tification], Christ contains both of them inseparably in himself. Do you wish, then, to attain righteousness in Christ? You must first possess Christ; but you cannot possess him without being made partaker in his sanctification, because he cannot be divided into pieces [1 Cor. 1:13].[17]

Salvation as union with Christ is everywhere in Calvin's theology. Union with Christ is the meaning and goal of the sacraments. Calvin defined baptism as "the sign of the initiation by which we are received into the society of the church, in order that, engrafted in Christ, we may be reckoned among God's children."[18] The meaning of the Lord's supper is, for Calvin, "this mystery of Christ's secret union with the devout."[19] The Heidelberg Catechism expresses Calvin's doctrine of the sacrament of the supper in Lord's Day 28:

> What is it to eat the crucified body and drink the shed blood of Christ?

> It is . . . to be so united more and more to his sacred body by the Holy Ghost, who dwells both in Christ and in us, that although he is in heaven, and we on the earth, we are nevertheless flesh of his flesh and bone of his bones.[20]

Union with Christ was also for Calvin the bliss and glory of eschatology. The bodily resurrection of the believer in the day of Christ will be "union with God . . . [as a] sacred bond." This union with God is "the highest good," as even the heathen philosopher Plato knew.[21] In raising his people from the dead, "[the Lord] will somehow make them to become one with himself." Calvin thought that "every sort of happiness is included under this benefit."[22]

If, as some in the later Reformed tradition, notably Herman Hoeksema, contended, union with Christ is the very nature,

---

17. Ibid., 3.16.1, 1:798.
18. Ibid., 4.15.1, 2:1393; emphasis added.
19. Ibid., 4.17.1, 2:1361.
20. Heidelberg Catechism, Q&A 76, in Schaff, *Creeds of Christendom*, 3:332–33.
21. Calvin, *Institutes of the Christian Religion*, 3.25.2, 2:988.
22. Ibid., 3.25.10, 2:1005.

or essence, of the covenant of grace, Calvin ascribed to the covenant the fundamental importance of being everlasting salvation itself.[23]

Calvin did not, in fact, definitively and consistently describe the covenant as union with Christ and fellowship with God. But there are compelling indications in Calvin that he viewed the covenant as essentially a relationship of fellowship with God in Christ.

First, Calvin called the union with Christ that he regarded as the essence of salvation and the highest good "wedlock": The union of the people of God with Christ is "that sacred wedlock through which we are made flesh of his flesh and bone of his bone [Eph. 5:30], and thus one with him."[24] "Wedlock" alludes to God's marriage to the church of both the Old Testament and the New Testament, and this marriage is the covenant, as Calvin well knew.[25] "Wedlock" is a living bond of communion in love.

Second, there are numerous, explicit statements in Calvin's writings that describe the covenant as essentially the relationship of fellowship in love between God in Christ and the elect church. Two such statements occur in Calvin's commentary on the great covenant passage in Jeremiah 31:31–34, God's promise of the new covenant with Israel and Judah—a promise fulfilled in Jesus Christ in the covenant of grace with the church, ac-

---

23. For Hoeksema's doctrine of the covenant as a bond of fellowship between God in Christ and the elect church, see his *Reformed Dogmatics* (Grand Rapids, MI: Reformed Free Publishing Association, 1966), 285–336 and his *Believers and Their Seed*. His insights concerning the nature of the covenant as a living bond of communion and concerning the importance of the covenant as the highest good and the supreme blessedness of salvation, rather than merely a means by which salvation is obtained, were much earlier than the publication dates of these two books might suggest. Hoeksema wrote *Believers and Their Seed* (in Dutch) in the 1920s. His dogmatics was the content of his instruction in the Protestant Reformed Seminary from its very beginning in the middle 1920s. In those days he had virtually all Reformed and Presbyterian theologians against him. All were teaching that the covenant is a contract and that it is merely the means by which the sinner may obtain salvation.

24. Calvin, *Institutes of the Christian Religion*, 3.1.3, 3:541.

25. Ezekiel 16 describes God's covenant with Old Testament Israel as marriage. Ephesians 5:22–33 extols the fulfillment of the covenant with the New Testament church as marriage—the *real* marriage. Revelation 19:7–9 prophesies the perfection of the covenant in the new world as the marriage of the "Lamb . . . and his wife."

cording to Hebrews 8–10. Calvin observed that the word "covenant" used by God in the promise of the new covenant was more "honorable" for Israel and Judah than the word "edict" would have been. The word "covenant" shows that God "deals with his own people more kindly" than does a king who imperiously places his people under edicts. "Covenant" means that God "descends and appears in the midst of them [his people], that he may bind himself to his people, as he binds the people to himself."[26]

Regarding the words "[I] will be their God, and they shall be my people" (Jer. 31:33), words that express what the covenant *is* and words that Calvin elsewhere called "the very formula of the covenant,"[27] Calvin explained, "Here God comprehends generally the substance of his covenant."[28]

Conception of the Covenant As a Contract

Most Reformed churches and theologians have not followed this lead of Calvin or allowed the covenant formula to determine their understanding of the essence of the covenant. Rather, they have viewed the covenant as a contract, or an agreement, or even as a bargain between God and men, as though the covenant were similar to a business deal.

The conception of the covenant as a contract is embedded deeply in the Reformed tradition. The English Puritan William Perkins defined the covenant as God's "contract with man, concerning the obtaining of life eternall, upon a certaine condition." Perkins added, "This covenant consists of two parts: Gods promise to man, Mans promise to God. Gods promise to man, is that, whereby he bindeth himselfe to man to be his God, if he performe the condition."[29]

---

26. Calvin, *Jeremiah*, 4:129.
27. Calvin, *Institutes of the Christian Religion*, 2.10.8, 1:434.
28. Calvin, *Jeremiah*, 4:133.
29. William Perkins, "A Golden Chaine," in *The Workes of . . . Mr. William Perkins*, vol. 1 (London: John Legatt, 1626), 32. It ought to be noted that Perkins by no means intended to separate covenant from election. His definition of the covenant immediately follows Perkins' assertion that the covenant is the outward meanes of executing the decree of Election (31).

The Presbyterian Sum of Saving Knowledge, a document drawn up at the time of the Westminster Assembly and often published with the Westminster standards, and thus influential in forming the doctrine of the covenant in the minds of Presbyterians, is crass. It calls the covenant God's "bargain" with the sinner and views the sinner's acceptance of God's "offer" of the covenant as the sinner's "closing" of the "bargain." "Let the penitent desiring to believe ... say heartily to the Lord ... 'I have hearkened unto the offer of an everlasting covenant of all saving mercies to be had in Christ, and I do heartily embrace thy offer. Lord, let it be a bargain.'"[30]

The popular Louis Berkhof defined the covenant of grace as "that gracious agreement between the offended God and the offending but elect sinner."[31] He described God and the sinner as "contracting parties."[32]

According to Klaas Schilder, "*Covenant* is the mutual *agreement* between God and his people, established by him himself, and maintained (according to his gracious work) by him himself and his people as two 'parties.'"[33] The parenthetical phrase "according to his gracious work," obscures but does not in the least blunt the force of Schilder's clear, bold statement that the covenant is maintained by God *and by his people*. This statement explains what Schilder meant by conditions of and in the covenant. Although the covenant is established by God alone (with every child of godly parents alike, Esau as well as Jacob), it depends for its continuance with a child and for its realization in the everlasting salvation of a child upon works that the child must perform. This implies that the covenant, its blessings, and salvation, though graciously established with and bestowed upon a child, can be lost. The men of the federal vision are doing nothing more or other than making explicit what lay (and lies) implicit in this

---

30. Sum of Saving Knowledge, in *The Subordinate Standards and Other Authoritative Documents of the Free Church of Scotland* (Edinburgh: repr. William Blackwood & Sons, 1973), 196.

31. Louis Berkhof, *Systematic Theology* (Grand Rapids, MI: Eerdmans, 1938), 277.

32. Ibid., 284.

33. Schilder, *Looze Kalk,* 66. The emphasis is Schilder's.

doctrine of the covenant and developing it—developing it in the open denial of justification by faith alone and of all the doctrines of grace confessed in the Canons of Dordt. A little earlier in the chapter in which he gave the definition of the covenant quoted above, *in the context of denying that election governs the covenant,* Schilder asserted that the covenant is conditional.[34]

The seriousness of this sterile conception of the covenant is not only that it sucks the life out of the covenant. A bond of communion in love, like earthly marriage, is vibrant, warm, interesting, and exciting; a contract is a cold, calculating, and lifeless business. But the notion of contract, or agreement, also inherently jeopardizes, indeed compromises, the grace of the covenant and its salvation. It does this in two ways. For one thing, contract makes the establishment and fulfillment of the covenant the cooperative work of God and the sinner. It takes two to draw up and ratify a contract; two parties hammer out and keep an agreement. For another thing, contract suspends the covenant, its salvation, and all its benefits upon stipulations, or conditions, that the sinner must perform.

The idea of the covenant as a contract militates against two fundamental aspects of the grace of God's covenant. First, the covenant is established, kept, and perfected by God alone. The history of Old Testament Israel demonstrates that the covenant is unilateral not only in its establishment, but also in its maintenance and fulfillment. That God, and God alone, maintains and fulfills the covenant that he, and he alone, established with Israel is the doctrinal message of Ezekiel 16. God unilaterally established the covenant with Israel: "I sware unto thee, and entered into a covenant with thee, saith the Lord God" (v. 8). God also unilaterally keeps and fulfills this covenant. After a long history of Israel's egregious, appalling unfaithfulness to her divine husband, when all that could be expected was God's angry or sorrowful acknowledgment of the breaking of the covenant by his people, God announced, "Nevertheless I will remember my covenant with thee in the days of thy youth, and I will establish unto thee an everlasting covenant" (v. 60). This everlasting covenant is the new covenant in Jesus Christ.

---

34. He used the word *verbondsvoorwaarden,* in ibid., 59.

The second aspect of the grace of God's covenant against which the contract conception militates is that the covenant (which, as Calvin noted, is "founded on Christ"[35]), the blessings it bestows, and the salvation it promises depend upon God alone. Concerning the redemption, regeneration, and sanctification of his chosen, covenant people, Jehovah declares that he does all these things, "not . . . for your sakes . . . but for my holy name's sake" (Ezek. 36:21–38).

This intrinsic opposition of the contract conception of the covenant to sovereign grace is boldly expressed, and clearly disclosed, today by zealous advocates of the contract conception in these words, which have become virtually a mantra: "Covenant is not identical with election." Granted, this determined opposition to sovereign grace in the covenant is subtly couched in deceptive terminology, suggesting that some Reformed theologians are so stupid as to *identify* the eternal decree and the historical working out of the decree. But what is meant by the mantra is that the covenant is not governed by God's eternal decree of election in Christ. The covenant of grace with its gracious promise, its establishment with a baptized baby by uniting him or her savingly to Christ, its bestowal of at least some of the blessings of salvation, its continuance with the child, and its realization in the everlasting salvation of the child is cut loose from divine election.

And this is the issue between two rival doctrines of the covenant in the Reformed tradition: on the one hand, a doctrine of the covenant as a gracious but conditional contract with all the baptized children of believing parents alike and, on the other hand, a doctrine of the covenant as a bond of communion with Christ that God graciously and unconditionally establishes, keeps, and perfects with the elect children only. The former denies, whereas the latter confesses, that election governs the covenant.

---

35. Calvin, *Harmony of the Evangelists*, 1:70.

Chapter 7

CALVIN'S DOCTRINE OF THE COVENANT: COVENANT AND ELECTION

In the theology of John Calvin, the covenant is always closely related to, indeed is inseparable from, election. The relation is that election governs the covenant.

Election: "Foundation and First Cause"

That election governs the covenant in Calvin's theology should surprise no one who has the least knowledge of Calvin's thinking. The saving grace of God in Christ, for John Calvin, as for all the reformers, *has its source in election and is, therefore, strictly determined by election.* The covenant bestows this saving grace of God in Jesus Christ, chiefly the saving grace of justification on the basis of the cross, as Paul teaches in Galatians 3. The justification of the Gentiles by faith is the grace that God promised when he established the covenant with Abraham: "And the scripture, foreseeing that God would justify the heathen through faith, preached before the gospel unto Abraham, saying, In thee shall all nations be blessed" (v. 8). If saving grace, particularly justification, has its source in, and is determined by, election (as Calvin devoted his life to proclaiming) and if the grace of the covenant is saving grace, chiefly justification (as no one denies), it follows that the covenant and its grace have their source in, and are governed by, election.

The reason that Calvin treated predestination after the doctrine of salvation in the 1559 *Institutes* was to emphasize that election is the source of all God's grace and salvation in Jesus Christ. Calvin explained:

> We shall never be clearly persuaded, as we ought to be, that our salvation flows from the wellspring of God's free mercy until we come to know his eternal election, which illumines God's grace by this contrast: that he does not indiscrimi-

nately adopt all into the hope of salvation but gives to some what he denies to others.

Calvin's definition of predestination follows:

> We call predestination God's eternal decree, by which he compacted with himself what he willed to become of each man. For all are not created in equal condition; rather, eternal life is foreordained for some, eternal damnation for others. Therefore, as any man has been created to one or the other of these ends, we speak of him as predestined to life or to death.[1]

In his "Treatise on the Eternal Predestination of God," Calvin contended with an opponent who, like the men of the federal vision today, taught that God chooses those who make good use of his grace, which he bestows on all: "He chose us out of all men, because He foresaw that that which was set before all men for their reception [that is, God's grace] would become peculiar to us, who alone would receive it."[2]

Against this "folly" Calvin responded, with reference to Ephesians 1:3–12, by declaring that all of God's grace and saving work in Jesus Christ have their source in and depend upon God's eternal election.

> God is said to have saved us "according to His good pleasure which He purposed in Himself" for this very reason, because, finding no *cause* in us, He *made Himself* the *cause* of our salvation. Is it for nothing, think ye, that the apostle repeats five times over that the whole of our salvation is the effect of, and dependent upon, that eternal decree, purpose and good pleasure of God? Is it with no intent whatever that the apostle declares that we were "blessed" in Christ because we were "chosen" in Christ? Does not the apostle refer all sanctification and every good work to the election of God, as waters are traced to their originating source? Does not Paul attribute it to the same grace that we are the "workmanship of God, created unto good works, which He

---

1. Calvin, *Institutes of the Christian Religion*, 3.21.1, 5, 2:921, 926.
2. John Calvin, "A Treatise on the Eternal Predestination of God," in *Calvin's Calvinism*, trans. Henry Cole (Grand Rapids, MI: Eerdmans, 1956), 153.

hath before ordained that we should walk in them"? Why did God choose us out, and separate us from the rest, but that we might know that we are what we are, and that we are blessed above all others by the free favour of God alone?[3]

Commenting on Ephesians 1:4, "According as he [God] hath chosen us in him [our Lord Jesus Christ] before the foundation of the world, that we should be holy and without blame before him," Calvin taught the same truth. Every saving grace and all the divine work of salvation have their origin in, depend upon, and are determined by God's eternal decree of election.

> The foundation and first cause, both of our calling and of all the benefits which we receive from God, is here declared to be his eternal election. If the reason is asked, why God has called us to enjoy the gospel, why he daily bestows upon us so many blessings, why he opens to us the gate of heaven— the answer will be constantly found in this principle, that *he hath chosen us before the foundation of the world* . . . This leads us to conclude, that holiness, purity, and every excellence that is found among men, are the fruit of election.[4]

Well aware of the alternative to viewing election as the source, foundation, and determination of God's grace and saving work, Calvin astutely concluded: "Election, therefore, does not depend on the righteousness of works, of which Paul here declares that it is the cause."[5]

That Calvin, whose whole ministry was devoted to the defense of election as the source of the grace of God in Christ Jesus, would place the grace of the covenant outside the government of election is unthinkable on the very face of it.

The fact is that when Calvin contended for the truth that the grace and salvation of God are governed by God's eternal predestination, he invariably appealed to Romans 9, which speaks of God's grace *in the covenant*—grace to Jacob but not to Esau,

---

3. Ibid., 154.
4. John Calvin, *Commentaries on the Epistles of Paul to the Galatians and Ephesians*, trans. William Pringle (Grand Rapids, MI: Eerdmans, 1957), 197–98.
5. Ibid., 199

both being sons of godly parents. Against the "sentiments" of Pighius—that "wild beast"—that "the mercy of God is extended to every one, for God wishes all men to be saved; and for that end He stands and knocks at the door of our heart, desiring to enter" (sentiments that in the twenty-first century widely pass for Calvinistic orthodoxy, and the rejection of which earns from this novel Calvinistic orthodoxy the opprobrium "hyper-Calvinistic"), Calvin appealed to Paul's assertion in Romans 9 that "out of the twins, while they were yet in the womb of their mother, the one was *chosen* and the other *rejected!* and that, too, without any respect to the works of either, present or future . . . but solely by the good pleasure of God that calleth!"[6]

How closely Calvin related covenant and election is evident in his introduction of predestination into the *Institutes:*

> In actual fact, the *covenant of life* is not preached equally
> among all men, and among those to whom it is preached,
> it does not gain the same acceptance either constantly or in
> equal degree. In this diversity the wonderful depth of God's
> judgment is made known. For there is no doubt that this
> variety also serves the decision of God's eternal election.[7]

For Calvin, not only is the covenant of life closely related to election, so that the truth of the latter must be spoken in the same breath with the reality of the former, but the covenant is also governed and controlled by election. And not only is the saving purpose and effect of the covenant (the covenant's gaining "acceptance") determined by election ("this variety . . . serves the decision of God's eternal election"), but even the *preaching* of the covenant to some and not to others is also determined by election ("the covenant of life is not preached equally among all men").

In the context of his consideration of the shameful degeneracy of the Jews in the Old Testament, an apostasy that might seem to imperil God's covenant with them, Calvin assured his

---

6. Calvin, *Calvin's Calvinism*, 152.
7. Calvin, *Institutes of the Christian Religion*, 3.21.1, 2:920–21; emphasis added.

readers that "[God's] freely given covenant, *whereby God had adopted his elect,* would stand fast."[8]

Calvin insisted that the promise of the covenant is for the elect only, so that God establishes the new covenant with the elect, and the elect only. Commenting on the outstanding prophecy of the new covenant in Jeremiah 31:31–34, Calvin wrote:

> This is that one of the two covenants which God promises that He will not make with any but with His own children and His own elect people, concerning whom He has recorded His promise that "He will *write* His law *in their hearts*" (Jer. 31:33). Now, a man must be utterly beside himself to assert that this promise is made to all men generally and indiscriminately. God says expressly by Paul, who refers to the prophet Jeremiah, "For this is the covenant that I will make *with them.* Not according to the covenant that I made with their fathers: but I will put My laws into their mind, and write them in their hearts" (Heb. 8:9–10).[9]

What makes this statement of Calvin concerning the government of the covenant promise by election even more weighty is that Calvin made the statement in refutation of Pighius' doctrine that God's grace is universal, that is, not governed by an eternal election of some in distinction from others. Calvin had just noted that Pighius contended that the grace of God is intended for, and therefore made available to (well-meaningly offered to, that is, with a sincere desire on God's part to save), all men, with appeal to 1 Timothy 2:4 and Ezekiel 18:23. These are the favorite texts of the novel Calvinistic orthodoxy of the twenty-first century, and explained and applied by this novel orthodoxy exactly as did the old Roman Catholic heretic Albertus Pighius. Pighius, who received rough treatment at the hands of Calvin, was born too soon. In the twenty-first century, Pighius would be the leading authority and spokesman of the novel Calvinistic orthodoxy, that is, of the doctrine that the saving grace of God both on the mission field and in the covenant is universal and resistible. To deny that election

8. Ibid., 2.6.4, 1:346; emphasis added.
9. Calvin, *Calvin's Calvinism,* 100–101.

governs the covenant is necessarily to confess that God's (saving) grace is wider than election, dependent for its efficacy upon the will or works of the sinner, and resistible—the doctrine of Pighius.

In the sphere of the covenant, election governs the preaching of the gospel with regard to its saving purpose and power. Commenting on Isaiah 54:13, "all thy children shall be taught of the LORD," Calvin declared, "The Gospel is preached indiscriminately to the elect and the reprobate; but the elect alone come to Christ, because they have been 'taught by God.'" Calvin added, "Therefore to *them* [the elect] the Prophet undoubtedly refers," which means that, for Calvin, Zion's children (for they are the children spoken of in Isaiah 54:13) are the elect, not all the physical offspring of Abraham.[10]

As this last citation shows, Calvin explained the seed of Abraham, the house of Israel, and the children of believers as the elect among the physical descendants of Abraham, among the physical inhabitants of Israel's house, and among the physical offspring of believers. It is a principle of Calvin's interpretation of the Old Testament that Galatians 3 and Romans 9 determine who the true children of Abraham and the legitimate house of Israel are—the children and house to whom God is gracious, to whom the covenant promise is directed, and with whom God establishes his covenant.

With reference to the fact that many of the natural descendants of Abraham were unbelieving and perished, which might seem to indicate the failure of God's covenant promise to Abraham, Calvin wrote: "[The apostle] by no means makes the fleshly seed the legitimate children of Abraham, but counts the *children of the promise* alone for the seed."[11] Having restricted the "legitimate children of Abraham" to the children of the promise, as the apostle does in Romans 9, Calvin was not content to identify these legitimate children as those who believe. With appeal to the apostle in Romans 9, Calvin insisted on identifying the "legitimate children"—the true seed of the covenant—as the elect: "[The apostle] ascends higher [than the faith of the children] into the mind of

---

10. John Calvin, *Commentary on the Book of the Prophet Isaiah*, trans. William Pringle (Grand Rapids, MI: Eerdmans, 1956), 4:146; emphasis added.

11. Calvin, *Calvin's Calvinism*, 56; emphasis added.

God, and declares that those were the children of promise whom God chose before they were born."[12]

When Calvin sometimes said that the covenant is established with all the physical offspring of Abraham (as he did), he invariably added that the covenant is not established with all *in the same way* and that there is, in fact, among the physical offspring of Abraham *"a twofold class of sons."* These two kinds of children of Abraham are determined by God's eternal predestination.[13]

---

12. Ibid. Throughout his commentaries on the Old Testament, Calvin practiced his hermeneutical rule of interpreting Old Testament Scripture, particularly the prophets, in the light of the teaching of Romans 9 and Galatians 3 that the children of the covenant are God's elect—Christ and those whom the Father gave him. One instance, among countless others, is Calvin's commentary on Zechariah 1:15. Calvin explained that the "little" displeasure of God with his sinful people "must be applied to the elect . . . for he speaks not of the reprobate and of that impure mass from which he purposed to cleanse his own house; but he hath respect to his covenant" (John Calvin, *Commentaries on the Twelve Minor Prophets,* vol. 5, *Zechariah and Malachi,* trans. John Owen [Grand Rapids, MI: Eerdmans, 1950], 47).

13. See his commentary on Genesis 17:7, in John Calvin, *Commentaries on the First Book of Moses Called Genesis,* trans. John King (Grand Rapids, MI: Eerdmans, 1948), 1:447–551. In strongly affirming the truth that all the physical offspring of Abraham are included in the *administration* of the covenant, Calvin used incautious, indeed erroneous, language, which at that early stage of the development of the doctrine of the covenant is to be expected. But he immediately set things straight regarding the fundamental issue by distinguishing two kinds of "sons" in the covenant, in accordance with God's eternal predestination. Summing up his explanation of the children of Abraham, Calvin wrote: "Here, then, a twofold class of sons presents itself to us, in the Church; for since the whole body of the people is gathered together into the fold of God, by one and the same voice, all without exception, are, in this respect, accounted children; the name of the Church is applicable in common to them all: *but in the innermost sanctuary of God, none others are reckoned the sons of God, than they in whom the promise is ratified by faith. And although this difference flows from the fountain of gratuitous election, whence also faith itself springs; yet, since the counsel of God is in itself hidden from us, we therefore distinguish the true from the spurious children, by the respective marks of faith and of unbelief"* (449; emphasis added). Calvin's final word is that, under the administration of the covenant, there are "true" children and "spurious" children and that this radical difference between the "twofold class" of children is determined by eternal predestination. This is the fundamental issue in the controversy between the two doctrines of the covenant that now comes to a head in the heresy of the federal vision. And this, the defenders of the doctrine of a conditional covenant made with all the children alike, and the men of the federal vision, reject.

Identifying the true, legitimate children of the covenant as the elect in Christ, Calvin was simply teaching what the apostle teaches in Galatians 3: The seed of the covenant to whom the promise was made and with whom the covenant was established is "Christ" (v. 16) and all those, but those only, who "[are] Christ's," ultimately because of divine election (v. 29).

Because the covenant has its source in and is governed by election, for Calvin the covenant is sure and steadfast. It depends upon the promising God, not upon the working children. It is founded upon Christ and his cross, not upon conditions performed by little children (or, for that matter, grown men and women). Its source is the gracious will of God in eternity, not the will of man.

Commenting on Lamentations 2:1, the prophet's lament over the destruction of Jerusalem and the seeming failure of the covenant because of the unfaithfulness of Judah, Calvin proclaimed: "Though men were a hundred times perfidious, yet God never changes, but remains unchangeable in his faithfulness; and we know that his covenant was not made to depend on the merits of men [that is, men's works]."[14]

The Covenant: Unconditional

That the covenant has its source in and is governed by election implies that the covenant is unconditional. As never before in the history of Reformed thought about the covenant, it is imperative today that theologians make unmistakably clear what they mean by the conditionality or unconditionality of the covenant. The meaning of unconditionality in the ages-long controversy over the covenant, culminating today in the life-or-death struggle of Reformed orthodoxy with the federal vision, is *not* that there is no necessary means by which God realizes his covenant with the elect, namely, faith. This means is the gift of God in the covenant (Eph. 2:8).

Neither is the meaning of unconditionality that the covenant is not "mutual." Of course, the covenant is mutual. The right conception of the covenant views it as a relationship of love in

---

14. Calvin, *Jeremiah*, 5:343.

which God befriends and saves his children in sovereign love and the children cleave to and serve God in thankful love. To "cleave . . . to . . . God" is their *part* in the covenant. [15] This is the language of the Reformed baptism form, which does not call a second, contracting *party* to perform conditions, carry out an agreement, or keep its end of a bargain. But in a lovely, apt, Spirit-influenced word, the form admonishes and obliges God's covenant children to do their part by cleaving to their Father.

Cleaving is not the activity of one who is negotiating an agreement, carrying out the stipulations of a contract, or keeping his end of a bargain. Cleaving is the activity of a child, responding spontaneously to a mother's tender love; of a woman drawn ineluctably by her husband's fervent love; and of a friend who finds his or her friend irresistibly dear. Cleaving is willing, ardent, thankful love desiring God and therefore seeking closer, ever closer, communion with the good, gracious, and desirable God who has first loved us in Jesus Christ. Cleaving is covenant mutuality. It differs radically from conditional, contractual mutuality.

The realizing of this mutuality and thus of our doing our part in the covenant is the efficacious work of the Spirit of the covenant Christ in God's covenant people, as the third and fourth heads of the Canons of Dordt make confessional for all churches and persons who call themselves Reformed.

Neither is the meaning of unconditionality that there are no demands in the covenant. There certainly are demands in the covenant, as God made perfectly clear when he established the covenant with Abraham: "Thou shalt keep my covenant therefore" (Gen. 17:9). Creedal, Reformed Christianity condemns the denial of demands in the covenant, as in the Christian life, as antinomianism. The willing performance of the demands by the covenant people, essentially the keeping of God's law, is an important aspect of God's own work of covenant salvation, as

---

15. "Whereas in all covenants there are contained two parts, therefore are we by God, through baptism, admonished of and obliged unto new obedience, namely, that we cleave to this one God, Father, Son, and Holy Ghost," etc. (Form for the Administration of Baptism, in *Confessions and Church Order*, 258).

the promise of Jeremiah 31:33 makes plain: "I will put my law in their inward parts," and as Augustine taught us long ago: "[O God], give what Thou commandest, and command what Thou wilt."[16]

In the past, orthodox champions of grace have sometimes inaccurately referred to the necessary means of the covenant, the essential mutuality of the covenant, and the fitting demands of the covenant as "conditions." Although their terminology was faulty, and even dangerous, their theology of the covenant was sound. The great covenant controversy, now coming to a head in the federal vision, is not strife about words.

The meaning of unconditionality is very simply that the gracious promise of the covenant, the gracious establishment of the covenant with one, and the gracious bestowal of covenant blessings (and union with Christ certainly is the covenant blessing par excellence) *are not wider in scope than election*. Rather, the grace of the covenant is determined by election.

The meaning of unconditionality is very simply that the realization of the promise with a child, the maintenance of the covenant with a child, and the child's everlasting salvation *do not depend upon something the child does, regardless that the child is said to perform the condition with the help of God*. Rather, the covenant and its salvation depend solely upon the sovereign will and grace of God.

The meaning of unconditionality is very simply that the explanation why some baptized children finally inherit eternal life in the day of Jesus Christ, whereas other baptized children do not inherit eternal life, *is not that, although all alike were the objects of the covenant favor of God and savingly united to Christ, some distinguished themselves from the others, showed themselves worthy of eternal life, or obtained eternal life, by their own work of believing and obeying*. Rather, the explanation is that God, in sovereign, discriminating grace, chose some unto eternal life in the covenant, whereas he reprobated others.

---

16. Augustine, "Confessions," 10.29, in *Nicene and Post-Nicene Fathers,* ed. Philip Schaff, vol. 1, *Confession and Letters of St. Augustin* (Grand Rapids, MI: Eerdmans, 1956), 153.

That some children of believers receive the gift of faith from God, and other children of believers do not receive it, proceeds from God's eternal decree.[17]

Calvin expressly declared that the covenant of grace with Abraham and Christ, which is the subject of the passage in Galatians 3 that Calvin was explaining, is unconditional. Having just repudiated the teaching that "salvation would be suspended on the condition of satisfying the law," Calvin stated, "He [the apostle in Galatians 3:18] immediately adds, *God gave it* [the inheritance, that is, the covenant promise], not by requiring some sort of compensation on his part, but by free promise; for if you view it as conditional, the word *gave* . . . would be utterly inapplicable."[18]

C. Graafland, who rejects Calvin's covenant doctrine, freely and correctly acknowledges that for Calvin election governs the covenant: "[Calvin] saw the decisive factor of the covenant locked up in the eternal, divine decree of election and reprobation. Because others (the humanists) did not want to know anything of this, Calvin lays even heavier stress on it."[19]

Covenant in Calvin is not a device with which to weaken, obscure, ignore, oppose, and in the end bury in utter oblivion God's decree of predestination. On the contrary, in the Reformed faith of John Calvin the covenant has its source in, serves, and is governed by the gracious election of God in Jesus Christ.

The great evil in the Reformed theology of the twenty-first

---

17. See Canons of Dordt, 2.6, in Schaff, *Creeds of Christendom*, 3:582.

18. Calvin, *Galatians and Ephesians*, 98; emphasis is Calvin's.

19. Graafland, *Van Calvijn tot Comrie*, 3:395. Such is their fear, if not detestation, of God's sovereign, gracious election in Jesus Christ that the defenders of a conditional covenant, among whom is C. Graafland, cannot describe the relation of election and covenant as taught by the defenders of an unconditional covenant otherwise than in pejorative words. In the quotation just given, Graafland speaks of the covenant's being "locked up" in the decree of election and reprobation, in Calvin's theology, like an unfortunate prisoner in a dank, dark cell. Elsewhere, Graafland (and many others) mournfully refers to election's "oppression" of the covenant and gravely alleges the unresolvable and threatening "tension" between covenant and election in the theology of those who affirm that election governs the covenant. Whatever else this astounding suspicion of God's election may indicate about these Reformed and Presbyterian theologians, it shows their radical difference from John Calvin.

---

century is not that some few *identify* covenant and election, to the praise of the electing God. Rather, the evil (and a great evil it is) is that many tear covenant and election apart, to the praise of willing and working man.

We covenant friends of God must live in covenant communion with Christ, enjoying the magnificent covenant blessings (chief among which is justification by faith alone), certain of our continuing in the covenant, trusting firmly in Jesus Christ, zealously performing the good works that are the demand of the covenant, and hoping without doubt for the eternal life and glory that will be ours at the coming of Christ—conscious ourselves that all of this is due to God's sovereign, gracious election and loudly testifying both to the ignorant world and to the dubious Reformed churches that the entire reality of the covenant has its source in and depends upon the electing God. That is, we ought to be conscious ourselves and testify to all and sundry that the covenant is God's covenant of divine grace, rather than a divine/human contract of (decisive) human conditions.

Then we also have confidence concerning our dear children and grandchildren that "the children of thy servants shall continue, and their seed shall be established before thee" (Ps. 102:28)

CALVIN'S DOCTRINE OF THE COVENANT: ELECT INFANTS IN THE COVENANT

In the controversy over the covenant that has endured and often raged in the Reformed tradition, the infant children of believing parents have figured prominently.

Infant Baptism

Indeed, the truth about the children of believers occasioned the distinctively Reformed development of the doctrine of the covenant at the time of the sixteenth-century Reformation of the church. Ulrich Zwingli, John Calvin, and others were compelled to treat the doctrine of the covenant by the Anabaptist refusal to baptize infants.

Again and again, controversy regarding the covenant erupted in the Reformed churches over the meaning of the Reformed baptism form concerning infants and over the right view of baptized children. This was the nature of the covenant controversy in the churches of the Secession in the Netherlands in the nineteenth century, of the covenant controversy in the RCN in the twentieth century, and of the covenant controversy in the Protestant Reformed Churches in the twentieth century.

Often, churches split over the issue of the right understanding of the inclusion of infants in the covenant of grace.

Today, the heresy of the federal vision in the conservative Reformed and Presbyterian churches of North America centers on the perennial questions: How are we to explain the baptism of the infants of godly parents? How are we to view baptized children? What is the meaning of God's covenant promise to the children of believers?

The fundamental issue in the controversy over the covenant in Reformed churches down the ages to the present is whether the sacrament of baptism is conditional grace to all the children or unconditional grace to the elect children only.

But other important issues also are involved. Does infant baptism mean nothing more than that the little children are formally set apart as special objects of evangelism—the evangelizing of those whose spiritual condition is no different from that of unregenerated heathens—so that in later life (often, *much* later life) they may be converted and saved? Are they, therefore, to be presumed to be, and viewed as, unregenerated, unsaved little vipers, until in maturity they show signs of regeneration and confess their faith? Are the children to grow up *viewing themselves as* little vipers? That is, is infant baptism, oddly, to be explained as teaching that God does *not* save infant children—*in their infancy?*

Or, does infant baptism mean infant salvation of the elect children of believers, as the divine rule, so that the children are to be reared from earliest childhood in the nurture and admonition of the Lord Jesus? Are they to be viewed, and to view themselves, not as little vipers, but as beloved sons and daughters of God? That is, does infant baptism signify infant salvation?

By no means is it accidental, much less unfortunate, that the great covenant controversy in the Reformed tradition has always swirled about the children of believers. God's own covenant promise has always included, and even emphasized, the child and the children.

The first promise of the gospel of the covenant laid emphasis on the woman's seed: God will put enmity between the woman's seed and the seed of the serpent. Everything depends on the woman's seed. He will crush the serpent's head, thus saving the woman and the rest of her children (Gen. 3:15).

The covenant promise to Noah encompassed his children: "And God spake unto Noah, and to his sons with him, saying, And I, behold, I establish my covenant with you, and with your seed after you" (Gen. 9:8–9). The same was, and is, true of the covenant established by promise with Abraham: "And I will establish my covenant between me and thee and thy seed after thee in their generations for an everlasting covenant, to be a

God unto thee, and to thy seed after thee" (Gen. 17:7). The Davidic covenant likewise looked to David's seed: "I will set up thy seed after thee, which shall proceed out of thy bowels" (2 Sam. 7:12). That individual child of David will also have children, to whom the covenant promise extends, according to Psalm 89:29: "His seed will I make to endure for ever."

That the new covenant, no less than the old covenant, includes the children of the godly, the Spirit made clear on the day that the old was fulfilled in the new: "The promise is unto you, and to your children, and to all that are afar off, even as many as the Lord our God shall call" (Acts 2:39).

The children of believers are dear to God. They are his children. Such is the greatness of his grace to those who fear him that he takes their children, naturally guilty and totally depraved, into the fellowship of his Son. Jesus, therefore, required the infant children to be brought to him as proper objects of his blessing and salvation, acknowledging them, *in their infancy,* as citizens of his kingdom. "Suffer little children [infants] to come unto me, and forbid them not: for of such is the kingdom of God" (Luke 18:16).

In his love of the little children of believers, God hates divorce (and the inevitable remarriage that follows divorce). Divorce is destructive, often eternally destructive, of the children. "The LORD, the God of Israel, saith that he hateth putting away [divorce]" (Mal. 2:16). The reason for this hatred of divorce, according to the prophet, is that he "seek[s] a godly seed" (v. 15). Godly children are the fruit of good rearing by married parents in a godly, peaceful, solid home.

Because of the inclusion of children in the covenant, when in the past, Reformed churches lived out of the covenant, they demanded good Christian schoolteachers for the children of the church and therefore good Christian schools. In Article 21 of the Reformed church order, the Synod of Dordt required that "the consistories shall everywhere see to it that there are good schoolteachers, who not only teach the children to read, to write, to speak, and the liberal arts, but also instruct them in godliness and in the Catechism."[1]

---

1. H. Bouwman, "Scholen" [Schools], in *Gereformeerd Kerkrecht* [Reformed

In light both of the inclusion of the children of believers in the covenant and of the controversy in the Reformed tradition over the right understanding of this inclusion, it will be profitable to hear Calvin on the subject of the covenant and the children of believers.

Of vital importance to Calvin was the inclusion in the new covenant of the infant children of believing parents. Scripture teaches the inclusion of infants inasmuch as the new covenant in Christ is one and the same covenant as the covenant established with Abraham, and the covenant with Abraham included Abraham's infant child and subsequent infant descendants (Gen. 17:7). "The covenant which the Lord once made with Abraham [cf. v. 14] is no less in force today for Christians than it was of old for the Jewish people."[2] If the new covenant excludes the children of the godly, whereas the Old Testament form of the covenant included them, "Christ by his coming lessened or curtailed the grace of the Father—but this is nothing but execrable blasphemy!"[3]

The New Testament abundantly corroborates the conclusive testimony regarding the inclusion of children based on the unity of the covenant. On the day of the revelation of the fulfillment of the covenant with Abraham, Acts 2:39 extends the covenant promise to the children of believers: "The promise is unto you, and to your children." "To the same point applies Peter's announcement to the Jews [Acts 2:39] that the benefit of the gospel belongs to them and their offspring by right of the covenant."[4] Nothing has changed in the new covenant with regard to the inclusion of children!

The incident of Jesus' reception and blessing of infant children, because "of such is the kingdom of God" (Luke 18:15–17), was extremely important to Calvin. Again and again, he appealed to the passage in Luke and to the parallel passages in Matthew 19 and Mark 10 in his defense of children in the

---

church polity], vol. 1 (Kampen: Kok, 1928), 518. The translation of the Dutch is mine.

2. Calvin, *Institutes of the Christian Religion*, 4.16.6, 2:1328.

3. Ibid.

4. Ibid., 4.16.15, 2:1337.

covenant and of infant baptism. Noting that the Greek word used in Luke 18:15 refers to "infants at the breast," Calvin argued, "If it is right for infants to be brought to Christ, why not also to be received into baptism, the symbol of our communion and fellowship with Christ?"[5]

In addition, there is the policy of the apostles to baptize households, which certainly included children. The repeated mention in the book of Acts of the apostles' baptizing of families renders "silly" the objection of the Anabaptists, as also of the Baptists of the present day, "that there is no evidence of a single infant's ever being baptized by the hands of the apostles."[6] According to the Baptists, all households, or families, in apostolic times happened to lack infants and young children.

Because God includes the children of believers in his covenant and because he directs the covenant promise to them, infant children of believers may be, and indeed *must be,* baptized. For Calvin, there is one compelling ground for infant baptism: the inclusion of infants in the covenant of grace.

> If the covenant still remains firm and steadfast, it applies no less today to the children of Christians than under the Old Testament it pertained to the infants of the Jews. Yet if they are participants in the thing signified, why shall they be debarred from the sign? . . . This one reason [for infant baptism], if no others were at hand, would be quite enough to refute all those who would speak in opposition.[7]

Basic both to Calvin's understanding of the unity of the covenant in both dispensations and to his insistence on the baptism of infants in the new dispensation was his conviction that circumcision, which was administered to infants in the old dispensation, had the very same spiritual significance that baptism has today.

> The promise . . . is the same in both, namely, that of God's fatherly favor, of forgiveness of sins, and of eternal life.

---

5. Ibid., 4.16.7, 2:1330. The Greek word is *brephee.*
6. Ibid., 4.16.8, 2:1331.
7. Ibid., 4.16.5, 2:1328.

Then the thing represented is the same, namely, regeneration. In both there is one foundation [namely, Christ] upon which the fulfillment of these things rests . . . We therefore conclude that, apart from the difference in the visible ceremony, whatever belongs to circumcision pertains likewise to baptism.[8]

Colossians 2:11–12 expressly teaches that baptism is the fulfillment of circumcision. Here Paul teaches that "baptism is for the Christians what circumcision previously was for the Jews."[9]

Rejection of infant baptism, therefore, is grave error. Calvin's attitude toward the Baptist teaching concerning the covenant and kingdom (excluding children) and practice concerning the sacrament (denying baptism to children) differed sharply from the conciliatory attitude of many Reformed theologians today. Those who reject infant baptism are "frantic spirits." Their teachings are "mad ravings."[10] By their erroneous doctrine of the sacrament of baptism, they are guilty of repudiating the sacrament itself, the pure administration of which is one of the marks of a true church. This is the force of Calvin's preferred name for them, not *Ana*baptists, which refers to their rebaptizing those who were baptized as infants (which is bad enough), but *Cata*baptists. This name expresses that they *oppose* the sacrament of baptism. They "ceaselessly assail this holy institution of God."[11] The implication is that only those who practice infant baptism honor the sacrament, administer it rightly, and are the true Baptists.

In addition to corrupting the sacrament, depriving Christ of many of the members of his covenant and citizens of his kingdom (all the children), and consigning children who die in childhood to perdition (since according to the Catabaptists they all die outside the covenant and church of Christ), those who reject infant baptism are guilty of the dispensational heresy: the denial of the unity of the old and new covenants. One cannot deny

---

8. Ibid., 4.16.4, 2:1327.
9. Ibid., 4.16.11, 2:1333.
10. Ibid., 4.16.1, 2:1324.
11. Ibid., 4.16.10, 2:1333.

infant baptism without holding that circumcision, the sign of the old covenant, had a different significance than baptism, the sign of the new covenant. And this necessarily implies two essentially different covenants.

Calvin warned the Catabaptists of his day, as he warns the Baptists of our day, that God threatens to "wreak vengeance upon any man who disdains to mark his child with the symbol of the covenant."[12]

Calvin's severe condemnation of the Baptist false doctrine and corresponding disobedient practice is confessional for all Reformed Christians: "We detest the error of the Anabaptists, who . . . condemn the baptism of the infants of believers, who, we believe, ought to be baptized and sealed with the sign of the covenant, as the children in Israel formerly were circumcised upon the same promises which are made unto our children."[13]

Infant Salvation

Inclusion of the infants in the covenant, signified by their baptism, meant for Calvin that the infant children are saved, are saved *in their infancy*. Regarding this crucially important truth, many Reformed and Presbyterian theologians and churches differ radically from Calvin. They hold the distinctly uncovenantal and essentially Baptist position that all the children of believers are unregenerated, are to be viewed as unregenerated, and must view themselves as unregenerated until they grow up and confess their faith or have a conversion experience.[14] This view explains in large part the conciliatory attitude of many Reformed theologians toward the Baptist error: Despite sprinkling a little water on the babies, the Reformed theologians share the fundamental Baptist conviction that children are outside of Christ; only adults belong to Christ and enjoy his salvation.

Calvin expressly denied the popular, contemporary Reformed

---

12. Ibid., 4.16.9, 2:1332. See the similar warning in Calvin's commentary on Genesis 17:14, "The uncircumcised man child . . . shall be cut off from his people; he hath broken my covenant" (*Genesis*, 457–59)

13. Belgic Confession, Art. 34, in Schaff, *Creeds of Christendom*, 3:427.

14. If *The Case for Covenantal Infant Baptism* is any indication, this position is now the majority position among Reformed theologians and churches.

notion that "children are to be considered solely as children of Adam until they reach an appropriate age for the second birth." This essentially Anabaptist, or Catabaptist, notion erroneously supposes that "spiritual regeneration . . . cannot take place in earliest infancy."[15]

Against this notion Calvin taught, as "God's truth everywhere," that God not only *can* regenerate the infants of believers in their infancy, but that he also *does* regenerate them in their infancy. Infants are alive in Christ by "communion with him," for "to quicken them he makes them partakers in himself." "Those infants who are to be saved (as some are surely saved from that early age) are previously regenerated by the Lord."[16] Toward the end of his defense of infant baptism, Calvin asserted that he had "already established . . . the regeneration of infants."[17]

In his response to the Anabaptist argument that infants are unable to repent and believe (something, Calvin observed, that the New Testament required of *adults* prior to their baptism in view of the apostles' work with adults), Calvin contended that "the seed of both [repentance and faith] lies hidden within them [infants] by the secret working of the Spirit."[18] In flat contradiction of the Reformed theologians today who make the holiness of 1 Corinthians 7:14 ("now are they [your children] holy") a mere outward, formal, vague setting apart of the children unto God—the Baptist "dedication" of the children to God—Calvin explained the holiness of the text as the inner, spiritual sanctifying of the children by the Spirit of Christ in their hearts: "newness of spiritual life . . . holy by supernatural grace."[19] Calvin thought that "the age of infancy is not utterly averse to sanctification."[20]

In support of the Spirit's salvation of infants, Calvin appealed both to the regeneration of John the Baptist in his mother's

---

15. Calvin, *Institutes of the Christian Religion*, 4.16.17, 2:1339.
16. Ibid.
17. Ibid., 4.16.26, 2:1349.
18. Ibid., 4.16.20, 2:1343.
19. Ibid., 4.16.31, 2:1355.
20. Ibid., 4.16.18, 2:1341.

womb and to the sanctification of Jesus in his infancy.[21] This appeal to unborn John and infant Jesus in support of his teaching that God sanctifies covenant children in their infancy puts beyond any doubt and all possibility of contradiction that by sanctification Calvin meant real, inner, Spirit-worked, spiritual holiness. The holiness of John, leaping in Elizabeth's womb at the presence of the Christ (in Mary's womb), and the holiness of baby Jesus were not a formal, external, *positional* holiness—a mere setting apart of the two children unto God in case God might someday will to work in them.

But the main argument of Calvin for infant salvation was the same as his chief argument for infant baptism: God's inclusion of infants in his covenant. If infants are included in the covenant, and therefore marked with the sign of the covenant, they receive the spiritual blessings of the covenant, *in their infancy.* For God to include them in his covenant and give them the sign of the covenant and its salvation but withhold from them the salvation of the covenant and the blessings represented by the covenant sign would be "mockery" and "trickery" on God's part. With specific reference to the salvation of the infants of godly Israelites under the old covenant, Calvin wrote:

> In early times the Lord did not deign to have them [infants] circumcised without making them participants in all those things which were then signified by circumcision [cf. Gen. 17:12]. Otherwise, he would have mocked his people with mere trickery if he had nursed them on meaningless symbols, which is a dreadful thing even to hear of.[22]

Inclusion of infants in the covenant *is* infant salvation. Infant baptism *means* infant salvation. The practice of infant baptism, professedly in obedience to the command of God, while denying infant salvation, makes God a mocker and trickster.

Closely related to his understanding of covenant membership as covenant salvation was Calvin's understanding of the covenant promise, particularly the extension of the promise to

---

21. Ibid., 4.16.17–18, 2:1340–41.
22. Ibid., 4.16.5, 2:1328.

the infant children of believing parents: "I will be the God of your (infant) children." The promise expresses not merely God's willingness, or desire, to save the infants, but also the certainty of the realization of the promise in the infants' salvation. In addition, the promise expresses that God will save the infants *as infants, in their infancy.*

Contending with his Roman Catholic adversaries, who thought that all unbaptized babies are lost, or at least not saved, and who, therefore, held that even women are permitted to baptize dying infants, Calvin quoted the covenant promise in Genesis 17:7: "I will establish my covenant between me and thee and thy seed after thee in their generations for an everlasting covenant to be a God unto thee, and to thy seed after thee." Calvin then explained the covenant promise concerning the children of believers thus: "Their [our babies'] salvation is embraced in this word. No one will dare be so insolent toward God as to deny that his promise of itself suffices for its effect."[23]

This line is of extraordinary importance, not only for its refutation of the Roman Catholic doctrine that the sacrament is necessary for the salvation of covenant children (as though the promise is insufficient for salvation), but also for its exposure of two prevalent errors concerning the covenant on the part of Reformed theologians and churches. One is the common teaching that baptized infants remain, and are to be viewed as, unsaved. On the contrary, "his promise of itself suffices for its effect," *in the infants.*

The other error is the widespread teaching that the covenant promise merely expresses God's willingness, or desire, to be the God of the children and save them, but that the "effect" of the promise, that is, the actual salvation of the children, is not assured and accomplished by the promise itself. The "effect" of the promise, it is widely held, is conditioned upon the faith and obedience of the children. On the contrary, "his promise of itself suffices for its effect."[24]

---

23. Ibid., 4.15.20, 2:1321.
24. A conditional promise is inherently powerless and therefore intrinsically worthless. A *divine* conditional promise is powerless and therefore worthless. It is

The inevitable objection against Calvin's doctrine of the salvation of infants by virtue of their being included in the covenant and by the power itself of the covenant promise was, in his day and is still today, that many infants of godly parents both under the old covenant and under the new covenant proved, and prove, to be unregenerate, reprobate, and lost. Calvin's an-

---

an axiom in theology that *conditio nihil ponit in re* (a condition establishes nothing in reality). Significantly, Martin Luther noted this truth in his great controversy with Desiderius Erasmus. Responding to Erasmus' appeal to a conditional sentence in one of the apocryphal books in support of conditional salvation, Luther observed that "a conditional statement asserts nothing indicatively" (Martin Luther, *The Bondage of the Will*, trans. J. I. Packer and O. R. Johnston [London: James Clarke, 1957], 151). Regarding the conditional statement to which Luther was referring, the conditional promise "If thou are willing to keep my commandments, and to keep continually the faith that pleaseth me, they shall preserve thee" establishes absolutely nothing concerning either the ability of the people to keep the commandments or the preservation of the people. Similarly, the covenant promise to every baptized child in "liberated" theology, "If you believe, I will save you," establishes absolutely nothing concerning either the child's actually believing or God's saving him.

That the covenant promise to children at baptism, according to Schilder, is nothing more than a conditional statement (which establishes nothing in reality) is acknowledged by S. A. Strauss in a volume by disciples and acolytes of Schilder celebrating and promoting his teachings. Strauss explains Schilder's teaching about the covenant promise this way: "In my baptism I receive a concrete address from God, a message that God proclaims to everyone who is baptized, personally: if you believe, you will be saved" (S. A. Strauss, "Schilder on the Covenant," in *Always Obedient: Essays on the Teachings of Dr. Klaas Schilder*, ed. J. Geertsema [Phillipsburg, NJ: P&R, 1995], 28–29). This is all that God says to every baptized child: "If you believe, you will be saved." One can hear the indignant response to this pitiful account of the covenant promise of God to the infants of believers (which establishes nothing in reality) coming down the years from the Secession theologian Simon van Velzen. Van Velzen responded to what was essentially the same description of the covenant promise of God at baptism by the two Reformed ministers K. J. Pieters and J. R. Kreulen. They described the covenant promise to all the baptized infants as Christ's testimony to them that they "can find in Me a rich righteousness, salvation, and honor in the way of faith." Van Velzen responded in amazement and indignation, if not in horror: "'Can find . . . in the way of faith?' Merely this? The believer says more, much more. As certainly as our children have been washed with water, they have the forgiveness of sins, for to them is promised redemption from sins by the blood of Christ, not less than to the adults (Heid. Cat., Q. 74) . . . Therefore they ought to receive the sign and the sacrament of that which Christ has done for them (Bel. Conf., Art. 34)" (see Engelsma, "The Covenant Doctrine of the Fathers of the Secession," in *Always Reforming*, 118–19). Schilder and his colleagues deliberately adopted the covenant doctrine of Pieters and Kreulen as their own.

---

swer to the objection was that the children included in the covenant by the covenant promise are the *elect* children of Abraham and of believing parents, and the elect children *only*. This was Calvin's clear teaching both in his doctrine that the grace of salvation for all who are saved, infants as well as adults, has its source in God's eternal election and in the quotations given earlier in this and the preceding chapters concerning the legitimate children of Abraham and the objects of the covenant promise.

In addition, running throughout Calvin's defense of infant baptism, in chapter 16 of book 4 of the *Institutes,* like the foundational theme of a symphony, is the repeated affirmation that the infants whose salvation in infancy Calvin was asserting are *elect* infants.

> In distinguishing the heirs of the Kingdom from the illegitimate and foreigners, we have no doubt that God's election alone rules as of free right.[25]

> Christ was sanctified from earliest infancy in order that he might sanctify in himself his elect from every age without distinction.[26]

> If those whom the Lord has deigned to elect received the sign of regeneration but depart from the present life before they grow up, he renews them by the power, incomprehensible to us, of his Spirit, in whatever way he alone foresees will be expedient. If they happen to grow to an age at which they can be taught the truth of baptism, they shall be fired with greater zeal for renewal.[27]

Practical Benefits

The truth of the inclusion of our children and grandchildren in the covenant, signified by infant baptism and implying their salvation in infancy, is of great comfort and practical benefit to both parents and children. One extremely important benefit of

---

25. Calvin, *Institutes of the Christian Religion,* 4.16.15, 2:1337.
26. Ibid., 4.16.18, 2:1341.
27. Ibid., 4.16.21, 2:1344.

this truth is that only this doctrine accounts for the salvation of those infants who die in their infancy, something Calvin heartily believed and taught. "When some of them [infants of believers], whom death snatches away in their very first infancy, pass over into eternal life, they are surely received to the contemplation of God in his very presence."[28]

Also, "God's boundless generosity" in extending his mercy to our children and grandchildren "floods godly hearts with uncommon happiness, which quickens men to a deeper love of their kind Father, as they see his concern on their behalf for their posterity."[29] Childless himself, Calvin nevertheless knew "how sweet . . . it [is] to godly minds to be assured . . . that they obtain so much favor with the Heavenly Father that their offspring are within his care."[30]

Then there is the huge benefit that the covenant membership and baptism of infants motivate parents diligently to instruct their covenant children in the ways of the covenant: "We feel a strong stimulus to instruct them in an earnest fear of God and observance of the law." Rejection of infant baptism inevitably results in "a certain negligence about instructing our children in piety."[31]

The effect of the Baptist negligence to instruct their children in piety (beginning with the failure to instruct the children in the fundamental piety that they are included in the covenant by God's mercy), on the one hand, and of the judgment of God upon the Baptist disobedience to God's command to administer the sign of the covenant to the children, on the other hand, is

---

28. Ibid., 4.16.19, 2:1342. Calvin was here appealing to the salvation of infants who die in infancy, which for him was incontrovertible, in support of his teaching that elect infants receive "some part of that grace which in a little while they shall enjoy to the full." His argument was that without the grace of regeneration infants who die in infancy could not "pass into eternal life." The Reformed faith has made this practical implication of the doctrine of infant membership in the covenant of grace confessional in the Canons of Dordt, 1.17: "Godly parents have no reason to doubt of the election and salvation of their children whom it pleaseth God to call out of this life in their infancy" (Schaff, *Creeds of Christendom*, 3:585).

29. Calvin, *Institutes of the Christian Religion*, 4.16.9, 2:1332.

30. Ibid., 4.16.32, 2:1359. Calvin's one child died in infancy.

31. Ibid.

the notable lack of a continuation of the covenant in the generations of Baptists. Baptist parents know nothing of the urgent petition of Reformed parents, "O God, cut us not off in our generations!"

The benefit for the baptized children themselves is that "being engrafted into the body of the church, they are somewhat more commended to the other members." Later, "when they have grown up, they are greatly spurred to an earnest zeal for worshiping God, by whom they were received as children through a solemn symbol of adoption before they were old enough to recognize him as Father."[32]

Presentation of their children for baptism is, therefore, a demand of the covenant upon believing parents: "Accordingly, unless we wish spitefully to obscure God's goodness, let us offer our infants to him, for he gives them a place among those of his family and household, that is, the members of the church."[33] The Reformed Church Order of Dordt makes Calvin's (and the Bible's) demand that infants be baptized law for Reformed churches. It grounds this law in the covenant. "The covenant of God shall be sealed unto the children of Christians by baptism, as soon as the administration thereof is feasible, in the public assembly when the Word of God is preached."[34]

In light of the doctrinal and practical importance of the truth of infant membership in the covenant and infant baptism, as well as of the clear, compelling biblical witness to it, there is only one explanation of the opposition to this truth, Calvin thought: "Satan is attempting [to take away from godly parents and the Reformed church this powerful testimony to God's grace and goodness] in assailing infant baptism with such an army."[35] By the twenty-first century, this army has swelled to enormous size with the addition of hosts of Baptists, fundamentalists, evangelicals, charismatics, and even, wonderful to relate, "Calvinistic Baptists!" By a sound confession of the truth of the covenant

---

32. Ibid., 4.16.9, 2:1332.

33. Ibid., 4.16.32, 2:1359.

34. Church Order of the Protestant Reformed Churches, Art. 56, in *Confessions and Church Order*, 397.

35. Calvin, *Institutes of the Christian Religion*, 4.16.32, 2:1359.

and an uncompromising condemnation of the Baptist error, Reformed and Presbyterian churches must withstand these hosts, who in their opposition to infant membership in the covenant and infant baptism are doing Satan's work.

Summary of the Reformed Tradition

Very early in their history when the Reformed churches in the Netherlands confessed that the covenant of grace has its source in, depends upon, and is governed by election, they were simply applying Calvin's teaching concerning election specifically to the covenant. In the covenant the objects of God's grace in Christ, particularly among the physical children of believers, are determined by election. In the covenant all the blessings of salvation, including union with Christ, regeneration, conversion, justification, sanctification, and perseverance, are bestowed and worked by the Spirit of Christ according to election. In the covenant God's grace depends upon his election. In the covenant, therefore, God's grace and saving work are sure, so that no one in whom God begins the work of salvation shall fall away and perish.

It is preposterous to suppose that the early Dutch Reformed churches, hearing and reading the gospel of grace as preached and written by Calvin, would have concluded that, although election is the source of grace and salvation, the grace and salvation of the covenant are excluded; although God's saving works in Christ depend upon election, in the covenant they depend upon something else (namely, a condition fulfilled by the children); although election determines the objects of grace, in the covenant many more are the objects of grace than the elect; although the grace of God in Christ is effectual and irresistible, in the covenant many successfully resist the grace once bestowed on them, so that they forfeit the grace and perish; although God's gracious gifts and calling are without repentance, in the covenant the gifts and calling of God can be, and often are, revoked.

Of course, the Reformed churches in the Netherlands, like the Reformed and Presbyterian churches everywhere in those glorious early days of the Reformation, alive by the gospel of salvation by sovereign grace as proclaimed especially by John Calvin, confessed the covenant of sovereign grace. This was simply the gospel of the Reformation applied to the covenant.

Chapter 9

A PREPOSTEROUS PROPOSAL

If it is preposterous to suppose that the Reformed churches in the Netherlands at the time of the Reformation would have excluded God's grace and salvation in the covenant from the gospel of the Reformation as taught especially by Calvin, it is still more preposterous to propose that Calvin himself did this. According to this preposterous proposal, whereas for Calvin the fact is that "among those to whom it [the gospel] is preached, it does not gain the same acceptance either constantly or in equal degree . . . For there is no doubt that this variety also serves the decision of God's eternal election,"[1] *in the covenant* (Calvin is said to have taught) this fact does not serve the decision of election, but rather serves the decision of the children. Whereas for Calvin "salvation flows from the wellspring of God's free mercy [in] his eternal election,"[2] *in the covenant* (Calvin is said to have taught) salvation flows from the fulfillment of a condition on the part of the covenant child. Whereas for Calvin God "does not indiscriminately adopt all into the hope of salvation but gives to some what he denies to others,"[3] *in the covenant* (Calvin is said to have taught) God indiscriminately adopts all the physical children of believers into the hope of salvation, gives his covenant grace to all alike, and denies the hope of salvation to none. Whereas for Calvin predestination is "God's eternal decree, by which he compacted with himself what he willed to become of each man," so that "eternal life is foreordained for some, eternal damnation for others,"[4] *in the covenant,* with re-

---

1. Ibid., 3.21.1, 2:921.
2. Ibid.
3. Ibid.
4. Ibid., 3.21.1, 2:926

gard to the physical children of godly parents, (Calvin is said to have taught) God has not eternally compacted with himself what is to become of each of them, eternal life for some, eternal damnation for others, but rather has a gracious will of salvation for all of them alike.

In short, whereas for Calvin the grace of God in Jesus Christ is particular, unconditional, and efficacious, *in the covenant* (Calvin is said to have taught) grace is universal, conditional, and resistible, indeed losable.

Lillback's Book

This is the proposal of the Presbyterian theologian Peter A. Lillback, who is president of Westminster Seminary (Philadelphia). By virtue of Westminster's reputation as a bastion of Reformed orthodoxy, Lillback's position as president lends weight to his theological writing among conservative Christians. As president of Westminster, Lillback has great influence on thousands of ministers and missionaries in many Reformed, Presbyterian, and evangelical churches worldwide. Because of the close association of Westminster with the Orthodox Presbyterian Church, Lillback is a powerful influence on that denomination. He is a member of the Presbyterian Church in America, so that his theological thinking influences many in this denomination as well.

In the book *The Binding of God* Lillback presents Calvin's doctrine of covenant and election as the divorcing of covenant and election.[5] Lillback's Calvin does not allow the eternal decree of election unto salvation to govern the grace of the covenant. On the contrary, he has the covenant of grace, conceived as grace for all the baptized children alike, dominate election. The book is, and likely is intended to be, scholarly support for the heresy of the federal vision. It effectively stops up the fountain, in the Reformed tradition, of the truth of the sovereignty of covenant grace.

The book is part of Baker Academic's prestigious series *Texts and Studies in Reformation and Post-Reformation Thought,*

---

5. Peter A. Lillback, *The Binding of God: Calvin's Role in the Development of Covenant Theology* (Grand Rapids, MI: Baker, 2001).

making the book even more of a threat to the gospel of sovereign (irresistible) grace in the covenant.

Lillback contends and attempts to demonstrate with many quotations from Calvin's writings, especially his commentaries, that Calvin taught a bilateral, conditional, and breakable covenant. "[There is] massive evidence for Calvin's . . . [adoption of the doctrine of a] bilateral, mutual, conditional, and breakable covenant."[6] "[For Calvin] the covenant is mutual, conditional, and potentially breakable."[7]

That is, regarding the children of Abraham and the children of believing parents, Calvin taught that God makes his gracious covenant promise to all the children alike, establishes his covenant of grace with all of them alike, and both promises and makes available covenantal "redemptive benefits" to all the children alike.[8] According to Lillback, Calvin taught that the saving, covenant grace of God in Jesus Christ is universal in the sphere of the covenant, that is, God is gracious to all the physical children of Abraham, Esau as well as Jacob, and to all the physical children of believers, those who finally perish outside the new Jerusalem as well as those who inherit the celestial city.

For Calvin, Lillback would have us believe, the covenant is conditional. Whether the promise is realized in the final salvation of a child, whether the covenant bond continues with a child, and whether a child keeps the redemptive benefits bestowed upon him depend upon works the child must do, namely, believe, keep on believing to the end of his life, and obey the demands of the covenant. Covenant grace and salvation are conditional, that is, they depend not on the electing God, but on the willing and working child. Therefore, they can be lost, and are lost in many cases. Many who were covenant saints in their infancy and childhood fall away to everlasting perdition.

From this presentation of Calvin's covenant doctrine, Lillback draws the astounding, if logical, conclusion that Calvin, unlike Luther, taught justification by faith and by the works of faith.

---

6. Ibid., 175.
7. Ibid., 264.
8. Ibid., 247.

Lillback's book is no unbiased piece of scholarship. It is part of a deliberate, massive effort on the part of Reformed Christianity worldwide to bury the eternal election of God, once and for all, in the tombs of the Canons of Dordt and the Westminster Confession of Faith (as well as the Heidelberg Catechism, the Belgic Confession, the Westminster catechisms, and virtually all the other Reformation creeds). The instrument by which this is being accomplished is the doctrine of the covenant. The covenant is divorced from election, so that God's covenant grace can be universal. The doctrine of the covenant becomes the wedge to dislodge every one of the doctrines of grace, beginning with justification by faith alone.

Now Calvin—the Calvin who devoted his life to the teaching that all of God's grace and saving work in Jesus Christ has its origin in, is governed by, depends upon, and is efficacious because of the eternal decree of election—is compelled to support a doctrine that flatly denies everything he gave his life for. The heart of Lillback's book is his contention that "Calvin's use of the covenant was not hampered [*sic*] because of his belief in the doctrines of sovereign election and reprobation."[9] In Calvin's theology, election does not govern the covenant. If it did, this would be *hampering* the covenant.

The use of the word "hampered" indicates the radical difference between the spirit of John Calvin and the spirit of Lillback and all his multitudes of allies. It is the difference between a humble submission to and trusting reliance on the sovereignly gracious will of God and a suspicious fear of and resentful hostility toward that will. For Lillback, to bring the covenant into close relation with God's election, above all to allow election to govern the covenant, would be to *hamper* the covenant.

God's will would *hamper* God's covenant!

It is not farfetched to imagine the earnest prayer of such as Peter Lillback: "O Lord, keep your eternal decree altogether away from my family, altogether away from my congregation, and altogether away from the universal, visible church

---

9. Ibid., 229.

over all the world! Be careful, O Lord, not to *hamper* our work in the covenant by your election!"

Rejecting election as governing the covenant, the vast movement of which Lillback is a prominent member subjects the covenant to the will and work of the members of the covenant, particularly the will and work of the children of godly parents. The covenant is conditional. Drawing the logical implication of this terrifying notion, the movement, at the forefront of which today are the men of the federal vision, teaches justification by faith and works. Having made Calvin a proponent of universal, conditional covenant grace, Lillback must declare (or, can now safely declare) that Calvin differed from Luther in teaching justification by faith and by the good works that faith performs.

In other words (and this is what Lillback fully intends, even though he does not mention the names), Calvin was a sixteenth-century Norman Shepherd and the theology of John Calvin was the early version of the theology of the federal vision.

John Calvin according to Lillback

Lillback's preposterous proposal is that Calvin cut the covenant loose from election. This allowed Calvin to teach a conditional covenant of grace with all circumcised Jews in the Old Testament and with all baptized Gentiles in the New Testament.

How Lillback goes about proposing this is deceptive.

He is forced to acknowledge that Calvin taught an eternal decree of election and that, somehow, in the end this election has something to do with final, everlasting salvation in the covenant. "[There is in Calvin a] secret election that infallibly secures salvation . . . Only secret election ratifies the covenant in the case of any individual."[10]

Lillback admits that, in view of God's eternal decree of election, "from God's eternal perspective it [the covenant in Calvin's theology] is unconditional."[11] "The covenant from God's vantage point is absolutely unconditional."[12]

---

10. Ibid., 309.
11. Ibid., 170.
12. Ibid., 169.

But God's "vantage point" and "perspective" are not the only "vantage point" and "perspective" for Calvin, according to Lillback. The "vantage point" and "perspective" that matter regarding the covenant, the "vantage point" and "perspective" that govern and control the covenant, covenant grace, covenant blessings, and covenant salvation, are the "vantage point" and "perspective" of man. "From man's vantage point, the covenant is conditional."[13] This "vantage point" perceives that "if the covenant people fail to keep their word [that is, fail to perform the conditions upon which the covenant promise, covenant grace, and the covenant itself depend], they shall lose the covenant blessings."[14]

In addition to the "secret election" of the eternal decree, there is another election. Lillback calls this other election a "general covenant election."[15] General covenant election is God's gracious choice in history of every circumcised physical descendant of Abraham in the Old Testament and of every baptized child of believing parents in the New Testament alike.

This is an election that establishes the covenant of grace with all the baptized infants alike, those who finally perish as well as those who finally inherit the new world. By virtue of this general covenant election all the baptized children alike are "really" in the covenant. "All who are generally elect are also in the covenant."[16] "Those who enter the covenant sphere by baptism, even if not secretly elected, are really in the covenant."[17]

In his general covenant election God graciously offers and promises covenant blessings and salvation to all those who are baptized. "The covenant is a general election that offers the promise of the benefits of the covenant."[18]

Indeed, the significance of the historical, general covenant election of all is that it gives to all alike the privilege, and therefore also the right, of claiming the redemptive blessings of the

---

13. Ibid.
14. Ibid., 170.
15. Ibid., 229.
16. Ibid., 217.
17. Ibid., 309.
18. Ibid.

cross of Christ, namely, justification and sanctification. "It is also the privilege of the person being baptized to claim the two redemptive benefits of the covenant."[19]

Still more, such is the power of the promise that issues from the general covenant election that, in a real sense, all baptized persons, those who will perish as well as those who finally will be saved, are put in possession of the blessings of the covenant. Those who fail to perform the conditions will "lose the covenant blessings."[20] "The Old Covenant people thanklessly rejected the promise and the benefits of the covenant that were theirs by right of general election."[21] Many people "turn away from their general election and the blessings of the covenant that have been sealed to them."[22]

Although the general covenant election of God, in the nature of the case, shows and brings (covenant) grace to all baptized persons alike, this grace is conditional and resistible. It does not irresistibly save. It does not irresistibly save all. It does not irresistibly save any. It is as resistible, as impotent, as the election from which it issues. Careful to state this deplorable characteristic of God's covenant election and covenant grace as favorably as possible, Lillback nevertheless, admits that the covenant grace that flows from his general covenant election is a weak and pitiful thing. "General election is not automatically [*sic*] efficacious in imparting spiritual benefits because God does not always give to all in the covenant the spirit of regeneration that enables perseverance in the covenant."[23]

One cannot but notice the nest of heresies in this statement. According to his general election, God imparts "spiritual benefits" to many who perish. Since these are benefits of the covenant of grace, they must be the grace of the covenant: union with Christ, the forgiveness of sins, and holiness. The precious graces and benefits of the covenant of God in Jesus Christ can be lost. The imparting of these "spiritual benefits" is evidently

19. Ibid., 247.
20. Ibid., 170.
21. Ibid., 226.
22. Ibid., 223.
23. Ibid., 216.

the beginning of salvation, since the problem is that those who have them do not persevere, that is, continue to the end in the salvation that was begun in them. But the beginning of the work of salvation by no means assures the end of the work.

And what does this statement say about this electing God? He begins a good work in some, indeed, in many, but fails to "perform it until the day of Jesus Christ."[24] In God's election, be it his general covenant election, he wills the covenant salvation of all, chooses all unto covenant salvation, and makes known to all his will for their covenant salvation. But then he changes his mind about them and his will toward them and decides on their everlasting perdition.

Behold, the inglorious, dependent, changeable god of the Lillback proposal!

And where does such a theology, such a doctrine of God, leave all of us, who are confident that God has begun a good work in us, that he has imparted "spiritual benefits" to us, but now must doubt whether the covenant grace at work in us might not be the inefficacious grace of a general covenant election?

The main point is that by Lillback's own admission the grace that proceeds from his general covenant election is inefficacious and resistible. It merely "enables" all baptized persons to perform the conditions upon which the covenant promise and everlasting covenant salvation depend. "It is also the privilege of the person being baptized to claim the two redemptive benefits of the covenant *to enable* him to keep such an imposing stipulation."[25]

Because the general covenant election and the covenant that it attempts to establish and maintain are conditional, it is possible that men and women break the covenant in the sense that the real, spiritual bond with Christ, once established, is severed. Men and women can, and do, lose the covenant blessings. Men and women can, and do, very really fall away from covenant salvation, once begun in them, to eternal perdition. Covenant saints can, and do, fall away, impenitently, finally, forever.

24. See Philippians 1:6, to the contrary.
25. Ibid., 247; emphasis added.

"There is covenant-breaking in the New era of the Church . . . It occurs in the converted nations when they turn away from their general election and the blessings of the covenant that have been sealed to them."[26] "The warnings [in Scripture of apostasy] are applicable to the elect [here, evidently, the reference is to the eternal decree] . . . because they . . . from the vantage point of human responsibility could apostatize."[27] "Even one who believes that he is truly elect may stumble and prove himself to be a hypocrite."[28]

Calvin himself feared that he might fall away from God and perish. In the context of apostasy, Lillback tells us that "he [Calvin] believed that he might stumble away from the covenant even though he was one of God's elect."[29] Lillback draws this totally illegitimate and perverse conclusion from the fact that Calvin prayed that God would grant that "we may never fall away from the true worship of thee." As though the prayer for a benefit, in this case preserving grace, implies the fear that God might very really withhold the benefit! According to this reasoning, every time the believer asks for forgiveness, he does so because he is afraid that God may hold his sins against him and damn him. Every time the believer beseeches God for deliverance from the devil, she does so because she is terrorized by the fear that God may give her over to the evil one to suffer with him in the everlasting flames.

How the possibility of the falling away of covenant saints comports with the testimony of the Westminster Confession of Faith—Lillback's Presbyterian creed—that "they whom God hath accepted in his Beloved, effectually called and sanctified by his Spirit, can neither totally nor finally fall away from the state of grace; but shall certainly persevere therein to the end, and be eternally saved,"[30] Lillback does not inform us.

Neither does he inform us how Calvin's (and, presumably, all believers') lifelong terror that he might apostatize is to be harmonized with Westminster's teaching that all true believers

---

26. Ibid., 223.
27. Ibid., 222.
28. Ibid., 225.
29. Ibid., 223.
30. Westminster Confession of Faith, 17.1, in *Subordinate Standards*, 26.

have the assurance of perseverance unto everlasting salvation.

> Such as truly believe in the Lord Jesus, and love him in sin-
> cerity, endeavoring to walk in all good conscience before
> him, may in this life be certainly assured that they are in
> the state of grace, and may rejoice in the hope of the glory
> of God; which hope shall never make them ashamed. This
> certainty is ... an infallible assurance of faith ... [that] we
> are sealed to the day of redemption.[31]

From his doctrine of a conditional covenant, originating in a
general covenant election (attributed by Lillback to Calvin), Lillback eagerly and approvingly draws the conclusion that Calvin
taught justification by faith and works. Whereas Luther excluded all human works from God's act of justifying the guilty sinner, Calvin, according to Lillback, included the good works of
the believing sinner himself.

Lillback lays the foundation for his assertion that Calvin
taught justification by faith and works in an inexcusable mis-
reading of Luther. "Luther taught the Christian to be ignorant
of the law."[32] The truth is that Luther taught the Christian to be
ignorant of the law with regard to the Christian's own obedience to the law *in the matter of justification*. In the matter of
the Christian's thankful, holy life, Luther taught the Christian
to obey the law.

In his great commentary on Galatians, Luther wrote:

> Therefore we should make every effort that *in the question
> of justification* we reject the Law from view as far as possi-
> ble and embrace nothing except the promise of Christ ... We
> are justified by faith alone ... You should learn, therefore,
> to speak most contemptuously about the Law *in the matter
> of justification* ... Apart from the matter of justification, on
> the other hand, we, like Paul, should think reverently of the
> Law. We should endow it with the highest praises and call it
> holy, righteous, good, spiritual, divine, etc.[33]

---

31. Westminster Confession of Faith, 18.1–2, in ibid., 27.
32. Lillback, *Binding of God*, 186.
33. Martin Luther, *Luther's Works*, vol. 26, *Lectures on Galatians 1535,
Chapters 1–4*, ed. Jaroslav Pelikan (St. Louis: Concordia, 1963), 365; emphasis added.

Luther expressly repudiated the conclusion some wrongly drew from his doctrine of justification apart from the law or slanderously charged against it, namely, that the doctrine implies the rejection of the law as a rule of life and, therefore, a careless, lawless life—antinomianism.

> When the free forgiveness of sins [justification by faith alone, apart from the law] is preached, those who are malicious soon slander this preaching, as in Rom. 3:8: "Why not do evil that good may come?" For as soon as such men hear that we are not justified by the Law, they immediately infer slanderously: "Then let us forget about the Law" . . . These are the spiteful and arrogant men who willfully distort Scripture . . ."to their own destruction," as 2 Peter 3:16 says . . . On the other hand, the weak . . . are offended when they hear that the Law and good works do not have to be done for justification. One must go to their aid and explain to them how it is that works do not justify, how works should be done, and how they should not be done. They should be done as fruits of righteousness, not in order to bring righteousness into being. Having been made righteous, we must do them; but it is not the other way around: that when we are unrighteous, we become righteous by doing them. The tree produces fruit; the fruit does not produce the tree.[34]

Luther scholar Paul Althaus' explanation of the law in Luther's theology exposes the falsity of Lillback's description of Luther as a virtual antinomian.

> Luther saw the commandments not only as a mirror in which he recognizes sin—although they certainly are and remain that even for the Christian—but beyond this as instruction about the "good works" God wants; and such instruction is necessary and wholesome for the Christian . . . Accordingly, Luther structured his *Treatise on Good Works,* which was designed to describe the Christian life, as an interpretation of the Decalog. The Ten Commandments have their place not only "before" but also "after" justification; thus they not only exercise the Christian in the theological function of

---

34. Ibid., 169.

the law but also lead him to a right knowledge of the good he ought to do according to God's will.

Although the phrase "the third use of the law," referring to the function of the law as a guide to the holy life of gratitude, does not occur in Luther as it does occur in Calvin, "in substance, however, it also occurs in Luther."[35]

Having misrepresented Luther, Lillback proceeds to oppose Calvin to Luther regarding the place of the law, that is, one's own obedience to the law, in the great matter of justification. According to Lillback, Calvin found a place for the believer's own good works in his justification by God. Calvin taught justification by works. Calvin taught that one's own good works are part of his righteousness with God in justification, albeit a "subordinate" part.

> Calvin affirms that there is a works righteousness that is imputed to the believer's works. This works righteousness in no way detracts from justification by faith alone, since it is a subordinate righteousness ... The righteousness of works is subordinate to the righteousness of justification ... Calvin is insistent that works have a proper place in the discussion of justification by faith alone.[36]

Of the utmost importance for grasping Lillback's astounding attribution of the doctrine of justification by faith and works to John Calvin is recognition of the fact that justification by faith and by the works of faith is the necessary implication (according to Lillback) of Calvin's alleged doctrine of a conditional covenant. The long quotation that follows makes this clear.

> What is particularly important to remember at this point is that Calvin's development of the idea of the acceptance

---

35. Paul Althaus, *The Theology of Martin Luther,* trans. Robert C. Schultz (Philadelphia: Fortress Press, 1966), 272–73. In keeping with this right analysis of Luther's view of the law in the life of the Christian, the Lutheran Althaus insists that it is "incorrect to assert that the position of the Decalog in the *Heidelberg Catechism*—after 'Redemption' and under 'Gratitude'—is specifically Reformed rather than Lutheran."

36. Lillback, *Binding of God,* 189, 192.

of men's works by God was expressed in terms of the covenant. The works were not seen as meritorious, but rather, God has promised to reward works with spiritual gifts, and this promise of the law is realized by the gracious gifts of the covenant. God in covenant has liberally forgiven the sin in men's works, and actually enabled those works by His Spirit. This idea he readily admits is the common doctrine of the Schoolmen [medieval, Roman Catholicizing theologians], except they developed their idea of the covenant of acceptance in terms of merit, instead of justification righteousness and its subordinate righteousness of the Holy Spirit. Here one sees Calvin as the historical bridge between the medieval Schoolmen's covenant doctrine and that of the later Calvinistic federal theologians. Calvin simply excises the medieval doctrine of merit from the covenant of acceptance and replaces it with the Reformation's justification by faith alone. *Consequently, Calvin occupies a middle ground between the Schoolmen and Luther on the issue of the acceptance of good works in relationship to justification.* Luther and Calvin are in full agreement against the scholastics regarding the issue of the unique instrumentality of faith and the non-meritorious character of all of human standing before God. *On the other hand, Calvin, in agreement with the Schoolmen and contrary to Luther, accepts the fact that God can by covenant receive the works of man. Calvin's doctrine of the acceptance of men's works by God is therefore an intermediate position between Luther and the medieval tradition.*[37]

Lillback's sketch of the purported covenant theology of John Calvin is, in fact, a full-scale drawing, and thus defense, of the theology of the federal vision: justification by faith and works, rooted in a conditional covenant of grace with all baptized persons alike, according to a historical, changeable election of God of all those who are baptized, and necessarily involving the real possibility of the falling away of those who are "really" in the covenant and share in the beginnings of covenant

---

37. Ibid., 308; emphasis added.

salvation. The sketch even sports the remarkable feature of the difference between Luther and Calvin on justification.

Severing Covenant from Election

The fundamental error in Lillback's presentation of Calvin's theology of the covenant is Lillback's severance of the covenant from election—election as the eternal decree (what Lillback persistently calls "secret election," leaving the impression that nothing can, or need, be known of it).

Instead, Lillback attaches the covenant closely, indeed, very closely, to his doctrine of a general covenant election. So closely does Lillback connect the covenant to the general covenant election that he is willing to *identify* the covenant with this election.

This is ironic. Against *identifying* the covenant with God's eternal, unconditional election, Lillback and his conditional covenant allies rage, as though this were mortal theological sin. But Lillback has no problem whatever with *identifying* the covenant of grace with a historical, conditional election. "One can identify covenant and election for Calvin only if 'common election' is identified with the covenant."[38]

The explanation is that identifying the covenant with a historical, general, conditional election puts covenant salvation in the hands of man. Identifying the covenant with God's eternal, gracious decree would put covenant salvation in the hands of God.

The relation between election as God's eternal decree and general covenant election as God's vacillating decision in history, Lillback studiously avoids defining.

Is the relation nonexistent, so that God has two contradictory wills concerning the same persons?

Or is the relation that God's eternal decree infallibly appointing certain baptized persons to glory depends upon the outcome of his historical, conditional will for the salvation of all those who are baptized? That is, does God's eternal decree depend upon the performance of the covenant conditions by humans?

There are reasons to believe that the latter is the case for Lillback.

---

38. Ibid., 226.

First, although he pays lip service to the nebulous reality of election as an eternal decree, the decree does not govern the covenant. The decree does not function regarding the covenant. The decree is irrelevant. In fact, if the decree were to be allowed to bear on the covenant, it would *hamper* the covenant. What governs the covenant and its salvation is the historical, general, conditional, covenant election.

Second, the hard, historical fact is that all those in the Reformed tradition who have been determined to extend covenant grace more widely than the particularity of the decree of election, but felt obliged to acknowledge an eternal decree, proposed that the decree of election is dependent on men's performance of the conditions of the historical election. The eternal appointment of men and women to everlasting life depends in one way or another on their faith and obedience. This was the doctrine of Arminius. This was also the doctrine of Amyraut.

Third, Lillback himself intimates that the relation between the eternal decree—"secret election"—and the historical decision—"general covenant election"—is that the former depends on the outcome of the latter, that is, on the performance or nonperformance of conditions by the members of the covenant.

According to Lillback, "the covenant creates an intermediate category of persons between those who are the ones rejected by God, and those who are elect."[39] There are persons who are neither eternally elected nor eternally reprobated. They are all simply elected with the general covenant election. If they perform the conditions of the covenant, they obtain their eternal election. If they fail to perform the conditions, they become eternally rejected (contrary to God's gracious will of historical election).

Whatever the relation between the two different elections may be, the doctrine of a historical, general, gracious, conditional, covenant election of all baptized children alike is heretical. The heresy is a form of the false doctrine of Arminianism.

A general, conditional election posits an election unto grace (covenant grace), blessings (covenant blessings), and salvation (covenant salvation) that is not an election unto everlasting life

---

39. Ibid., 309.

and glory. The Canons of Dordt reject this error as an aspect of the Arminian heresy.

> The Synod rejects the errors of those . . . Who teach that there are various kinds of election of God unto eternal life: the one general and indefinite, the other particular and definite; and that the latter in turn is either incomplete, revocable, non-decisive, and conditional, or complete, irrevocable, decisive, and absolute. Likewise: that there is one election unto faith and another unto salvation, so that election can be unto justifying faith without being a decisive election unto salvation . . . For this is a fancy of men's minds, invented regardless of the Scriptures, whereby the doctrine of election is corrupted, and this golden chain of our salvation is broken: and whom he foreordained, them he also called; and whom he called, them he also justified; and whom he justified, them he also glorified (Rom. 8:30).[40]

According to the Canons,

> there are not various decrees of election, but one and the same decree respecting all those who shall be saved both under the Old and New Testament; since the Scripture declares the good pleasure, purpose, and counsel of the divine will to be one, according to which he hath chosen us from eternity, both to grace and to glory, to salvation and the way of salvation, which he hath ordained that we should walk therein.[41]

Lillback's doctrine of a general covenant election proposes that there is some other source and fountain of grace, blessing, and salvation than the eternal, unconditional decree. The Canons of Dordt deny this, affirming that the sole source and fountain of all the grace of God in Jesus Christ, blessing, and salvation is the eternal decree.

> Election is the fountain of every saving good; from which proceed faith, holiness, and the other gifts of salvation, and

---

40. Canons of Dordt, 1, Rejection of Errors 2, in *Confessions and Church Order*, 159–60.
41. Canons of Dordt, 1.8, in Schaff, *Creeds of Christendom*, 3:583.

finally eternal life itself, as its fruits and effects, according to that of the Apostle. 'He hath chosen us [not because we were, but] that we should be holy and without blame before him in love' (Eph. 1:4).[42]

Calvin's Resisting the Proposal

Calvin resists this scholarly, audacious, monstrous reconstruction of his confession of the gospel of grace with reference particularly to the covenant.

When he defines predestination in the final, authoritative edition of his *Institutes* as God's eternal decree by which he determined the eternal destiny of "each man," Calvin includes every child of believing parents. Children of believers are included in the category "each man."[43] For Calvin, predestination governs the covenant with respect to God's being gracious to some children but not to other children; with respect to God's willing eternal life for some children but eternal damnation for other children; and with respect to God's granting the communion of the covenant, with all its blessings of salvation, to some children while withholding this union with Christ and the blessings of salvation from other children.

Similarly, when Calvin writes in the final, authoritative edition of his *Institutes* that "our salvation flows from the wellspring of God's free mercy" having its source in "his eternal election," he includes the salvation of the children of believers.[44] So closely is the covenant related to election that election is the source of the salvation of everyone saved in the covenant, particularly every regenerated child of believers.

And when Calvin immediately adds that it is God's "eternal election, which illumines God's grace by this contrast: that he does not indiscriminately adopt all into the hope of salvation but gives to some what he denies to others," he includes God's dealings in the covenant.[45] God's election governs the covenant in that he does not indiscriminately adopt all the physical chil-

42. Canons of Dordt, 1.9, in ibid.
43. Calvin, *Institutes of the Christian Religion*, 3.21.5, 2:926.
44. Ibid., 2:921.
45. Ibid.

dren of believers into the hope of salvation, but gives to some children what he denies to other children. Thus eternal election illumines God's grace *in the covenant* by this contrast.

Let Lillback, the federal vision, and all those today who like to portray Calvin as having taught that the covenant is "not hampered" by the eternal decree frankly tell the Reformed public, if they dare, that whenever and wherever Calvin teaches predestination he intends to exclude from consideration the covenant, God's grace in the covenant, and the saving work of God in the covenant. Why, the ungodly world that has read Calvin would laugh them out of court! In the Reformed world, this now passes for lofty scholarship.

That Calvin certainly held that predestination governs the covenant is evident from the fact that, again and again, when Calvin defended double predestination, election and reprobation, as the source of God's giving grace to some and of his withholding grace from others and as determining the salvation of some and the damnation of others, he appealed to Romans 9:10–13: "And not only this; but when Rebecca also had conceived by one, even by our father Isaac; (For the children being not yet born, neither having done any good or evil, that the purpose of God according to election might stand, not of works, but of him that calleth;) It was said unto her, The elder shall serve the younger. As it is written, Jacob have I loved, but Esau have I hated."

But this passage, concerning God's loving election of Jacob and his rejection of Esau in hatred, is not about God's grace and saving work on the mission field among the heathen. Rather, the passage concerns God's dealings with twin grandsons of Abraham, to whom God had made the covenant promise "I will be the God of your seed." The passage teaches the extremely close relation of predestination *and the covenant*. It teaches that predestination governs *the covenant*. And Calvin appealed to this passage, more than to any other, in grounding his doctrine of the eternal decree.

One instance of such an appeal is found in Calvin's defense of eternal predestination against his Roman Catholic opponent Pighius. Pighius denied Calvin's teaching that God's eternal election is the unconditional source and cause of salvation. Pighius maintained, on the contrary, "the fiction that grace is offered equally to all, but that it is ultimately rendered effectual by the will of man, just as each one is willing to receive it." Calvin responded: "Now let that memorable passage of Paul (Rom. 9:10–13) come forth before us. This passage alone should abundantly suffice to put an end to all controversy among the sober-minded and obedient children of God."[46]

Election Governs the Covenant

But Calvin did more than merely refer to Romans 9:10–13 in support of a general teaching that predestination governs God's salvation of sinners. Gifted interpreter of Holy Scripture that he was, Calvin recognized that the passage teaches that predestination governs the *covenant, covenant* grace, the objects of grace *in the covenant,* and *covenant* salvation. Thus he explained the passage to the confounding of Albertus Pighius—and Peter Lillback. Having called Pighius' attention to "that memorable passage of Paul" (Rom. 9:10–13), Calvin continued:

> It was, indeed, a very great difficulty, and a formidable obstacle, in the way of the weak when they saw the doctrine of Christ rejected by nearly all these very persons whom God had appointed the heirs of His everlasting covenant. The apostles had all along preached that Jesus was the Messiah of God. But the whole of this nation, to whom the Messiah had been promised, opposed and rejected Him . . . The apostle, therefore, enters into the battle with the Jews in this manner: he by no means makes the fleshly seed the legitimate children of Abraham, but counts the children of promise alone for the seed. Now he might have counted the seed according to their faith. And that indeed would have been consistent, when, in reference to the promise, he was stating the difference between the genuine and the spurious offspring; and that, indeed, he had before done. But now he ascends higher into the mind of God, and declares that

---

46. Calvin, *Calvin's Calvinism,* 50–51, 55.

those were the children of promise whom God chose before they were born. In proof of which he cites that promise
which was given by the angel to Abraham, "At this time
will I come, and Sarah shall have a son (as if the apostle
had added, before Isaac was conceived in the womb, he was
chosen of God). And not only this (saith the apostle), but
when Rebecca also had conceived by one (embrace), even by
our father Isaac (for the children being not yet born, neither
having done any good or evil, that the purpose of God according to election might stand, not of works, but of Him
that calleth), it was said unto her, The elder shall serve the
younger. As it is written, Jacob have I loved, but Esau have
I hated" (Rom. 9:10).[47]

Calvin taught that election governs the covenant.

So does election govern the covenant that election determines
which of the children of believing parents are children of the
promise and the real seed of Abraham. Accordingly, Calvin
added, election determines which children receive "the blessing
of God and the covenant of eternal life."[48] In the case of Jacob
and Esau, Calvin wrote, "*both* the children could not be heirs
of the covenant at the same time, which covenant had already,
by the secret council [*sic*] of God, been decreed for the *one*."[49]

The implication of the apostle's doctrine in Romans 9:10–13
concerning election's governing the covenant, Calvin observed,
is that "the váin fiction of Pighius concerning universal grace
falls to the ground at once."[50] Likewise falls to the ground the
vain fiction of the men of the federal vision, as of all who divorce the covenant from election, that grace is universal in the
sphere of the covenant, bestowed by God on all the physical
offspring of believers alike, but dependent for its staying power
and saving effect upon the will and work of the children.

Also in his sermons on Genesis 25–27, preached around
1560, shortly before his death, Calvin brought the eternal decree into the closest relation with the covenant. The relation

---

47. Ibid., 56.
48. Ibid., 59.
49. Ibid.
50. Ibid., 58.

is that predestination governs the covenant, determining with whom the covenant is established and who are saved in the covenant. Explaining Genesis 25:23, God's word to Rebecca concerning the violent struggle in her womb, "the elder shall serve the younger," Calvin preached to his congregation in Geneva:

> Albeit God had established his covenant with Abraham, yet notwithstanding he would declare that this was not all, to have made offer of his grace: but that it behooved that he chose according to his liberty, such as he thought good, and that the rest should remain in their cursed state. And therefore Saint Paul allegeth this place to apply it to the secret election of God [in Rom. 9:10–13], through which before the foundation of the world, he chose those as seemed good unto him.[51]

Of great significance in this quotation is Calvin's use of Romans 9:6–33, particularly verses 10–13, to explain the history of the covenant in the Old Testament. In theological terms, for Calvin Romans 9:6–33 was the *hermeneutical key* to the understanding of the covenant with Israel in the Old Testament. "They are not all Israel, which are of Israel . . . Jacob have I loved, but Esau have I hated." Election determined who were the real "seed of Abraham" and the true "Israel" with whom God established his covenant (vv. 6–7, 13). Election governed the covenant.

By no means did Calvin find the truth that election governs the covenant only in Romans 9. He saw the close relation between election and the covenant also in Jeremiah 31:31–34, where God promises to make "a new covenant with the house of Israel, and with the house of Judah" (v. 31).

> Certain is it that the gift of conversion is not common to all men; because this [the "new covenant" promised in Jeremiah 31:31–34] is that one of the two covenants which God promises that He will not make with any but with His own children and His own elect people, concerning whom He has recorded His promise that "He will *write*

51. John Calvin, *Sermons on Election and Reprobation* (Audubon, NJ: Old Paths Publications, 1996), 27–28.

147

His law *in their hearts*" (Jer. 31:33). Now, a man must be utterly beside himself to assert that this promise is made to all men generally and indiscriminately. God says expressly by Paul, who refers to the prophet Jeremiah, "For this is the covenant that I will make *with them*. Not according to the covenant that I made with their fathers: but I will put My laws into their mind, and write them in their hearts" (Heb. 9:9–10). Surely, to apply this promise to those who were worthy of this new covenant, or to such as had prepared *themselves* by their *own* merits or endeavours to receive it, must be worse than the grossest ignorance and folly; and the more so, as the Lord is speaking by the prophet to those who had before "stony hearts."[52]

Lillback's Logic

There are two other considerations that refute Presbyterian theologian Lillback's learned liberation of the covenant from election in the theology of John Calvin, in Lillback's book *The Binding of God*. There is, first, the implication that Lillback himself draws from Calvin's supposed doctrine of a covenant of universal, but conditional, grace. The implication is that Calvin, unlike Luther, taught justification by faith and works.

Lillback's logic, in contrast to his theology, is sound. If the covenant, divorced from election, is conditional, justification—the outstanding benefit of the covenant—is partly by works, namely, the conditions that the sinner performs. If Calvin taught a conditional covenant, that is, a covenant divorced from election, he taught justification by faith and works. This logic is ironclad.

But the force of this ironclad logic also works the other way. If Calvin, like Luther, in fact taught justification by faith alone, Calvin did *not* teach a conditional covenant, but a covenant governed by election.

Thus Lillback's own logic demolishes his thesis that Calvin taught a conditional covenant. For it is incontrovertible that Calvin was one with Luther—*perfectly* one with Luther—in teaching justification by faith alone. Hear Calvin on justification in the final, authoritative, 1559 edition of his *Institutes*,

---

52. Calvin, *Calvin's Calvinism*, 100–101.

where the exact subject in view is the issue of whether justification is by faith and the good works faith performs, or by faith alone, altogether apart from any and all works of the justified sinner.

> But a great part of mankind imagine that righteousness is composed of faith and works. Let us also, to begin with, show that faith righteousness so differs from works righteousness that when one is established the other has to be overthrown . . . Farewell, then, to the dream of those who think up a righteousness flowing together out of faith and works. The Sophists [Roman Catholic theologians], who make game and sport in their corrupting of Scripture and their empty caviling, think they have a subtle evasion. For they explain "works" as meaning those which men not yet reborn do only according to the letter by the effort of their own free will, apart from Christ's grace. But they deny that these refer to spiritual works. For, according to them, man is justified by both faith and works provided they are not his own works but the gifts of Christ and the fruits of regeneration. For they say that Paul so spoke for no other reason than to convince the Jews, who were relying upon their own strength, that they were foolish to arrogate righteousness to themselves, since the Spirit of Christ alone bestows it upon us not through any effort arising from our own nature. Still they do not observe that in the contrast between the righteousness of the law and of the gospel, which Paul elsewhere introduces, all works are excluded, whatever title may grace them [Gal. 3:11–12] . . . Moreover, we shall see afterward, in its proper place, that the benefits of Christ—sanctification and righteousness—are different. From this it follows that not even spiritual works come into account when the power of justifying is ascribed to faith.[53]

Calvin taught justification by faith alone, apart from any and all works of the sinner. Therefore, by Lillback's own logic, Calvin must have taught a covenant that is unconditional, because it is governed by gracious election.

Lillback is hoist with his own petard.

---

53. Calvin, *Institutes of the Christian Religion,* 3.11.13–14, 1:743–44.

Westminster against the Preposterous Proposal

The second consideration that weighs against Lillback's presentation of Calvin as having taught a covenant of universal, conditional grace and therefore as having taught justification by faith and the works of faith is that there is not a hint of this teaching in the Reformation creeds. So heavy and pervasive was the influence of Calvin on the writing of the Reformation creeds that, if Calvin did indeed teach what Lillback asserts he taught, the creeds would certainly contain this doctrine.

However, nothing of this supposed teaching of Calvin, concerning a covenant of universal, conditional grace, implying justification by faith and works in the covenant, is found in the Reformation creeds.

Rather, the creeds teach the very opposite.

I limit myself to the Westminster standards, which are the official confessions of Presbyterian Lillback.

Why, if for Calvin the covenant is not governed (or, in Lillback's term, "not hampered") by election, does the Westminster Larger Catechism answer the question, "With whom was the covenant of grace made?" as it does: "The covenant of grace was made with Christ as the second Adam, and in him with all the elect as his seed"?[54]

Why, if Calvin in accordance with his supposed doctrine of a conditional covenant taught justification by faith and works, does the Westminster Confession of Faith define justification as it does?

> Those whom God effectually calleth he also freely justifieth; not by infusing righteousness into them, but by pardoning their sins, and by accounting and accepting their persons as righteous: not for any thing wrought in them, or done by them, but for Christ's sake alone; nor by imputing faith itself, the act of believing, or any other evangelical obedience to them, as their righteousness; but by imputing the obedience and satisfaction of Christ unto them, they receiving and resting on him and his righteousness by faith; which faith they have not of themselves, it is the gift of God.[55]

---

54. The Larger Catechism, Q&A 31, in *Subordinate Standards*, 57.
55. Westminster Confession of Faith 11.1, in Schaff, *Creeds of Christendom*, 3:626.

And why, if Calvin was so determined not to allow election to *hamper* the work of salvation in the covenant, does the Westminster Confession of Faith deliberately locate the source of covenantal justification (I remind the reader that Westminster grounds the blessings of salvation, specifically justification, in the covenant of grace, which Westminster has treated in chapter 7) in God's eternal election? "God did, from all eternity, decree to justify all the elect."[56]

In view of the influence of Calvin on the Westminster standards, the answer is plain: Calvin did not teach the doctrines Lillback ascribes to him; Calvin taught the opposite.

"Dung . . . [and] Rubbish"

What accounts then for the many quotations Lillback has diligently compiled especially from Calvin's commentaries that seemingly teach a conditional, breakable covenant with all the children alike of godly parents, that is, a covenant that is *not* governed by election?

It must freely be acknowledged that Lillback has found such statements in Calvin's voluminous writings.

About some, even many, of these statements of Calvin that seemingly teach a conditional covenant, two observations blunt the force that Lillback ascribes to them. First, the fact that Calvin taught a "mutual" covenant does not imply that he taught the conditional covenant of Lillback, the men of the federal vision, and the RCN (lib.).

The covenant of grace is mutual in the sense that it is a bond of fellowship between God in Christ and the elect church.

The covenant is also emphatically mutual in the sense that there are two parts in the covenant, God's part, which is his redemption and renewal of us, and our part, which is our solemn calling, or duty, to love, reverence, trust, and obey God. Our part in the covenant is the demand of the covenant upon us (which God also graciously works in us).

This truth of mutuality differs radically from the notion of conditionality that holds that the realization of the covenant

---

56. Westminster Confession of Faith, 11.4, in ibid., 3:627.

promise supposedly made to all alike, the continuation of the covenant supposedly made with all alike, and the perfection of covenant salvation supposedly begun with all alike depend upon the faith and obedience of the children.

The second observation that renders Lillback's use of many of Calvin's statements suspect is that the word "condition" did not always have the same meaning for Calvin that it does in the covenant theology of Peter Lillback and the men of the federal vision. For Lillback and the federal vision "condition" means a work of the member of the covenant upon which the covenant depends. Often Calvin used the word "condition" to express that a certain act is the necessary way in which God would realize his covenant, or that a certain activity is the necessary way in which the member of the covenant, by the grace of God, abides in and enjoys the covenant.

This being said, there remain quotations of Calvin that Lillback can point to as supporting the doctrine of a conditional, breakable covenant. These statements contradict other statements of Calvin affirming that the covenant is unconditional and unbreakable. More importantly, these statements contradict the massive, overwhelming testimony of Calvin's theology as a whole. But Lillback has found statements in Calvin's writings that support the doctrine of a conditional, breakable covenant. This cannot be denied.

About these statements, two further observations are in order. Both were the observations of the reformers Luther and Calvin regarding similar efforts of enemies of the gospel of grace to find support for their heresies in the writings of the church fathers. When Pighius appealed to statements in the early church fathers contradicting Calvin's teaching on predestination, Calvin responded as follows:

> Since the authority of the ancient Church is, with much hatred, cast in my teeth, it will perhaps be worth our while to consider at the commencement how unjustly the truth of Christ is smothered under this enmity, the ground of which is, in one sense, false, and in another frivolous. This accusation, however, such as it is, I would rather wipe off with the

words of Augustine than with my own; for the Pelagians of old annoyed him with the same accusation, saying, that he had all other writers of the Church against him. In his reply he remarks that before the heresy of Pelagius, the fathers of the primitive Church did not deliver their opinions so deeply and accurately upon predestination, which reply, indeed, is the truth. And he adds: "What need is there for us to search the works of those writers, who, before the heresy of Pelagius arose, found no necessity for devoting themselves to this question, so difficult of solution? Had such necessity arisen, and had they been compelled to reply to the enemies of predestination, they would doubtless have done so." This remark of Augustine is a prudent one, and a wise one. For if the enemies of the grace of God had not worried Augustine himself, he never would have devoted so much labour (as he himself confesses) to the discussion of God's election.[57]

What Augustine said to the Pelagians, and Calvin to Pighius, applies to Lillback's quotations from Calvin supporting a conditional, breakable covenant. Calvin did not confront the erroneous doctrine of a covenant of universal, conditional, resistible (saving) grace. The doctrine of the RCN (lib.), of the men of the federal vision, and of Peter Lillback simply was not an issue in Calvin's day. Men were not employing the doctrine of the covenant to destroy and bury predestination. The fact is that Calvin did not concentrate on, develop, or systematize the doctrine of the covenant. This would be the task of a later age. To cast in the teeth of contemporary defenders of the gospel of sovereign grace in the covenant statements by Calvin to the contrary is, as Calvin put it, "frivolous."

The other observation about Lillback's quotations of Calvin in support of a conditional, breakable covenant is that made by Luther concerning Erasmus' collection of statements by various biblical scholars in favor of free will. "They have defiled the gold with dung," charged Luther. And then he turned on Erasmus: "But the gold should not be equated with the dung and thrown away with it, as you are doing. The gold must be re-

---

57. Calvin, *Calvin's Calvinism*, 36–37.

claimed from their hands, the pure Scripture must be separated from their own rotten rubbish."[58]

Lillback must learn to distinguish the dung and rubbish in Calvin from the "gold . . . and pure Scripture." Then he must "reclaim" and deliver to the Reformed community the gold and pure Scripture in Calvin, discarding the dung and rubbish.

Rather than doing the opposite.

---

58. Luther, *Bondage of the Will*, 85.

Chapter 10

GRAAFLAND ON COVENANT AND ELECTION IN CALVIN

In his magisterial study of the origin and development of the covenant in Reformed Protestantism, the Dutch theologian C. Graafland acknowledges that in Calvin's theology election governs the covenant of grace.[1]

"Locked Up in the Decree"

At the outset of his study of Calvin's doctrine of the covenant, Graafland recognizes that the fundamental issue in understanding Calvin's doctrine of the covenant, as it is the fundamental issue in the entire development of the doctrine of the covenant in Reformed Protestantism, is the "relation between covenant and election."[2] For Calvin, says Graafland, "election is the heart of God's church. This has the result that when Calvin speaks about the covenant, he does so in direct connection with election."[3]

According to Graafland, Calvin "allows the covenant to be governed by election. The covenant is *merely* 'means' for the realizing of election. Election is the main thing, and the covenant stands in the service of election."[4] Indeed, for Calvin, the covenant is governed by the double decree of predestination and is the means of both salvation and damnation.

> The covenant as means of salvation and damnation [in Calvin's theology] still has an important function. Not for nothing is the covenant called God's "means" by which he performs his work of salvation. If it finally is fulfilled in or must give way to the relentless electing and reprobating ac-

---

1. Graafland, *Van Calvijn tot Comrie.*
2. Ibid., 1:81.
3. Ibid., 1:82.
4. Ibid., 1:131; see also 1:148.

tion of God on the ground of his eternal counsel, it still has fulfilled an important function, exactly in the service of the execution of God's counsel. That function appears then to be as well a positive one as a negative one. It is positive for the elect. The covenant with its offer of salvation and the summons (demand) to enter into it gives to the elect the way along which they, by recognition of their own weakness and unworthiness, are made receptive to the need of God's Spirit in order to come to faith and salvation. For the reprobate this same covenant with the same offer of salvation and demand to believe has the function to expose their obstinate disobedience and thus to render them guilty before God, who on the ground of this disobedience is then also just in the execution of his decree of reprobation, which was taken already from eternity, and in his actual condemnation [of them].[5]

Graafland sums up Calvin's view of the covenant this way:

The most characteristic aspect of this vision [of the covenant by Calvin] appeared to be that in it election and covenant stand in an intense relation of tension. Calvin tries to do maximum justice to the historical dealing of God with Israel and the Christian church in this world, but with this he yet repeatedly allows this history as it were to be dominated by eternity. It is the tension between the "unreal" (time) and the "real" (eternity), in which the first ["unreal time"] is the vehicle of the last ["real eternity"]. This structure Calvin has worked out in his doctrine of the covenant, according to which the intrinsic worth of the covenant appears to lie in this, that it is the "means of salvation," the means for the realizing of the salvation that has been considered and decreed by God from eternity and that realizes itself throughout time in order (anew) to flow out into eternity (the eternal, heavenly life).[6]

The Dutch Reformed theologian returns to Calvin's doctrine of the covenant at the very end of his three-volume study of the

---

5. Ibid., 1:169.
6. Ibid., 2:7.

doctrine of the covenant in Reformed Protestantism. He emphasizes even more strongly and bluntly that in Calvin's theology
election governs the covenant.

> Calvin proceeds to subject the doctrine of the covenant to
> the doctrine of election. The covenant is part of election,
> and indeed in this sense, that the covenant is viewed as very
> definitely *under* election [Graafland plays on the Dutch
> word for "part" in the preceding phrase, "The covenant is
> part of election." The Dutch word is *onderdeel.* The Dutch
> is "*Het verbond als* onder-*deel wordt gezien.*" Graafland
> emphasizes that for Calvin the covenant is very definitely
> subjected to election]. Election is the main thing, and within
> the framework of election the covenant receives its place as
> the general form of election. This general election serves to
> the end of realizing special election.

Graafland continues:

> [Calvin] saw the decisive factor of the covenant locked up
> in the eternal, divine decree of election and reprobation. Be-
> cause others (humanists) did not want to know anything of
> this, Calvin lays even heavier stress on it.[7]

Criticism of Lillback

Graafland is sharply critical of Peter Lillback's presentation
of Calvin's doctrine of the covenant as divorced from, or,
as Lillback conceives it, "not hampered" by, election.[8] Lillback's comparison of the covenant doctrine of Bullinger and
the covenant doctrine of Calvin is "drastically deficient," according to Graafland. Lillback states that Calvin "stands in
full union" with Bullinger on the covenant. The truth is that
whereas Bullinger treats the doctrine of the covenant without
any mention of election, "this . . . is for Calvin impossible."
"When Calvin speaks about the covenant, he does that in a direct connection with election."[9]

---

7. Ibid., 3:395.
8. Lillback, *Binding of God,* 229.
9. Graafland, *Van Calvijn tot Comrie,* 1:82.

Still more devastating is Graafland's criticism of Lillback for proposing that Calvin viewed election as governed by the covenant.

> It is noteworthy [writes Graafland] that Calvin exactly in his commentary on Romans 9–11 speaks frequently about the covenant (39 times). For P. A. Lillback this is a proof that Calvin's doctrine of election is governed by the covenant . . . It will actually become plain in the continuation of our investigation [of Calvin's doctrine of the covenant] that the truth of the matter is precisely the other way round, namely, that from this study it appears that Calvin's doctrine of the covenant stands entirely in the service of his doctrine of election. With regard to Calvin's exposition of Genesis 17, it is plain in any case that (in contradiction of the judgment of Lillback) Calvin's doctrine of the covenant is full of references to election.[10]

Graafland exposes Lillback's forcing of Calvin's doctrine of the covenant into the mold of a doctrine of the covenant that is liberated from God's election.

> A striking gap in the study of P. A. Lillback of Calvin's doctrine of the covenant is the virtually complete lack of attention paid to the pneumatological [having to do with the work of the Spirit of Christ] dimension of the covenant, which is exactly of decisive significance for Calvin. The cause of this is to be found in the fact that he [Lillback] one-sidedly emphasizes the mutuality and conditionality of the covenant in Calvin. Also by this pneumatological deficiency, the relation between covenant and election in Calvin is not correctly understood by him [Lillback].

What Graafland finds strangely and seriously lacking in Lillback's study, Graafland supplies, as the teaching of Calvin: "The positive reply [to God's offer of grace] in connection with the covenant takes place by the accompanying working of the Spirit as fruit of God's election."[11]

---

10. Ibid., 1:88.
11. Ibid., 1:150.

Looking for Covenant Deliverance to Saumur!

What makes Graafland's honest analysis of Calvin's doctrine of the covenant especially compelling is that Graafland himself wants nothing of a covenant governed by the eternal decree. Graafland is as opposed to election's governing the covenant as are Peter Lillback, the men of the federal vision, and the disciples of Klaas Schilder and Benne Holwerda. Graafland indicates his own opposition to Calvin's doctrine of the covenant in typical contemporary Dutch Reformed fashion. Graafland speaks of the "shadow" that election casts over the covenant. Election "threatens" the covenant. There is "tension" in Calvin between election and covenant (this "tension" describes Graafland's feeling, not Calvin's).[12]

To one important chapter, Graafland gives the worrisome title, "*Het verbond onder druk van de verkiezing*" (The covenant under [oppressive] pressure of election).[13]

Oh, that dangerous, frightening, troublesome decree of election!

Such is Graafland's opposition to a doctrine of the covenant that has the covenant governed by election that when, at the very end of his study, he looks about for a doctrine of the covenant that will allow the Reformed churches to "break through" this "oppressive" covenant doctrine, he proposes the covenant doctrine of Saumur. "In my view the Saumur doctrine of the covenant has made a serious attempt to give a new and liberating perspective."[14]

In order to *liberate* the covenant from the *oppressive* decree of election, the Reformed churches must turn to the theology of Amyraut!

Amyraldism!

This was the teaching that God conditionally elected all men without exception, that Christ conditionally died for all men without exception, and that God is conditionally gracious to all men without exception. God's decisive election of a man to sal-

---

12. Ibid., 3:395–96.
13. Ibid., 1:147.
14. Ibid., 3:402.

vation (in distinction from his earlier conditional election), and therefore the final salvation of everyone who is saved, depend squarely upon that man's performance of the condition of faith.

Graafland is right. The covenant theology of Saumur will certainly *liberate* the covenant from election. This is exactly what the Saumur school intended, in deliberate opposition to the Canons of Dordt. And the purpose was to bring God's election into bondage to the will and work of the sinner in the covenant.

In this context, Graafland makes the telling observation that "in the recent past it has been particularly K. Schilder who in his own way has pursued this track [of the doctrine of the covenant of Saumur]."[15] Again, Graafland is right. Both Saumur and Schilder cut the covenant loose from election. Both Saumur and Schilder extend the gracious covenant, the gracious promise of the covenant, the grace of the covenant, and the gracious benefits of the covenant more widely than only to the elect. And both Saumur and Schilder make the covenant grace of God in Jesus Christ dependent upon the faith and obedience of the sinner. That is, both Saumur and Schilder teach universal, conditional, resistible grace in the covenant.

This was not Calvin's doctrine of the covenant, as Graafland freely acknowledges. It was not Calvin's doctrine of the covenant because such a doctrine of the covenant violently contradicts the gospel of salvation by grace alone proclaimed by the sixteenth-century Reformation of the church.

Luther's Suspicion of Covenant

In his zeal for the glory of God in the gospel of sovereign grace, Luther, who in his early years emphasized the covenant, came to give the covenant a minimal place in his teaching. The reason was that the medieval theologians had seized upon the doctrine of the covenant to teach that man and God cooperate in salvation. For Luther the promise of God, rather than the covenant, served to express the sheer sovereignty and grace of God's salvation of sinners.

---

15. Ibid., 3:403.

With Luther we see the covenant increasingly recede into the background and eventually disappear from his horizon . . . Luther came increasingly to the insight that the word "covenant" was not the most felicitous expression to describe God's gracious workings of salvation in Christ. It does not declare the gracious character of salvation in Christ plainly and radically enough . . . This becomes understandable especially when we have an eye for the nominalist background [in medieval theology] out of which Luther's theological existence proceeded . . . In nominalism also the covenant (*pactum*) played a great role. But [in nominalism] this conception [of the covenant] has exactly the tendency, within the framework of the sovereign self-limiting of God, to confer a positive and creative significance upon man and his merits. In ecclesiastical and spiritual practice, this meant that the emphasis fell on the cooperation of man in his own salvation. It is particularly this essentially semi-Pelagian feature that accompanied medieval thinking about the covenant. Exactly against this [semi-Pelagian heresy], Luther was determined to turn with his theology of the cross, [the gospel] of God's grace alone, through the death of Christ.[16]

We may disagree with Luther's reaction against the semi-Pelagian corruption of the doctrine of the covenant. Indeed, we do disagree with Luther's reaction, as does the Reformed tradition, although we understand his reasons for the reaction. The covenant of grace is too prominent in Scripture, too important for the life of the church and Christian, too precious to Christ, too fundamental for God's revelation of himself, to be allowed to fade into the background of the teaching of the church. The doctrine of the covenant must be central. But it must be the doctrine of a covenant governed by election. Only this is a covenant doctrine that is faithful to, indeed an essential aspect of, the gospel of grace. Only this doctrine of the covenant does justice to Luther's valid concerns.

---

16. Ibid., 1:39–40; see also 48–49.

Chapter 11

BAVINCK ON COVENANT
AND ELECTION

The Dutch Reformed theologian Herman Bavinck is universally held in high esteem as a Reformed dogmatician. Bavinck taught as his own belief, the position of the Reformed tradition, and the doctrine of Scripture that election and covenant are closely related. Treating explicitly of covenant and election in his Reformed dogmatics, Bavinck wrote that election is the source and fountain of the covenant. This is Bavinck's own figure: "The covenant of grace is the channel by which the stream of election flows toward eternity."[1]

Bavinck on Sovereign, Covenant Grace

Election governs the covenant; the covenant is God's execution in history of his elective will of salvation in eternity. "Election only and without qualification states who are elect and will infallibly obtain salvation; the covenant of grace describes the road by which these elect people will attain their destiny."[2]

---

1. Herman Bavinck, *Reformed Dogmatics*, vol. 3, *Sin and Salvation in Christ,* ed. John Bolt, trans. John Vriend (Grand Rapids, MI: Baker, 2006), 229. The editor of the English translation of Bavinck's dogmatics rightly gives this section of the dogmatics the heading "Covenant and Election." Here Bavinck states not only his own definitive theological thinking on the subject, but also what he considers to be the biblical and Reformed (and for Bavinck "Reformed" means creedal) doctrine concerning the relation of covenant and election. With specific reference to the relation of covenant and election, Bavinck explains the relation clearly, precisely, and thoroughly, if briefly. This passage is decisive regarding Bavinck's understanding of the relation of covenant and election. One may fill out this explanation from other places in Bavinck. But all efforts to weaken and even contradict Bavinck's doctrine in this passage by references to other writings of Bavinck, sometimes ignoring this passage—the *locus classicus* on the subject—come to ruin on the rock of this passage.

2. Ibid.

"The elect . . . [are] gathered into one under Christ as their head in the way of the covenant."[3]

Basic to this conception of the relation of election and covenant is the recognition of Jesus Christ as head of the covenant of grace, as Adam was head of the covenant of creation. For Bavinck, Jesus Christ is "head of the covenant of grace," as well as "its mediator."[4] This means that "the covenant of grace has been made with Christ."[5] In and through Christ, the head of the covenant, the covenant "reaches out also to his own."[6] "His own" are all those whom the Father has given to Jesus in the decree of election (John 6:37, 39; John 10:29; John 17:2, 6, 9, 11, 24).

In support of his teaching that God has made his covenant with Christ, as head of the covenant, and in him with his own, Bavinck appeals to Galatians 3:29: "If ye be Christ's, then are ye Abraham's seed."[7] This text depends on Galatians 3:16, which teaches that God made the promise of the covenant to Abraham's seed, Jesus Christ.

Of course, election and covenant are different. Bavinck does not identify them. No Reformed theologian has ever identified them. When opponents of Bavinck's teaching that election and covenant are closely related, as a fountain to its stream, charge those who confess this close relation with *identifying* covenant and election, what they really intend to deny, and to root out of the Reformed churches, is the teaching that election *governs* the covenant.

Invariably, an examination of the mantra "covenant and election are not identical" will show that those who sound the mantra mean "election does not govern the covenant."

Election is the divine decree in eternity appointing Jesus Christ as head of the church and, in Christ, choosing a certain number of persons to redemption as the body of Christ. The covenant is God's structured bond of union and communion with Christ and his people in history, in which living relationship God works out the salvation of the church and its members.

---

3. Ibid., 232.
4. Ibid., 229.
5. Ibid.
6. Ibid.
7. Ibid., 224.

The difference that Bavinck emphasizes is that, whereas in election the members of the church are passive, in the covenant the Spirit of Christ makes the elect members of the church active. This activity includes that they "consciously and voluntarily consent to this covenant."[8]

This is what Bavinck means by the covenant's becoming "bilateral."[9] He does not mean that a covenant that was originally established unilaterally, by God alone, now becomes dependent for its maintenance and perfection upon the will and work of the member of the covenant. This is indeed what many Reformed theologians mean by their teaching that the covenant is unilateral (one-sided) in its establishment but bilateral (two-sided) in its maintenance. This is to teach that, whereas the beginning of the covenant with a human is sovereign grace, the maintenance and perfection of the covenant are a cooperative effort of God and men. This is to teach that, whereas the establishment of the covenant depends solely upon God, the maintenance and perfection of the covenant depend upon the sinner. This is to teach that, whereas the beginning of the covenant and its salvation is God's work, in the end the covenant and its salvation are the work of man himself.

Bavinck will have none of this. "The doctrine of the covenant maintains God's sovereignty in the entire work of salvation . . . Into that entire work of salvation, from beginning to end, nothing is introduced that derives from humans. It is God's work totally and exclusively; it is pure grace and undeserved salvation . . . This doctrine of the covenant . . . purely and fully maintains God's sovereignty in the work of salvation."[10]

God not only unilaterally establishes the covenant, but he also unilaterally maintains the covenant: "The covenant of grace . . . is indeed unilateral: it proceeds from God; he has designed and defined it. *He maintains and implements it. It is a work of the triune God and is totally completed among the three Persons themselves.*"[11]

---

8. Ibid.
9. Ibid., 230.
10. Ibid., 228–29.
11. Ibid., 230; emphasis added.

When Bavinck speaks of the covenant's becoming bilateral (after its unilateral establishment with a person), he means that once God establishes his covenant with a child, a woman, or a man, that person becomes active by the grace of the covenant and is commanded to be active. Bavinck tells us that this is what he means by the bilateral character of the established covenant:

> It [the covenant] is destined to become bilateral, to be consciously and voluntarily accepted and kept by humans in the power of God . . . The covenant of grace does not deaden human beings or treat them as inanimate objects . . . It does not kill their will but frees them from sin.[12]

By the covenant's bilateral character, Bavinck has in mind what orthodox Reformed theologians have taught as the mutuality of the covenant. The covenant is a bond of mutual love and fellowship between God in Christ and God's covenant friends. It is like the marriage of the Christian man and the Christian woman.

By the covenant's bilateral character, Bavinck has in mind what the Reformed baptism form teaches when it declares that the covenant of grace, unilaterally established, maintained, and perfected by the triune God, contains "two parts." Members of the covenant have a part in the covenant. Our part is "new obedience, namely, that we cleave to this one God, Father, Son, and Holy Ghost."[13]

By the covenant's bilateral character, Bavinck has in mind exactly what the Protestant Reformed Churches declare about the covenant of grace in their Declaration of Principles (concerning the covenant):

> The sure promise of God which He realizes in us as rational and moral creatures not only makes it impossible that we should not bring forth fruits of thankfulness but also confronts us with the obligation of love, to walk in a new and holy life, and constantly to watch unto prayer.[14]

---

12. Ibid.
13. Form for the Administration of Baptism, in *Confessions and Church Order*, 258.
14. Declaration of Principles, in ibid., 426. See also the appendix in *Covenant and Election*.

That the covenant friends of God undertake their side of the bilateral covenant, that they actively enter into the mutuality of the covenant (as a loved and loving wife in a good marriage), that they do their part, that they carry out their obligation in the covenant to love their covenant God—this is due to the sovereign grace of the covenant working in them.

Bavinck thinks so. "Into that entire work of [covenant] salvation, from beginning to end, nothing is introduced that derives from humans. It is God's work totally and exclusively."[15] "The covenant of grace . . . re-creates the whole person and, having renewed it by grace, prompts it, freely and independently, with soul, mind, and body, to love God and to dedicate itself to him."[16]

Covenant and election are different in important respects. They are not different in respect of sovereign grace. Covenant grace is as sovereign as is the grace of election. They are the one, saving grace of the triune God in Jesus Christ. And the grace of God in Jesus Christ is sovereign.

Neither are covenant and election different, in the judgment of Herman Bavinck, with regard to their extent. That is, for Bavinck the grace of election and the grace of the covenant are coterminous. The grace of the covenant is not wider than election. The covenant grace of God is for the elect and for the elect only. Bavinck expresses this fundamental harmony of election and covenant in these words: "The two [election and covenant] are not so different that election is particular while the covenant of grace is universal."[17]

What Bavinck states concerning the particularity of both election and covenant applies to the physical, baptized offspring of godly parents. Evidently, Bavinck *intended* that his statement concerning the particularity of the gracious covenant apply specifically to the children of godly parents. One essential aspect of the particular covenant is the inclusion of the children of believers. "It [the covenant] is never made with a solitary individual but always also with his or her descendants. It is a covenant from generations to generations."[18]

---

15. Bavinck, *Reformed Dogmatics*, 3:229.
16. Ibid., 230.
17. Ibid., 229.
18. Ibid., 231.

A few pages after he has insisted that the covenant, like election, is "particular," at the end of his treatment of covenant and election, with explicit appeal to the distinction in Romans 9:6–23 between two kinds of children of Abraham, Bavinck will affirm that the covenant is established with the elect, and with the elect only.

According to Herman Bavinck, it is not true that, whereas election embraces only some of the physical offspring of Abraham, of Isaac and Rebecca, and of believing parents today, the covenant embraces all of the physical offspring without exception. Covenant is not the welcome doctrinal instrument by which Reformed and Presbyterian theologians who detest the particularity of election may broaden and universalize the saving grace of God in Jesus Christ. Covenant is not a doctrine with which to shove election far, far into the background of Reformed preaching and teaching, until finally it disappears altogether.

Election and covenant do not differ in this respect: that, whereas election is particular regarding grace toward the children of believers, the covenant of grace is universal with regard to circumcised or baptized children.

That Bavinck means by the particularity of the covenant that the covenant of grace is established, maintained, and perfected with the elect, and the elect only, is evident, not only from the statement itself, but also from what immediately follows. Immediately, Bavinck declares that the covenant is "made with Christ [and] . . . his own."[19]

Bavinck clearly sees that any extension of the grace of the covenant beyond the limits of God's election necessarily implies the heresy of free will. If covenant grace is wider than election, *covenant grace is resistible.* Some toward whom God has a gracious attitude, desiring to save them, or upon whom God bestows grace as a covenant power, resist this grace, and go lost. Implied is that whether one is saved by covenant grace depends, not upon the grace itself (for many who are objects of this grace are not saved by it), but upon his own decision, his own will. Extending covenant grace more widely than election necessarily introduces the heresy of salvation by the free will of the sinner into the gospel of the covenant.

19. Ibid., 229.

Repudiating the idea that election and covenant differ regarding the extent of their grace, Bavinck adds, in the same sentence: "that the former [election] denies free will and the latter [the covenant] teaches or assumes it, that the latter takes back what the former teaches." The complete sentence reads as follows: "The two [election and covenant] are not so different that election is particular while the covenant of grace is universal, *that the former denies free will and the latter teaches or assumes it, that the latter takes back what the former teaches.*"[20]

Bavinck on the Unconditionality of the Covenant

Neither are election and covenant different with regard to their unconditionality. As a Reformed theologian, Bavinck held unconditional election. As a Reformed theologian, Bavinck also confessed that the covenant of grace is unconditional. Because the issue of the unconditionality or conditionality of the covenant is controversial in the Reformed churches, and because the vast majority of Reformed theologians like to leave the impression that the Reformed tradition overwhelmingly has taught that the covenant is conditional, dismissing the doctrine of the unconditional covenant as a "radical" aberration, it will be profitable to hear Bavinck on the issue.

> In the beginning, Reformed theologians spoke freely of "the conditions" of the covenant. But after the nature of the covenant of grace had been more carefully considered and had to be defended against [Roman] Catholics, Lutherans, and Remonstrants [Arminians], many of them took exception to the term and avoided it.[21]

Bavinck continues: "In the covenant of grace, that is, in the

---

20. Ibid.; emphasis added.
21. Ibid. I insert the word "Roman" in the quotation. The translator erred. Neither here nor elsewhere in his dogmatics did Bavinck refer to the Roman Catholic Church as the "Catholic" Church. Here the Dutch original has the word *Roomschen* (Romish) (see Herman Bavinck, *Gereformeerde Dogmatiek*, vol. 3, 2nd revised and expanded ed. [Kampen: Kok, 1910], 241). The Roman Catholic Church is not the catholic church of Christ. It is not even *a* catholic, or universal, church; it is a *Roman* church. This was Bavinck's conviction.

gospel, which is the proclamation of the covenant of grace, there are *actually . . . no conditions*." He explains: "For God supplies what he demands. Christ has accomplished everything . . . and the Holy Spirit therefore applies [everything]."[22]

Bavinck denies, absolutely, that the covenant is conditional in the proper sense of the term "condition," namely, a decision or work of a member of the covenant upon which the covenant and its salvation depend. Bavinck denies, absolutely, that the covenant is conditional in the sense that the member of the covenant must make a decision or perform a work that is decisive for the maintenance of the covenant. Bavinck denies, absolutely, that the covenant is conditional in the sense that by performing a demand a member of the covenant makes himself to differ from others who, like himself, are objects of the covenant grace of God.

> He [God] made it [the covenant of grace] . . . with the man Christ Jesus . . . And in him, who shares the divine nature and attributes, this covenant has an unwaveringly firm foundation. It can no longer be broken: it is an everlasting covenant. It rests not in any work of humans but solely in the good pleasure of God, in the work of the Mediator, in the Holy Spirit, who remains forever. It is not dependent on any human condition; it does not confer any benefit based on merit; it does not wait for any law keeping on the part of humans. It is of, through, and for grace. God himself is the sole and eternal being, the faithful and true being, in whom it rests and who establishes, maintains, executes, and completes it. The covenant of grace is the divine work par excellence—his work alone and his work totally. All boasting is excluded here for humans; all glory is due to the Father, Son, and Holy Spirit.[23]

Whoever cannot say "Amen" to this, from the bottom of his or her heart, is no Reformed Christian.

Bavinck will speak only of the "conditional form" of the administration of the covenant: "In its administration by Christ, the covenant of grace does assume this demanding conditional

---

22. Ibid., 230; emphasis added.
23. Ibid., 225–26.

form."[24] By a conditional form, Bavinck refers, among other constructions, to the biblical exhortations and admonitions that use the conjunction "if": "If thou shalt hearken unto the voice of the LORD thy God" (Deut. 30:10); "If ye through the Spirit do mortify the deeds of the body, ye shall live" (Rom. 8:13).

By acknowledging a conditional *form* of the administration of the covenant, Bavinck does not give back with the left hand the error that he has just taken away with the right hand. A conditional form of the administration of the covenant is not the same as a conditional covenant. The conditional form of the administration of the covenant does not mean, for Bavinck, demands for a human work upon which the covenant depends, or for a human work that must make impotent covenant grace effectual in the case of the one performing the work.

The conditional form of the administration of the covenant rather refers to God's dealings with "humans in their capacity as rational and moral beings . . . to treat them as having been created in God's image; and also . . . to hold them responsible and inexcusable; and, finally, to cause them to enter consciously and freely into this covenant and to break their covenant with sin."[25]

That for Bavinck this conditional form of the administration of the covenant does not mean a conditional covenant is confirmed by his affirmation of the covenant's unilateral character, in the very next sentence after his explanation of the covenant's conditional form. "The covenant of grace, accordingly, is indeed unilateral."[26]

A unilateral covenant is an unconditional covenant—a covenant accomplished from beginning to end, with regard to every aspect of it, by God alone. It is a covenant dependent from beginning to end, with regard to every aspect of it, upon God alone.

The covenant of grace is as unconditional as is gracious election.

Bavinck's exposition and defense of the unconditionality of the covenant ought to give twenty-first-century Reformed theologians and churches pause. Bavinck gives the lie to the popular

---

24. Ibid., 230; emphasis added.
25. Ibid.
26. Ibid.

notion that the doctrine of the unconditional covenant has no place in the Reformed tradition or, at least, no place anywhere near the center of this tradition.

On the contrary, Bavinck suggests that those who freely, indeed vehemently, contend for a conditional covenant have not very "carefully considered" the nature of the covenant of grace. Nor, evidently, are they concerned to defend the covenant of grace "against [Roman] Catholics, Lutherans, and Remonstrants [Arminians]." On the other hand, those theologians and churches who take exception to the term *conditions* (of the covenant), rather than being reproached as hyper-Calvinists, or ignored as beyond the pale, ought to be credited with having carefully considered the nature of the covenant of grace and with a zeal for defending the gospel of grace against its foes.

Most importantly, Bavinck indicates the seriousness of the issue of the unconditionality or conditionality of the covenant. At stake is the gospel of free, sovereign (that is, unconditional) grace itself. For the "gospel . . . is the proclamation of the covenant of grace."[27] The doctrine of the unconditional covenant is the good news of grace. The doctrine of a conditional covenant is the false gospel of salvation by the will and works of the sinner. That is, the doctrine of a conditional covenant is the Arminian theology of the covenant.

Bavinck on Membership in the Covenant

God makes his covenant with the elect in Christ, and with the elect alone. The elect, and the elect alone, are members of the covenant. Bavinck teaches this in the statement "The covenant of grace has been made with Christ . . . [and with] his own."[28] He reiterates and explains this when he comes to the matter of covenant membership at the conclusion of his treatment of covenant and election.

Bavinck sharply distinguishes two essentially different kinds of connections to the covenant of grace. There is the vital membership in the covenant itself of a true and living faith. This

---

27. Ibid.
28. Ibid., 229.

membership affords participation in the blessings of the covenant. There is also, in radical distinction, a membership merely in the covenant's "earthly administration." This is the connection to the covenant of those who lack true faith. This membership does "not share in the covenant's benefits."

Here is Bavinck's statement of the distinction: "It is self-evident, therefore, that the covenant of grace will temporarily—*in its earthly administration and dispensation*—also include those who remain inwardly unbelieving and do not share in the covenant's benefits."[29]

There are those (Bavinck is thinking especially of baptized children of believers) who are "*in* the covenant," but not "*of* the covenant."[30] This is a strong statement of the qualitative difference between the two kinds of connections to the covenant. In the original language of his dogmatics, Bavinck uses two Latin expressions: "*de foedere*" (of the covenant) and "*in foedere*" (in the covenant).[31]

Some (baptized children) are "of" the covenant. The covenant is the origin of their true, spiritual life; they are born again by the covenant promise. They share the essence of the covenant. They belong to the covenant. The covenant identifies them. The covenant determines their life, experience, and behavior.

Other (baptized children) are merely "in" the covenant. By natural birth to believing parents; by the administration to them of the sacrament of the covenant; by their training under the word of God in a godly home, a true church, and a Christian school; more or less by their outward conduct (at least for a while); and even by their profession of faith (which does not arise from the heart), they are closely related to the covenant, as closely as a human can be without being "of" the covenant. But they are never part of it. Nor is it ever part of them.

The difference is that between a genuine, healthy cell of the human body and a foreign substance in the bloodstream.

---

29. Ibid., 231; emphasis added.
30. Ibid., 232.
31. Bavinck, *Gereformeerde Dogmatiek*, 3:244. In the original, the phrase reads as follows: "*Schoon niet* de foedere, *zijn zij toch* in foedere." Bavinck adds: "*en zullen zoo eenmaal geoordeeld worden*" (and will thus one day be judged).

In accordance with these two distinct kinds of covenant connections, Bavinck speaks of "the external and internal sides" of the one covenant of grace.[32]

Regarding covenant membership, therefore, Bavinck denies that all the baptized offspring of believers are in the covenant in the same way. Indeed, Bavinck denies that all the children are members of the covenant. If some children have membership merely in the covenant's "earthly administration," they are not members of the covenant in its essence.

What determines and governs these two connections to the covenant is God's predestination. When Bavinck distinguishes the two radically different connections to the covenant as belonging to the covenant, for some, and merely being "*in* the covenant," that is, being in the "earthly administration" of the covenant, for others, he obviously has his eye on Romans 9:6. In this passage, the apostle distinguishes two kinds of physical offspring of Abraham. Some are merely "of Israel," that is, in Bavinck's words, they are in the "earthly administration" of the covenant. Others "are . . . Israel," that is, in Bavinck's expression, they are "of the covenant." And in Romans 9:6–23, the apostle accounts for the two distinct connections to the covenant by appeal to eternal predestination: "that the purpose of God according to election might stand" (v. 11).

But Bavinck does not leave to implication, clear and necessary as the implication may be, that the two essentially different connections to the covenant "proceed from God's eternal decree," as Canons 1, Article 6 puts it. In explanation of the reality that some are merely "*in* [the earthly administration of] the covenant," whereas others are "*of* the covenant," Bavinck appeals, explicitly, to divine election.

> Here on earth they [those who are merely in the administration of the covenant] are connected with the elect in all sorts of ways, and the elect themselves . . . can as an organism only be gathered into one under Christ as their head in the way of the covenant.[33]

---

32. Ibid., 232.
33. Ibid.

Those who are connected to the covenant by vital membership in the covenant itself—in the very essence of the covenant—are the elect, and election determines their covenant membership. That Bavinck should teach this is nothing strange. For he was a Reformed theologian. And the Reformed faith confesses that faith, which is the living bond of union with Christ and, thus, fellowship with the triune God—the covenant in essence—proceeds from God's eternal election. "That some receive the gift of faith from God . . . proceeds from God's eternal decree."[34]

Those whose connection is merely the "external side" of the covenant, membership only in the "earthly administration" of the covenant, for Bavinck are the nonelect, the reprobate from eternity. This nonelection, or reprobation, determines their exclusion from the covenant. That Bavinck should teach this is nothing strange, for he was a Reformed theologian. And the Reformed faith confesses that the nonreception of faith, whether on the part of a contemporary heathen in the depths of San Francisco or on the part of a baptized child of godly Reformed parents, proceeds from God's eternal reprobation. "That . . . others do not receive it [faith], proceeds from God's eternal decree."[35]

Herman Bavinck repudiates the covenant doctrine that refuses to relate covenant membership to predestination, that deliberately banishes predestination from consideration in the matter of covenant membership, that will not find the source of covenant membership in God's election.

Bavinck condemns the covenant doctrine that teaches that all the baptized children of godly parents are in the covenant in the same way, at least, originally, at baptism.

Bavinck exposes the doctrine of the covenant that rejects the teaching of two essentially different connections to the covenant as being altogether outside and contrary to the Reformed tradition.

Bavinck not only approves of but also insists upon the distinction between two kinds of connections to the covenant, whether the distinction is called internal/external; covenant/administration of the covenant; or of the covenant/in the covenant.

---

34. Canons of Dordt, 1.6, in Schaff, *Creeds of Christendom*, 3:582.
35. Canons of Dordt, 1.6, in ibid.

How the distinction is phrased is of no great significance. The distinction itself is fundamental. To disallow the distinction is to fly in the face of the Reformed tradition; to reject the apostolic doctrine in Romans 9:6–23; and, necessarily, to introduce the Arminian heresy into the Reformed doctrine of the covenant.

This last, the theology of the federal vision is demonstrating clearly and practicing with a vengeance.

Mysterious Bias

In light of the history of the doctrine of the covenant in Reformed Protestantism, particularly Dutch Reformed Protestantism, and in light of the covenant doctrine of the highly regarded Bavinck, it is a mystery why contemporary Reformed theologians so violently react against a doctrine of the covenant that closely relates the covenant and election, and relates them in such a way that election governs the covenant. These theologians assail such a doctrine of the covenant as illegitimate. Their dismissal of the *identification* of the covenant and election (which is their pejorative way of describing a doctrine of the covenant in which election governs the covenant) leaves the impression that this doctrine of the covenant has had no place in the Reformed tradition. But at the very least it must be acknowledged by every knowledgeable, honest scholar that the teaching that the covenant is governed by election has had a prominent, powerful, honorable place in the Reformed tradition.

Chapter 12

THE COVENANT AND CHRIST:
OUT OF THE DECREE

It is fitting that this study of covenant and election conclude with a brief account of the biblical and Reformed doctrine of the covenant in the whole of its revelation.

Dominating, unifying, and illuminating the grand biblical truth of the covenant is the triune God's eternal decree of election. But the election that governs, unifies, and illumines the covenant is not, primarily, God's choice of his church. Rather, it is God's choice of Jesus Christ. The great issue in the ages-long controversy in the Reformed churches over the covenant that now comes to a head in the heresy of the federal vision is Jesus Christ. The issue "covenant and election" is, at bottom, the issue "covenant and Christ."

If the Reformed churches will understand the election that is related to the covenant as the divine choice and appointment of Jesus Christ, surely, even at this late hour, they will perceive the necessity of confessing that election governs the covenant.

Covenant with Abraham's Seed

God established the covenant of grace, in history, with Jesus Christ. It is a fundamental error with regard to the doctrine of the covenant to relate Jesus Christ to the covenant only by having him carry out the covenant will of God on behalf of the people of God. Jesus is not only the mediator of the covenant through whom God has fellowship with and saves his people and through whom the people of God commune with and serve God. Jesus Christ is also head of the covenant of grace. The triune God has made the covenant with the man Jesus Christ, the eternal Son of God in human nature. Jesus Christ is the representative of the people of God. He is also the source and fountain for the people of the spiritual life and the benefits of salvation that belong to the covenant.

According to Galatians 3:16, when God spoke his covenant promise to Abraham and his seed, he addressed the promise to Jesus Christ. "Now to Abraham and his seed were the promises made. He saith not, And to seeds, as of many; but as of one, and to thy seed, which is Christ." Verse 19 repeats that God made the covenant promise to Jesus Christ: The law was added to the promise "because of transgressions, till the seed [Jesus Christ] should come to whom the promise was made."

This Galatians passage refers specifically to Genesis 13:15 ("to thee will I give it [the land], and to thy seed for ever") and to Genesis 17:8 ("and I will give unto thee, and to thy seed after thee, the land wherein thou art a stranger, all the land of Canaan, for an everlasting possession; and I will be their God"). But if "seed" in these covenant promises was Jesus Christ, as Galatians 3:16 and 19 say it was, "seed" in all the covenant promises was centrally Jesus Christ. Even though "seed" in Genesis 17:7 broadens out to include all those humans who belong to Jesus Christ, it refers primarily to Jesus Christ. "I will establish my covenant between me and thee and thy seed after thee" means "I will establish my covenant between me and Jesus Christ."

God spoke his covenant promise to Jesus Christ. By this promise, God established his covenant with Jesus Christ. The covenant was established with Abraham by virtue of its establishment with Abraham's great seed, Jesus Christ.

That Galatians 3:16 and 19 teach the establishment of the covenant with Jesus Christ by God's address of the promise to him is made explicit by what follows in the chapter. Verse 17 explains God's address of the covenant promise to Christ as God's confirming the covenant in Christ: "And this I say, that the covenant, that was confirmed before of God in Christ . . ." "Confirmed" means established. Literally, the text reads: "And this I say, that the covenant, that was *established* before *unto* Christ . . ."

The covenant promise to Christ established the Abrahamic covenant, which is the one covenant of grace, with Christ as personal head of the covenant.

Because Christ is the head of the covenant, as Galatians 3:16 and 19 teach, Christ determines membership in the covenant. All those, but those only, who are Christ's are the seed of Abraham with whom God makes his covenant, and heirs of the promise, which God made to Christ. This is the conclusion about membership in the covenant that Galatians 3:29 draws from the truth that God made the covenant promise to Christ: "And if ye be Christ's, then are ye Abraham's seed, and heirs according to the promise."

Davidic Covenant

The outstanding feature of the Davidic covenant was its revelation that the covenant of grace is established with one man, the seed, or son, of David, the Messianic king.

The Davidic covenant was a distinct administration in the Old Testament of God's one covenant of grace.

The historical account of the establishment of this covenant is 2 Samuel 7:11–17. The prophet Nathan announced to David, when David was thinking of building the temple, that Jehovah God would set up David's seed after him and that this son of David would build the house of God. God would "stablish the throne of his [the coming son of David] kingdom for ever" (v. 13). Significantly, that son of David would also be the Son of God: "I will be his father, and he shall be my son" (v. 14).

The inspired commentary on this administration of the covenant is Psalm 89.

The covenant with David made known, progressively, the riches of the truth of the covenant of grace in several respects. They include the truth that the covenant, which is essentially the fellowship in love of God and his people, as revealed in the covenant formula, "I will be their God, and they shall be my people," takes form as an everlasting kingdom. Also, the man by whom Jehovah God will establish the covenantal kingdom, or "kingdomly" covenant, will be a physical descendant of King

David. "I will set up thy seed after thee, which shall proceed out of thy bowels, and I will establish his kingdom" (2 Sam. 7:12).

The typical fulfillment of this covenant promise was King Solomon, who built the earthly house of God. The spiritual reality is Jesus, the Messianic king, who builds the true and lasting house of God in his own resurrection body, which marvelously expands by the Spirit to include the church. That the promised son of David and son of God in view in the Davidic covenant is Jesus Christ, the angel made known in the announcement to Mary of Jesus' birth. "He shall be great, and shall be called the Son of the Highest: and the Lord God shall give unto him the throne of his father David: And he shall reign over the house of Jacob for ever; and of his kingdom there shall be no end" (Luke 1:32–33).

Zacharias heralded the birth of Jesus not simply as the fulfillment of the Davidic covenant, but as the fulfillment of the Davidic covenant *as a special administration of the covenant of grace made by God with Abraham and his seed.* That is, the coming of Jesus Christ into the world was God's realization of the covenant of grace with Abraham and his seed in the distinct form that was promised to David.

When Zacharias declared that the Lord God "hath raised up an horn of salvation for us in the house of his servant David" (Luke 1:69), he identified Jesus as the fulfillment of the Davidic covenant of 2 Samuel 7.

When the old priest, now become also a prophet, added that in Jesus God remembered "his holy covenant; The oath which he sware to our father Abraham" (Luke 1:72–73), he identified Jesus as the fulfillment of the covenant of grace established with Abraham and his seed in Genesis 12–22.

The outstanding characteristic of the Davidic covenant was that, just as he had done in the Abrahamic covenant, God established it with Jesus Christ, the true seed of David. This is emphasized in the divine commentary on the Davidic covenant, Psalm 89. Jehovah made the Davidic covenant "with my chosen" (v. 3). Verse 28 declares, "my covenant shall stand fast with him," that is, with the man who is the real David and who also will cry unto God, "Thou art my father" (vv. 20, 26). God made his covenant, in its Davidic form, with Jesus Christ. He did not make it directly with those called the "children" of the Messiah in verse 30, but with the Messiah himself.

Because God established the covenant with the Messiah himself and because God established the Davidic covenant by solemn, oath-bound promise ("I have sworn unto David my servant" (v. 3), the Davidic covenant is unbreakable—absolutely unbreakable. This is God's own word: "My covenant will I not break" (v. 34). The Hebrew word translated "break" by the Authorized Version means loose or dissolve.

God will not dissolve the covenant with Jesus Christ. Because Jesus Christ appears in the covenant not by himself alone, but as the head of a certain number of chosen covenant people—the citizens of his kingdom and the members of his nation—the covenant is unbreakable also with regard to all of the Messianic king's people. These people are prominently in view in Psalm 89. Knowing the joyful sound of the gospel of the Messianic king, they are "blessed," and they will walk in the light of God's countenance (v. 15). God's righteousness will exalt them (v. 16). There is certainty about their salvation, "for . . . the Holy One of Israel is our king" (v. 18).

The Messianic king has "seed" (v. 29) and "children" (v. 30). Their everlasting salvation is sure: "His seed also will I make to endure for ever" (v. 29).

Even though the king's children sin, and sometimes grievously, they do not, they cannot, dissolve the covenant. For the covenant depends on God, and God will not dissolve it. His faithfulness is at stake (v. 33). If he allows his covenant to be dissolved, his covenant promise is a lie. "My covenant will I not break, nor alter the thing that is gone out of my lips. Once have I sworn by my holiness that I will not lie unto David" (vv. 34–35).

The amazing explanation of the unbreakable covenant in view of the guilt and depravity of the people whom Jesus Christ represents is the astonishing God-forsakenness of the Messiah himself, as prophesied in Psalm 89:38–45. This section of the psalm describes the lifelong suffering and accursed, shameful death of Jesus Christ. If ever in all the long history of redemption the covenant of God has been broken, God himself broke it once—in his dealings with the Messiah, especially in the crucifixion of Jesus.

Psalm 89:38–39 speak of God's making void the covenant of his servant in wrath: "But thou hast cast off and abhorred, thou hast been wroth with thine anointed. Thou hast made void the covenant of thy servant." The word translated "made void" by the Authorized Version in verse 39 is not the same as that used in verse 34, where God promises never to "break" the covenant. God dealt with Jesus Christ as though he abhorred the covenant with him. In fierce anger, he cast Jesus off—the opposite of the fellowship that is the essence of the covenant. Jesus experienced this casting off, this voiding of the covenant with himself, and cried out in the agony of it, "My God, my God, why hast thou forsaken me?" (Matt. 27:46).

The reason for the voiding of the covenant with God's own Messiah himself was exactly the headship of Messiah of the Davidic covenant. As head of the covenant, Messiah represented a guilty people before a righteous God. By his wrath with his anointed, God propitiated in the Messiah the divine wrath against the covenant people.

By voiding the covenant with Jesus Christ individually, God realized his promise never to dissolve the covenant with Christ and his children. By voiding the covenant in the soul of Jesus Christ, God made the covenant with Christ and the elect church sure and everlasting.

Covenant Headship in Romans 5

Clear and conclusive biblical testimony to the fundamental truth concerning the covenant of grace, that God established the covenant with Jesus Christ as head of the covenant, is Romans 5:12–21. The passage compares Adam and Jesus Christ as the two men in history who had (and in the case of Christ, has) the position of covenant head of the human race. Romans 5:12–21 teaches the federal, or covenant, headship of the first Adam with regard to the entire human race, Jesus alone excepted. As covenant head of the race, Adam rendered the race guilty by his disobedience concerning the tree of knowledge. In Adam "all have sinned" (v. 12). The reference is to the imputation of the guilt of Adam's sin to all the race, as verse 18 makes plain: "by the offence of one judgment came upon all men to condemnation."

Romans 5:14 calls Adam the "figure [literally the type] of him that was to come," that is, of Jesus Christ. As Adam was covenant head, referring especially to his being the legal representative of the entire race, so Jesus Christ is covenant head of the new human race of the elect. This headship of the covenant, and only this headship of the covenant, accounts for the fact that the righteousness of Jesus Christ comes "upon all men unto justification of life" by imputation (v. 18).

Covenant headship explains that "by one man's disobedience many were made sinners," that is, made sinners legally by imputation. Likewise, covenant headship explains that "by the obedience of one shall many be made righteous," that is, made righteous legally by imputation (v. 19).

As God established the covenant of creation with Adam personally and directly, and with the race only in their head Adam, so God has established the covenant of grace with Jesus Christ, as covenant head, and with the new human race of the elect from all nations only in him. And this determines which humans are included in the covenant of grace and who the "all men" of Romans 5:18 are: all those, but those only, who are in Christ.

Source of the Covenant in the Decree

The establishment of the covenant with Jesus Christ in history has its source in God's eternal counsel. More specifically, it has its source in the decree of election. So close is the relation of covenant and election. So essential is the dependency of covenant upon election.

That the covenant of God with Jesus Christ and, in Christ, with the new human race has its origin in the decree of election is evident simply from the fact that the covenant is, contains, and bestows salvation. Scripture teaches that "the fountain of every saving good" is the divine decree of election, as the Canons of Dordt summarize Scripture.[1]

In addition, Scripture reveals that God's establishment of the covenant with Jesus Christ in history was decreed in the counsel of election. As the Canons of Dordt state, "the new covenant," which Christ "confirmed by the blood of the cross," was the "sovereign counsel and most gracious will and purpose of God the Father."[2]

The explanation of the covenant's source in eternity as an agreement, even a bargain, between the first and second persons of the Trinity is utterly mistaken. First, there is not a shred of biblical evidence for such a bargain between two of the persons of the Godhead. The main passage adduced in support of such a bargain, Zechariah 6:13, which speaks of "the counsel of peace . . . between them both," refers to the union of the royal and priestly offices in the coming "Branch," that is, the Messiah. It has nothing whatever to do with a bargaining of Father and Son.

Second, it is altogether unfitting that the first and second persons strike up agreements, as though two persons of the Godhead (usually leaving the third person—the Holy Ghost—sitting on the sideline) were two parties in the great work of salvation, rather than the one Savior God, with the Holy Ghost, planning Christ and the covenant with one mind and one will.

Third, the source in eternity of the establishment of the covenant in time must not be conceived as a pretemporal analogue of the supposed historical reality: two divine persons striking a conditional agreement that is thought to correspond to a conditional agreement between God and Jesus Christ or between God and sinners. But the source in eternity of the historical covenant was a divine decree of the one God, Father, Son, and Holy Ghost, just as all history is the unfolding of the eternal counsel. When the apostle traces "all things" back to the "will" of God, "according to his good pleasure which he hath purposed in himself," he certainly does not exclude Jesus Christ and the

---

1. Canons of Dordt, 1.9, in ibid., 3:583.
2. Canons of Dordt, 2.8, in ibid., 3:587.

covenant of grace with his church (Eph. 1:9–10). On the contrary, Jesus Christ and his church are at the very center of the "all things" purposed by the divine, eternal decree: "[God] hath chosen us in him [Jesus Christ]" (v. 4).

Fourth, the conception itself of the covenant as a conditional agreement between two parties, which then is projected backward into the relations of two persons of the Trinity, is erroneous. The covenant is not a cold, calculating, graceless contract. Covenant life is not the anxious performing of stipulated conditions, on our part, and the dutiful performing of stipulated conditions, on God's part. But the covenant is sweet communion between God and his people in Jesus Christ.

> *In sweet communion, Lord, with Thee*
> *I constantly abide;*
> *My hand Thou holdest in Thy own*
> *To keep me near Thy side.*
> *To live apart from God is death,*
> *'Tis good His face to seek;*
> *My refuge is the living God,*
> *His praise I long to speak.*[3]

Covenant life is wholly free, undeserved expression of love and bestowal of salvation toward us, on God's part, and wholly grateful outpouring of love, praise, and service toward God, on our part. The *Psalter* discloses the deepest wellsprings of the Christian's life with God, as well as the sovereign digging of these wellsprings by the unconditional love of God.

> *What shall I render to the Lord*
> *For all His benefits to me?*
> *How shall my soul by grace restored*
> *Give worthy thanks, O Lord, to Thee?*

---

3. Number 203, stanzas 1 and 5, in *The Psalter with Doctrinal Standards, Liturgy, Church Order, and added Chorale Section,* reprinted and revised edition of the 1912 United Presbyterian *Psalter* (Grand Rapids, MI: Eerdmans, 1927; rev. ed. 1965), 171. The *Psalter* accurately versifies Psalm 73.

His saints the Lord delights to save,
Their death is precious in His sight;
He has redeemed me from the grave,
And in His service I delight.
Within His house, the house of prayer,
I dedicate myself to God;
Let all His saints His grace declare
And join to sound His praise abroad.[4]

There must be an origin in eternity of the covenant of grace with Jesus Christ. It is inconceivable that Jesus Christ and the covenant of grace are the natural product of the historical process, or that they are a desperate, last-ditch attempt by God to salvage something from the wreckage when his plan with the human race had gone seriously awry.

The origin in eternity of the covenant of grace with Jesus Christ is the triune God's decree of Jesus Christ, the eternal Son in human flesh, as head of the covenant of grace and, thus, God's friend and servant in history. This decree, choosing Jesus Christ in love and appointing him head of the covenant of grace with regard to all whom God would give him as his people, is the first and fundamental aspect of the decree of election. God chose Jesus Christ first. Jesus Christ is *the* elect of God. And he is *the* elect not only individually, but also, and especially, as head of the covenant of grace and head, therefore, of the new human race.

The importance of confessing the close relation of election and covenant is that this confession honors Jesus Christ, as God wills Jesus Christ to be honored.

The seriousness of denying the relation of covenant and election is that this denial dishonors Jesus Christ.

The Old Testament Scripture describes the Messiah as God's elect with specific reference to his headship, mediatorship, and realization of the covenant. Regarding the Messiah

---

4. Number 311, stanzas 1, 3, and 5, in ibid., 271. This is a versification of Psalm 116.

with whom Jehovah God has made the covenant, Psalm 89:3 calls him "my chosen."

In Isaiah 42:1, Jehovah puts his servant, the Messiah, in the limelight, calling him "mine elect." The thought of the prophet is that the Messiah is God's one and only elect. The multitude of the others who are chosen are elect only in him—an extension of the election of the Messiah. This election of the Messiah concerns the covenant of God with his people. Isaiah 42:6 adds to the introduction of the Messiah as God's elect by saying that Jehovah chose this man "for a covenant of the people." The following verses describe the salvation and blessings of this covenant in language that the New Testament applies to the ministry of Jesus: "a light of the Gentiles; to open the blind eyes, to bring out the prisoners from the prison, and them that sit in darkness out of the prison house" (vv. 6–7).

So intimately are election and the covenant related in the Messiah that, as he himself is *the* elect of God, so also is he the covenant. The meaning of Isaiah 42:6 is that, in accordance with God's election of the Messiah, God gave him to be the covenant. In his human nature, personally united with the eternal Son, glorified in the resurrection in the way of the atoning death of the cross, Jesus Christ himself *is* the covenant. In himself, as God become flesh, he is the union and communion of God and man that is the covenant of grace.

Although he is the covenant, he is not the covenant for himself alone. Verse 6 of Isaiah 42 adds "of the people." That is, "I the LORD . . . give thee [Messiah] for a covenant of the people." This people includes "the Gentiles." Of which people he is the covenant is determined by the election that appointed Messiah as head of the covenant.

It is evident that to cut the covenant loose from election, invariably with the purpose of extending covenant grace and salvation more widely than elect men and women, is necessarily to wreak havoc with the relation of election and covenant in Jesus Christ himself.

The New Testament also locates the origin of Jesus Christ and his saving work, which is the establishment and perfection of the covenant of grace, in God's eternal decree, specifically, the decree of election.

Ephesians 1:4 teaches that God chose the church in eternity ("before the foundation of the world") "in him," that is, in the "Christ," who is "our Lord Jesus Christ" (v. 3). If God chose the church in Christ, Christ was in the decree prior to its choice of the church. Christ was in the decree as the man elected by the triune God to glorify God as head, husband, and savior of the church. As Ephesians 2:12 indicates, the elected Christ's saving work in the world would be covenant work. According to Ephesians 2:12, when in time past we Gentiles were "without Christ," we were "strangers from the covenants of promise." If prior to our salvation we were "strangers from the covenants of promise," Christ's salvation of us is the work of making us at home in the covenant, that is, making us members of the covenant by uniting us to himself. To this covenant work he was appointed by God's choice of him as head of the covenant in the decree of election "before the foundation of the world" (Eph. 1:4).

The fullest, clearest, and most compelling revelation in all of Scripture that the origin of the covenant of grace with Christ in history is the election of Christ in the eternal decree is Colossians 1:13–23. The source of the "dear Son" of God, who has "translated us into the kingdom" of Jesus Christ (which is not essentially different from the covenant), is the eternal decree in which this Jesus Christ is "the firstborn of every creature" (vv. 13–15). Obviously, Jesus is not the firstborn of every creature in time. Neither is he the firstborn of every creature according to his divine person. According to his eternal person, he is the only begotten. As the eternal Son, he does not belong in the category of the creature.

Jesus Christ is the firstborn of every creature in his human nature—as a man. The man Jesus, as the Christ of God, is first not in time, but in the eternal decree. He is first in the decree both in the order of the decree and in primacy. This means that God willed all other creatures, including the first Adam, the speaking serpent, the tree of knowledge, and, indeed, Lucifer, who would become Satan, after and for the sake of Jesus Christ. "All things were created . . . for him" (v. 16). "It pleased the Father [this is decretal language] that in him [our Lord Jesus Christ, in whom we have redemption through his blood, even the forgiveness of sins] should all fulness dwell" (v. 19).

God set his good pleasure on Jesus Christ in the counsel not by himself alone, but as "head of the body, the church" (v. 18). This implies that God decreed Jesus Christ as the man who would establish the covenant with this church. It was the Father's pleasure, in the decree, that Jesus Christ reconcile the church to himself by his death (vv. 21–22). Reconciliation is a covenant word and reality: harmonious fellowship with God in restored peace.

God's choice and appointment of Jesus Christ purposed the realization of the covenant with the entire creation. "It pleased the Father . . . by him [Jesus Christ] to reconcile all things unto himself . . . whether they be things in earth, or things in heaven" (vv.19–20). The apostle has his eye on the covenant with Noah. The covenant of grace does not include only elect humanity. It extends to the entire, vast creation of heaven and earth, plants and animals. Paul enlarges on this aspect of the covenant with Christ in Romans 8:19–22.

Jesus Christ as the head of the covenant, and therefore the covenant of grace with man and with the rest of creation, are conceived in the womb of the decree of election. The Canons of Dordt are soundly and profoundly biblical when they attribute both the election of "a certain number of persons" and the (covenant) salvation of the elect in time to God's appointment of Jesus Christ in the decree of election.

> Election is the unchangeable purpose of God, whereby, before the foundation of the world, he hath . . . chosen . . . a certain number of persons to redemption *in Christ, whom he from eternity appointed the Mediator and head of the elect, and the foundation of salvation.*[5]

---

5. Canons of Dordt, 1.7, in Schaff, *Creeds of Christendom,* 3:582; emphasis added.

Fifty years before the Canons of Dordt, at the very dawn of the distinctively Reformed reformation of the church, the Scottish Confession of Faith likewise affirmed that the source of Christ as the mediator of the covenant and head of the church is the decree of election. Speaking of the "mediator" and with specific reference to the covenantal union of the divine and human natures "in Christ Jesus," the Scottish Confession declared:

> This wonderful union between the Godhead and the humanity in Christ Jesus did arise from the eternal and immutable decree of God from which all our salvation springs and depends.[6]

The Scottish Confession immediately added, in the chapter headed "Election":

> The same eternal God and Father, who by grace alone chose us in his Son Christ Jesus before the foundation of the world was laid, *appointed him to be our head, our brother, our pastor, and the great bishop of our souls.*[7]

---

6. The Scottish Confession of Faith, 7, in Arthur C. Cochrane, ed., *Reformed Confessions of the 16th Century* (Philadelphia: Westminster Press, 1966), 168; emphasis added. This confession is also found in Schaff, *Creeds of Christendom*, volume 3, but in the old English.

7. The Scottish Confession of Faith, 8, in ibid.; emphasis added.

Chapter 13

THE COVENANT AND CHRIST: ADAM AND NOAH

Covenant with Adam

God's election of Jesus Christ as head of the covenant of grace determines the meaning of the covenant of creation with Adam in paradise.

Regardless that Genesis 1–3 does not use the term *covenant* to describe the relation between God and Adam, Scripture puts beyond all doubt that the creator established a covenant with Adam.

From the moment on the sixth day that Adam breathed, stood upright, and knew God his maker in love, Adam was in the special, close relationship of fellowship with God that is the essence of the covenant between God and humans, as revealed in Scripture. The relationship was that of son and Father, for Adam was the son of God (Luke 3:38) and thus God's image (Gen. 1:26–27). God made the covenant with Adam by his creation of him in the image of God. The covenant with Adam is rightly called the covenant of creation.

As a Father with his son (and, of course, with Eve as his daughter), God walked and talked with Adam in the cool of the day (Gen. 3:8). God and his human creature were friends.

In this covenant relationship, Adam had the privilege and calling to serve his Father and sovereign out of pure love and simple gratitude. He must carry out his calling by obedience to the covenantal demands. Adam was God's friend; he was also God's servant. Adam was called to cultivate and guard[1] the garden of Eden (Gen. 2:15). Since obedience—sheer, unquestioning, humble, trusting obedience—is always the calling of man in

---

1. *Guard* is the right translation of the word translated as "keep" by the Authorized Version. Always the covenant calling includes watchfulness against the foe.

the covenant, God tried Adam with the perfectly lawful and utterly easy prohibition against eating of the tree of the knowledge of good and evil. "And the LORD God commanded the man, saying . . . of the tree of the knowledge of good and evil, thou shalt not eat of it: for in the day that thou eatest thereof thou shalt surely die" (vv. 16–17).

This negative command was not the establishment of the covenant. No covenant is established by a command, much less by a negative command. Rather, the command presupposed an already existing covenant between the commanding God and his duty-bound son and servant. In the biblical covenants, the human friend of God is always also an obedient servant. Adam, the servant, must serve his Lord also by heeding the prohibition against eating the fruit of one tree in the garden. So doing, he would earn nothing; nor by his labor, or better, his refraining, could he climb to a higher condition of life than that in which he was created.

The first Adam was made a "living soul"; he could never become for himself and the race a "quickening spirit" (1 Cor. 15:45). "The first man [was] of the earth, earthy"; he could never become, or make the race, "heavenly" (vv. 47–49). Only the "last Adam," the "second man," the "Lord from heaven," could himself become, and make the new human race, "spiritual" and "heavenly" (vv. 45–49).

The notion (popular though it has become, and now shrilly insistent that the denial of the notion is a main form, perhaps even the only form, of covenant heresy) that by not eating Adam could have earned, or otherwise obtained, the higher life and glory of man now found in the incarnate and risen Jesus Christ is false. It is an imposition on the text. It flatly contradicts the wise and good purpose of God with the negative command, namely, that by Adam's willful, wicked, foolish disobedience, that servant of God might come who alone could earn for himself and others and create in his own human nature immortal, heavenly, and eternal life.

Heeding the serious negative command of God simply because it was a divine command, without any rhyme or reason as man might judge, Adam must demonstrate his perfect serv-anthood and magnify the awesome sovereignty of his God in the covenant.

In the covenant Adam was head both of the human race that would come from him and his wife and of the earthly creation. He had authority over the race and the earth. Such was his posi-tion of headship in the covenant that his disobedience to, and falling away from, God would be the ruin both of the race and of the earth with all its creatures. Romans 5:18 teaches that Adam's disobedience rendered all men guilty and therefore under con-demnation: "Therefore as by the offence of one judgment came upon all men to condemnation; even so by the righteousness of one the free gift came upon all men unto justification of life." Adam was the legal representative of the race. Romans 8:20 teaches that Adam's transgression plunged the entire earthly creation into the vanity of corruption and death: "For the crea-ture was made subject to vanity, not willingly, but by reason of him who hath subjected the same in hope." Adam was legal representative of the earthly creation, so that the creation shared the guilt of Adam. God gave Adam knowledge of his responsible position when he blessed Adam and Eve with the fruitfulness of their sexual relationship in posterity and installed them as king and queen over all the earth. "And God blessed them, and God said unto them, Be fruitful, and multiply, and replenish the earth, and subdue it: and have dominion over the fish of the sea, and over the fowl of the air, and over every living thing that moveth upon the earth" (Gen. 1:28). Adam knew himself to be head of the covenant of creation.

Especially two passages of Scripture confirm the witness of Genesis 1–3 that God established a covenant with Adam in paradise.

The first is Hosea 6:7: "But they [Ephraim and Judah, that is, all Israel] like men have transgressed the covenant: there have they dealt treacherously against me." The Hebrew word trans-lated "men" in the Authorized Version is *"adam."* *Adam* in He-brew can be either the generic word for mankind, or the proper name of the first man. Here, contrary to the conclusion of the translators of the Authorized Version, the meaning is Adam, the first human. The correct translation is: "But they like Adam have transgressed the covenant." The text describes the disobedience of Adam in paradise as a transgression, or violation, of a covenant. This makes explicit what is implicit in the historical narrative, namely, that the relation between God and Adam was a covenant.

Hosea 6:7 demands the translation "Adam." First, it would be mere redundancy for the prophet to have declared that the men of Israel violated the covenant "like men." How else could they transgress the covenant? Second, even if the translation "like men" is adopted, the text would still teach that Adam's sin was transgression of a covenant. For "men" transgressed the covenant in the first father of the race, Adam. In addition, the accusation of dealing treacherously with God certainly applies to the deed of Adam in eating the forbidden fruit. He betrayed God's world, God's human race, himself as God's own son and servant, and, as to his intention, God himself to God's great enemy.

The other passage of Scripture that confirms the witness of Genesis 1–3 that Adam was in a covenant relation with God in paradise is Romans 5:12–21. The testimony of this passage is incontrovertible. Adam stood in such a relation to the entire race, which would proceed from him, that his disobedient act was imputed by God to the race. "By the offence of one judgment came upon all men to condemnation" (v. 18). "By one man's disobedience many were [legally] constituted sinners" (v. 19; my translation of the Greek).

Adam was the head of the race, in the sense of the legal representative. This is federal, or covenant, headship.

Romans 5:14 affirms that in this important respect—covenant headship—Adam was the "figure," literally the type, of Jesus Christ. The covenant headship of Adam was a divinely designed, historical type of the covenant headship of Jesus Christ.

The covenant with Adam in paradise was not a conditional agreement between God and Adam by which Adam could have merited, matured into, or obtained in any way whatever for himself and the race the higher, better, spiritual, immortal, eternal, and heavenly life that Jesus Christ has merited, obtained, and entered into for himself and elect humanity by his incarnation, death, and resurrection.

This understanding of the covenant with Adam, which shows its colors by preferring to call this covenant a covenant of works, is a serious error. It is in conflict with fundamental truths of Reformed theology. It has done grave damage to the Reformed faith's confession of salvation by grace alone.

For one thing, God's covenants with men are not conditional agreements or bargains. God does not bargain with his human creatures. Of a mutual agreement between God and Adam in the narrative in Genesis, there is not so much as a hint. God established a covenant with Adam, unilaterally. The nature of that covenant was fellowship in love. In the relation of the covenant, God simply commanded obedience as the reasonable service of himself by his highly favored son and friend.

Adam did not agree to this covenant. He received it with thankfulness and joy. Adam did not accept the stipulations, much less counter the divine demands with stipulations of his own. He submitted to them. And then he rebelled against one of them.

For another thing, Adam could not merit anything with God, certainly not the eternal life that Jesus Christ earned by his lifelong obedience and, especially, by his redeeming death. The notion of merit is basic to the conception of the covenant with Adam as a conditional covenant of works. By obedience Adam is supposed to have been able to earn a better, indeed a much better, life and a greater, indeed a much greater, glory. God would have owed this to the working Adam.

But mere man cannot merit! Mere man can never do more than is required of him, so as to deserve anything from God. "When ye shall have done all those things which are commanded you, say, We are unprofitable servants: we have done that which was our duty to do" (Luke 17:10).

Nor could God have permitted Adam to merit anything with him, certainly not eternal life. This is the defense of their doctrine by those who teach that Adam could have merited spiritual, heavenly, eternal life—the very life that Christ Jesus has obtained for his people. God, they contend, allowed Adam to merit eternal life *by virtue of the pact, or covenant.*[2] But God could not allow Adam to merit with him, whether by virtue of the covenant or by virtue of Adam's natural abilities. For God cannot allow himself to be indebted to mere man. God cannot put himself in the position in which he is obliged to man, rather than man's being obliged to him. If Adam could have merited eternal life, God conceivably would have owed Adam and the race eternal life. Eternal life would have been wages paid to a deserving human race.

This is absolutely impossible.

This is inconceivable.

Those who argue that God put Adam in a position in which he really could have merited eternal life, be it by divine condescension, are saying that it is conceivable that the human race might have obtained eternal life from God *as a debt owed to them.* Everlastingly (it is conceivable), the race might have sung a paean of praise to themselves: "We earned this! God owed this to us! Our work merited the highest and best God made available to us! Salvation is of man!"

Those who insist on a covenant of works as an arrangement by which Adam could have merited eternal life have no fundamental objection against man's earning salvation—the highest life and glory—by his own works. No doubt, they freely acknowledge that it did not work out. No doubt, they deny that it is any longer possible for fallen man to merit. No doubt, they sincerely confess that now only Jesus Christ merits salvation. No doubt, they criticize Rome for its doctrine of merit. But they themselves believe, and strenuously defend, that once man— mere man, man apart from Jesus Christ—could very really have merited eternal life. The idea is not repugnant to them.

From this notion arise, and have already arisen, threats to the Reformed faith and its gospel of grace. If God could al-

---

2. See Cornelis P. Venema, "Recent Criticisms of the 'Covenant of Works' in the Westminster Confession of Faith," *Mid-America Journal of Theology* 9, no. 2 (1993): 165–98.

low man to merit by virtue of his condescending covenant in paradise, why can he not also allow man to merit by virtue of a condescending covenant still today? This is the siren song of Rome. Calvin notes that the Roman Catholic Church grounds its doctrine of meritorious works in the alleged provisions of God's covenant. That is, Rome teaches that the good works of sinners are meritorious not intrinsically, but by virtue of the covenant. "They [Roman Catholic theologians] maintain that works are meritorious of salvation, not by their intrinsic worth, but by the acceptance of God, (to use their own phrase,) and on the ground of a covenant."[3]

Also, if the covenant with Adam was a conditional agreement in which man's works earned, or otherwise obtained, life and glory with God as a matter of human merit and divine debt, why cannot also the covenant of grace be viewed as a conditional agreement in which the good works of the human members of the covenant contribute to their justification and make them worthy of eternal life?

The deathblow to this doctrine of a covenant of works, however, is the truth of God's eternal election of Jesus Christ as head of the covenant of grace. Having chosen Jesus Christ as the one man who would establish the covenant with the human race of the elect out of all nations, God would not, indeed could not, also appoint Adam as a covenant head who might conceivably realize his covenant with the human race by earning, or otherwise obtaining, eternal life for all humans. God is not a whimsically paradoxical deity. He did not elect Adam and Christ. He did not elect Christ in case Adam should fail. He chose Christ Jesus.

Christ is first and preeminent in the counsel of God, as we have seen in Colossians 1. God decreed Adam as head of the covenant of creation not independently of Christ, nor as a competitor of Jesus Christ, but for the sake of Jesus Christ and the covenant of grace, which Jesus Christ, and Jesus Christ only, could and would realize.

God created Adam merely as a "figure," or type, of Jesus

---

3. Calvin, *Galatians and Ephesians*, 97.

Christ, the real covenant head (Rom. 5:14). The figure is not on a par with the reality, does not compete with the reality, and surely is not in a position to outdo the reality—in this case take the entire human race to the heights of life and glory, whereas Jesus Christ takes only some to these heights. Rather, the figure faintly pictures, serves, and then gives way to the reality.

Adam faintly pictured the coming Christ by his headship of an inferior covenant—in the words of 1 Corinthians 15—a covenant of merely natural, earthy life and glory.

Adam must serve the covenant purpose of God in Jesus Christ by his disobedience. Although the blame was truly and wholly Adam's and Satan's, who tempted him, and not at all God's, the covenant disobedience of Adam was decreed and governed by God in the service of Jesus Christ and the covenant of grace.

In the past the avowed enemies of the Reformed faith raged against this explanation of Adam's covenant transgression as "determinism," "fatalism," and "blasphemy." This doctrine, they charged, makes God the "author of sin." The Arminians harped on this string in their opposition to the confession of the sovereignty of God by the Reformed churches at the time of the Synod of Dordt.[4] Today, it is likely that nominally Reformed theologians will make these accusations.

The Reformed response is not a hasty retreat from, or the slightest compromise of, the confession that God decreed Adam and his covenant of creation, including Adam's transgression of the covenant, strictly on behalf of Christ and his covenant of grace. "All things were created . . . for him," including Adam, the serpent, and the tree of knowledge (Col. 1:16). Having purposed in eternity to "gather together in one all things in Christ [not in Adam]," God "worketh all things after the counsel of his own will," including the covenant disobedience of Adam (Eph. 1:10–11).

In the article on providence, the Belgic Confession affirms

---

4. The recent penetrating study of the theology of James Arminius by William den Boer makes plain that the charge against the Reformed doctrine of sovereign predestination that it makes God "the author of sin" was the main "argument" of the Remonstrants at the time of—and at—the Synod of Dordt. See William den Boer, *God's Twofold Love.*

that God, "after he had created all things, did not forsake them, or give them up to fortune or chance, but . . . he rules and governs them, according to his holy will, so that nothing happens in this world without his appointment." That the phrase "nothing happens in this world without his appointment" has particular reference to the disobedience of Adam and, by this disobedience, to the fall of the race is evident from what immediately follows: "Nevertheless, God neither is the author of, nor can be charged with, the sins which are committed." The explanation is that "his power and goodness are so great and incomprehensible, that he orders and executes his work in the most excellent and just manner even when the devil and wicked men act unjustly." [5] The Reformed believer curbs his overly curious, and sometimes defiant, reason with this meek spirit of faith:

> And as to what he [God] doth surpassing human understanding we will not curiously inquire into it further than our capacity will admit of; but with the greatest humility and reverence adore the righteous judgments of God which are hid from us, contenting ourselves that we are disciples of Christ, to learn only those things which he has revealed to us in his Word without transgressing these limits. [6]

This view of the covenant with Adam as serving Christ and the covenant of grace is by no means unknown in the Reformed tradition. Herman Witsius wrote this about the relation of the covenant with Adam and the covenant with Christ:

> But it pleased God, according to the riches of his unsearchable wisdom, to lay this breach of the legal covenant [Adam's transgression of what Witsius called the "covenant of works"] as a foundation for his stupendous works; for he took occasion to set up a new *covenant of grace;* in which he might much more clearly display the inestimable treasures of his all-sufficiency, than if every thing had gone well with man according to the first covenant. [7]

---

5. Belgic Confession, Art. 13, in Schaff, *Creeds of Christendom,* 3:396–97.

6. Belgic Confession, Art. 13, in ibid.

7. Herman Witsius, *The Economy of the Covenants between God and Man: Comprehending a Complete Body of Divinity,* vol. 1, trans. William Crookshank

Likewise, Herman Bavinck held that "God, who knows and determines all things and included also the breach of the covenant of works [the covenant with Adam] in his counsel when creating Adam and instituting the covenant of works, already counted on the Christ and his covenant of grace."[8]

The covenant with Adam was not an administration of the covenant of grace in Jesus Christ. There were fundamental differences between the covenant with Adam and the covenant of grace. The covenant with Adam was not a relationship with sinners; was not mediated by Jesus Christ; was not founded in the blood of the cross; did not deliver men and women from death to life; was not a revelation of the love of God toward guilty, depraved men and women that gives the only begotten Son for them. If it should not be named a covenant of works, neither should the covenant with Adam be called a covenant of grace.

The covenant of grace in Jesus Christ was revealed and established for the first time in the promise of the gospel to Adam and Eve in Genesis 3:15: "I will put enmity between thee [Satan, in the serpent] and the woman, and between thy seed and her seed; it shall bruise thy head, and thou shalt bruise his heel." Enmity between Satan's brood of the reprobate ungodly and the woman's family of the elect implies friendship between the woman's family and God. This friendship is the essence of the covenant of grace, which is salvation. God established the covenant by promise: "I will put." God assured the full realization of the covenant by promise: "It [the seed of the woman, who is Jesus Christ] will bruise thy [Satan's] head."

The notion of a conditional agreement, or bargain, whether in explanation of this first establishment of the covenant of grace or in explanation of the realization of the covenant, is simply excluded—is absurd. Adam and Eve stood before God as guilty and totally depraved. God established his covenant of grace, and assured its realization, by gracious

---

(London: R. Baynes, 1822; repr. Escondido, CA: The Den Dulk Christian Foundation, 1990), 164.

8. Bavinck, *Reformed Dogmatics*, 3:228.

promise in the seed of the woman, who is Jesus Christ.

Inasmuch as God established covenant friendship with himself for guilty, depraved sinners—Adam, Eve, and the woman's children—and inasmuch as God established the covenant in the seed of the woman, who is God's own Son in human flesh, Jesus Christ, the covenant was revealed as gracious.

The nature of the covenant with Adam and its relation to the covenant of grace with Christ are indicated by Romans 5:14, which calls Adam the "figure" of Christ. In his covenant headship, Adam was a type of Christ. Similarly, God's covenant with him was typical of the real covenant with Christ. In the inferior quality of a type, the covenant with Adam was humanity's communion with God in an individual head.

By virtue of his headship, Adam violated the covenant of creation not only for himself, but also for all his posterity. The entire human race, Jesus only excepted, suffer the consequences of Adam's disobedience to the end of time: original guilt, total depravity of nature, and physical death in all its aspects.

Although the consequences of the violation of the covenant of creation are in force throughout history, that typical covenant is not, and cannot be, renewed or reinstated. So did Adam break that distinct form of covenant that it is forever discarded and useless with regard to any right and saving relation of humans with God. In the eternal wisdom of God, that covenant—a type—gave way to the reality, the covenant of grace in Christ Jesus. When the reality has come, as it did in the promise of Genesis 3:15, there is no possibility of the return of the type.

Adam fell into the arms of Christ, and Christ was waiting, according to eternal election.[9]

Covenant with Noah

The word "covenant" occurs first in the Bible in the account of the salvation of Noah and his family from the wicked world

---

9. For a more complete explanation of the covenant of creation and a more thorough critique of the explanation of that covenant as a covenant of works, see David J. Engelsma, "The Covenant of Creation with Adam," *Protestant Reformed Theological Journal* 40, no. 1 (November 2006): 3–42.

by the baptizing waters of the flood. "With thee [Noah] will I establish my covenant" (Gen. 6:18).

Following the lead of Abraham Kuyper, most contemporary Reformed theologians (but not most orthodox Reformed theologians of the past) explain the covenant with Noah as a covenant of common grace. It is a different covenant from the covenant of grace in Jesus Christ. Jesus Christ is not the head and mediator of this covenant. This covenant is not confirmed by the atoning blood of the cross. This covenant does not bestow the blessings of salvation that are in Jesus Christ. This covenant does not save the church, or build the kingdom, of Jesus Christ. This covenant does not honor Jesus Christ. Indeed, this covenant has nothing to do with Jesus Christ, except that, in a polite gesture toward Jesus Christ, it is said to preserve a world that, in addition to its main purpose—culture! culture! culture!—enables Jesus Christ to do his saving work.

According to Kuyper, the covenant with Noah is not "a covenant of *particular* [grace], but . . . a covenant of *common* grace."[10] "This Noahic covenant is *not* saving . . . [and may not be] identified with the other covenants [in Scripture], but [must be] viewed as separate, as a covenant of an entirely different kind."[11] The "*content* [of the covenant with Noah] . . . lies wholly within the sphere of *natural* life, has in view *temporal* and not eternal benefits, and holds as much for unbelievers as for those who fear God."[12]

In his *Dictaten Dogmatiek* Kuyper denies that the common grace covenant with Noah is related to Jesus Christ as the "mediator of redemption." Rather, the connection is strictly to Christ as "the mediator of creation," that is, to

---

10. Abraham Kuyper, *De Gemeene Gratie*, vol. 1, *Het Geschiedkundig Gedeelte* [Common grace . . . the historical installment] (Kampen: Kok, n.d [the original edition of the three-volume work on common grace was published in 1902–04]), 22. This and following quotations from Kuyper's *De Gemeene Gratie* are my translation of the Dutch. The work has not been translated. The emphasis is Kuyper's in this and the following two quotations.

11. Ibid., 34.

12. Ibid., 26.

Christ exclusively as he is the eternal Son and Word of God.[13]

"The great purpose of God with his common grace [in the covenant with Noah]," wrote Kuyper, "is to restrain bestiality and make possible a development of human culture. In this he shows his love of mankind, indeed his love of the universe."[14]

Such is the importance, in his main work on common grace (*De Gemeene Gratie*), of Kuyper's explanation of the covenant with Noah that if Kuyper's understanding of this covenant is mistaken, his entire theory of common grace suffers a mortal blow.

The covenant of grace with Noah, it is vehemently asserted by Reformed theologians at the beginning of the twenty-first century, accomplishes a great purpose of God with creation and history alongside his purpose with Jesus Christ. This purpose is the forming of a good, even God-pleasing, indeed Christian culture by the cooperation of believers and unbelievers.

Ominously, this covenant unites the seed of the serpent and the seed of the woman of Genesis 3:15. Three chapters after he had put enmity—hatred and warfare—between God-fearing believers and ungodly unbelievers, God supposedly established a covenant of friendship and union between believers and unbelievers. The covenant of common grace with Noah unites believers and unbelievers by a shared grace of God. It unites them in a great good work: "Christianizing" society, the nation, and the world.

In the most bizarre twist imaginable, the climax of the common grace covenant with Noah, according to Abraham Kuyper, the premier theoretician of this covenant, will be the glorious culture of the kingdom of Antichrist. Presumably, believers will have helped in the forming of this dazzling kingdom of the beast.[15]

---

13. Abraham Kuyper, *Dictaten Dogmatiek* [Dictated dogmatics], vol. 3, *Locus de Providentia, Peccato, Foedere, Christo* [Locus concerning providence, sin, covenant, Christ], 2nd ed. (Grand Rapids, MI: B. Sevensma, n.d. [vol. 1 bears the date 1910]), "*Locus de Foedere*," 129. All quotations from *Dictaten Dogmatiek* are my translation of the Dutch. The work has not been translated.

14. Ibid., 128.

15. "The closing scene in the drama of common grace can be enacted only through the appearance on stage of the man of sin ... 'Common grace' ... leads

The fundamental criticism of the explanation of the covenant with Noah as a covenant of common grace is that it is a covenant that does not begin and end with Jesus Christ. It is a covenant that leaves Jesus Christ out altogether. Indeed, on Kuyper's reckoning, it is a covenant of a grace of God that establishes the kingdom of Satan, in opposition to the kingdom of God's dear Son. God's two graces work at cross-purposes with each other: his special grace favors Christ; his common grace opposes him. His special grace builds the kingdom of Christ; his common grace builds the kingdom of Antichrist.

The truth is that God has one purpose with creation and history. This purpose is Jesus Christ and the covenant of (special) grace in him. This is the significance of the choice of Jesus Christ first in the decree of election, which decree is first in the eternal counsel of God. "He [the dear Son of God, in whom we have redemption in his blood] is before all things" (Col. 1:17). "All things were created . . . for him" (v. 16).

The theology of a covenant of common grace is insulting to Jesus Christ, who must have the preeminence not only in the saving of the church, but also in the providential directing of history. "Who is the beginning . . . that in all things he might have the preeminence" (v. 18).

The covenant with Noah was an early administration of the covenant of grace in Jesus Christ, revealed first in the mother covenant promise of Genesis 3:15. "My covenant," in the first mention of the word "covenant" in the Bible, in Genesis 6:18, has the sense of "my one and only covenant." The covenant

to the most powerful manifestation of sin in history . . . At the moment of its destruction, Babylon—that is, the world power which evolved from human life—will exhibit not the image of a barbarous horde nor the image of coarse bestiality but, on the contrary, a picture of the highest development of which human life is capable. It will display the most refined forms, the most magnificent unfolding of wealth and splendor, the fullest brilliance of all that makes life dazzling and glorious. From this we know that 'common grace' will continue to function to the end. Only when common grace has spurred the full emergence of all the powers inherent in human life will 'the man of sin' find the level terrain needed to expand this power" (Abraham Kuyper, "Common Grace," in *Abraham Kuyper: A Centennial Reader*, ed. James D. Bratt [Grand Rapids, MI: Eerdmans, 1998], 180–81).

with Noah was a covenant founded on the righteousness of the bloody sacrifice of Jesus Christ, foreshadowed by Noah's altar and sacrifice (Gen. 8:20–22).

The salvation of Noah and his family—*and the animals*—in the ark was no mere physical preservation of the human race and animals from a natural calamity by a common grace of God. *By* the waters of the flood (not *from* the waters of the flood), God accomplished the spiritual salvation of Noah and his family— the elect human race of eight souls at that time—from sin and damnation—the corrupt world of the ungodly, which had filled its cup of iniquity and upon which the wrath of God would fall. The water by which the church was saved, for Noah and his family were the church, was the abundant sprinkling of the blood of Jesus Christ upon the ark and its cargo. The grace that delivered Noah from the wicked world and its destruction was the precious, particular favor of God in Jesus Christ.

This is the explanation, in 1 Peter 3:20–21, of the deliverance of Noah and his family:

> ... when once the longsuffering of God waited in the days of Noah, while the ark was a-preparing, wherein few, that is, eight souls were saved by water. The like figure whereunto even baptism doth also now save us (not the putting away of the filth of the flesh, but the answer of a good conscience toward God), by the resurrection of Jesus Christ.

By the flood Noah was not ushered into a world that had merely been preserved for continued use by the surviving human race. But Noah stepped out into a new form of the creation, cleansed of its unrighteousness, typically. Second Peter 3:1–10 compares the deliverance, in time past, of the church of eight souls into a new form of the earthly creation to the deliverance, in the future, of the church into a new heaven and a new earth, by the coming fire. "The world that then was, being overflowed with water, perished . . . We, according to his promise, look for new heavens and a new earth, wherein dwelleth righteousness" (vv. 6, 13). It is not common grace that brings the people of God into a new world of righteousness.

In addition, Genesis 9:16 calls the covenant with Noah "everlasting," which is true only of the covenant of grace of which Jesus Christ is head and mediator.

The meaning of the covenant with Noah was that it revealed the vast design of God with his covenant of grace in Christ and the greatness of the glory of Jesus Christ as head of the covenant. In its final outworking the covenant in Christ will incorporate not only the entire human race, in the elect of all nations and peoples, but also the entire creation of God—the earth itself, its various nonhuman creatures, and heaven. Regarding heaven, Jesus Christ will in this respect also outstrip Adam. Adam was head of the earthly creation. Jesus is head of heaven and earth.

Reflecting on the covenant with Noah, John exclaims concerning God's love for the "world"—the *kosmos* in the Greek—the universe, especially the earthly area of the universe, including not only the new human race of the elect out of all nations, but also the earth, the heaven, and the nonrational creatures they contain (John 3:16).

Paul puts the meaning of the covenant with Noah beyond all doubt, and any controversy, when he speaks of the hope of creation for the coming of Christ and the fullness of covenant salvation at his coming.

> The earnest expectation of the creature [or creation] waiteth for the manifestation of the sons of God. For the creature [or creation] was made subject to vanity, not willingly, but by reason of him who hath subjected the same in hope. Because the creature [or creation] itself also shall be delivered from the bondage of corruption into the glorious liberty of the children of God. For we know that the whole creation groaneth and travaileth in pain together until now (Rom. 8:19–22).

This passage is the authoritative New Testament commentary on the covenant with Noah.

Romans 8:19–22 expresses the hope not of the people of God, but of nonrational creation. Four times in the passage the Greek has the same word, referring to the world God made in the beginning, exclusive of rational, moral, personal beings.

Three times the Authorized Version translates the word as "creature," with reference to the individual entities that make up the world—earth and heaven; sun, moon, and stars; plants and animals. The fourth time, the Authorized Version correctly renders the Greek word as "the creation": "the whole creation" (v. 22).

The hope of creation—its expectation of, and longing for, a great good for itself in the future—is not for mere preservation of itself under the curse of God as long as history lasts. The present, history-long condition of creation is its "vanity" in the "bondage of corruption" from which creation desires to be liberated (vv. 20–21).

The hope of creation is certainly not the dazzling development of its powers in the kingdom of Antichrist. That God's grace—*any* grace of God—should realize itself in the kingdom of Satan is sheer absurdity. Indeed, the theory—Kuyper's theory of common grace, enthusiastically embraced by most of Reformed Christianity in the twenty-first century—borders on blasphemy: the grace of God produces the demonic glory of the kingdom of Antichrist and Satan!

But the hope of creation is the coming of Jesus Christ, for it is the coming of Christ that brings about the "glorious liberty of the children of God" (v. 21). The hope of creation is the same as the hope of the church. Creation will share in the "glorious liberty of the children of God." At his coming Christ will fully deliver the church from the corruption of death, which is due to sin, by raising the bodies of the elect into the likeness of the glorious liberty of his own resurrection body. At the same time, having reduced the whole creation to its basic elements by fire, Christ will recreate the earth and heaven God made in the beginning as the new world of righteousness and peace. The curse will be lifted. Death will be no more in this renewed world. Creation will be free to serve the purpose God had for it from the beginning: it will be the home and workplace of Christ and his elect church, the site of the Messianic kingdom.

Creation will share in the covenant salvation of Jesus Christ. That creation has hope—*this* hope—is due to the grace of

God toward creation. This grace is a free favor of God toward a creation that shares in the guilt of man's transgression of the covenant of creation with Adam. It is an almighty power that will deliver from vanity, corruption, and death. But the grace of God toward creation that once, in a garden "eastward in Eden" (Gen. 2:8; Gen. 3:17–19), subjected creation to vanity "in hope" (Rom. 8:20) is not some common grace of God. According to its proponents, common grace and its work end with the coming of Christ. But the grace of God for his creation taught in Romans 8:19–22 will work an everlasting renewal.

Common grace, according to its advocates, is a favor and power of God for creation that are radically different from his saving favor and power in the crucified and risen Jesus Christ. But the grace of God for his creation taught in Romans 8 is the very grace that one day raises the bodies of the children of God and gives them their "glorious liberty."

The hope of the creation and its several creatures is Jesus Christ. This is according to the eternal counsel of God concerning the creation. "It pleased the Father that . . . having made peace through the blood of his cross, by him to reconcile all things unto himself" (Col. 1:19–20).

By the covenant with Noah, God assured the creation of its participation in the salvation of Jesus Christ.

Alas, much of Reformed Christianity has forgotten.

Chapter 14

THE COVENANT AND CHRIST: OLD COVENANT AND NEW

The old and new covenants, compared by the Holy Spirit in Hebrews 8–10, are the covenant made by God with the nation of Israel at Sinai and the covenant made by God with the church at the coming of Jesus Christ. The covenant in Christ Jesus is the "new covenant," which implies that the "first" covenant, that is, the covenant made with Israel at Sinai, is "old": "In that he saith, A new covenant, he hath made the first old" (Heb. 8:13). Lest anyone suppose that the old covenant can continue alongside the new covenant (as millions of dispensationalists do, in fact, suppose), the Spirit adds: "Now that which decayeth and waxeth old is ready to vanish away."

The new covenant is "better" than the old: "He [Jesus Christ] is the mediator of a better covenant, which was established upon better promises" (v. 6).

This new covenant is God's relationship with his believing church. It is founded upon the blood of Jesus Christ (Heb. 9:12–14). It writes the law upon the hearts of believers by the sanctifying work of the Spirit of Christ (Heb. 10:14–17). It gives believers spiritual communion with God in the "holiest" (v. 9), which communion is enjoyed in the assembling of believers and their children in the weekly services of public worship on the Lord's day (v. 25).

In setting forth the similarity and, especially, the difference between the old and the new covenants, Hebrews 8–10 sheds light on the prophecy of the establishment of a new covenant with Israel in Jeremiah 31:31–34, as the quotation of the passage in Hebrews 8:8–12 shows.

> Behold, the days come, saith the Lord, when I will make a
> new covenant with the house of Israel and with the house

of Judah: Not according to the covenant that I made with their fathers in the day when I took them by the hand to lead them out of the land of Egypt; because they continued not in my covenant, and I regarded them not, saith the Lord. For this is the covenant that I will make with the house of Israel after those days, saith the Lord; I will put my laws into their mind, and write them in their hearts: and I will be to them a God, and they shall be to me a people: And they shall not teach every man his neighbour, and every man his brother, saying, Know the Lord: for all shall know me, from the least to the greatest. For I will be merciful to their unrighteousness, and their sins and their iniquities will I remember no more.

With regard to both covenants, their source is the election of Christ.

Old Covenant with Israel

God made a covenant with the nation of Israel at Sinai. When Israel was about to enter Canaan, Moses reminded the nation of this: "The LORD our God made a covenant with us in Horeb. The LORD made not this covenant with our fathers, but with us, even us, who are all of us here alive this day. The LORD talked with you face to face in the mount out of the midst of the fire" (Deut. 5:2–4). The outstanding feature of this covenant was the burdening of Israel with many laws. Ten commandments were inscribed on tables of stone; hundreds more were written in a book.

The old covenant with Israel was the same in essence as the covenant of grace that God made with Abraham and his seed, Jesus Christ, and that God would realize and fulfill in the new covenant with his church in Christ. The old covenant was an older form of the new covenant; the new covenant is the fulfillment (not a replacement) of the old covenant.

That the old covenant and the new covenant are essentially the same covenant, Jeremiah made plain in his great prophecy of the new covenant. Just as the essence of the old covenant was the fellowship of God and his people, expressed in the covenant formula, "I will be your God, and you will be my people," so also this will be the essence of the new covenant: "[I] will be their God, and they shall be my people" (Jer. 31:33).

The essential oneness of the covenant with Israel and the covenant with the church is confessional for Reformed Christians. Significantly, the Reformed confessions make the clearest and strongest statements of the unity of the covenant in connection with their defense of infant baptism. The essential oneness of the two covenants hinges on the essential oneness of circumcision and baptism and is maintained only by the doctrine and practice of infant baptism.

Are infants also to be baptized?

Yes; for since they, as well as their parents, *belong to the covenant* and people of God, and both redemption from sin and the Holy Ghost, who works faith, are through the blood of Christ promised to them no less than to their parents, they are also by Baptism, *as a sign of the covenant,* to be ingrafted into the Christian Church, and distinguished from the children of unbelievers, *as was done in the Old Testament by Circumcision, in place of which in the New Testament Baptism is appointed.*[1]

We detest the error of the Anabaptists, who are not content with the one only baptism they have once received, and moreover condemn the baptism of the infants of believers, who, we believe, ought to be baptized and sealed with the sign of the covenant, as the children in Israel formerly were circumcised upon the same promises which are made unto our children . . . Moreover, what Circumcision was to the Jews, that Baptism is to our children. And for this reason Paul calls Baptism the *Circumcision of Christ.*[2]

Among Reformed theologians, who agree on the unity of the covenant, however, there are explanations of the Sinaitic covenant that detract from the truth that the election of Christ as head controls the covenant of grace in all its administrations.

---

1. Heidelberg Catechism, Q&A 74, in Schaff, *Creeds of Christendom,* 3:331; emphasis added.

2. Belgic Confession, Art. 34, in ibid., 3:427–28.

One teaching has it that the covenant with Israel was in some respect or other a reinstatement, or renewal, of the covenant of works with Adam in paradise. The reason for this understanding of the covenant with Israel is the prominence of the law in this covenant.

This teaching is a direct attack on Jesus Christ. First, inasmuch as those who hold this view regard the covenant of works with Adam as an arrangement by which Adam could have merited with God, the reestablishment of the covenant of works by the Sinaitic covenant necessarily would have introduced the possibility of merit. No doubt, once again the defense of merit would be God's condescending permission of merit by virtue of the terms of the covenant. But any and every introduction of merit by mere man, to say nothing of *sinful* man, into the administration of the covenant jeopardizes grace and therefore Jesus Christ.

Second, the teaching that the covenant with Israel was a renewal of the covenant of works refuses to recognize that the covenant with Adam was never intended by God as a way for man to achieve the blessedness of eternal life—*by man's works.* Rather, according to the counsel of God, the covenant with Adam was strictly subservient to Jesus Christ, who alone could merit, obtain, and enter into eternal life.

When the covenant with Adam had served its purpose, in the way of Adam's disobedience, the covenant of creation was finished, except, of course, for its lasting, adverse consequences. It can no more be resurrected, reinstated, or renewed than Adam himself can be brought back onto the scene in his pristine state.

Certainly, the law of God for Adam in paradise is affirmed and detailed in the ten commandments. God has only one law for his human creatures: love me perfectly and love your neighbor as yourself. But the permanency of the one law of God in no wise implies a renewal of the covenant of creation.

There is also the peculiar explanation of the covenant with Israel that, although one aspect of that covenant was gracious and therefore unconditional, namely, spiritual salvation from sin by Jesus Christ, who was represented by the sacrificial system, there was also an aspect of the covenant with Israel that was conditional and meritorious. The aspect that is proposed as conditional and meritorious was Israel's inheritance of the land and enjoyment of the earthly blessings of peace, harvest, and long life.

Whatever of the covenant with Israel is regarded as conditional, that is, dependent not on the grace of God in Jesus Christ, but on the works of the Israelites themselves, and therefore meritorious, was outside of Jesus Christ. The conditional, meritorious aspect would have been a covenant apart from Jesus Christ within a covenant that was in Jesus Christ. But God had no covenant apart from Jesus Christ, least of all a mini-covenant lurking within the outstanding administration of the covenant of grace in the Old Testament. The whole of the covenant with Israel in the Old Testament was an administration of the covenant of grace with the seed of Abraham, who is Christ.

Besides, the land of Canaan was not some material good in addition to and alongside the spiritual blessedness of salvation in Jesus Christ. Canaan was a type of the new, heavenly world that Jesus Christ would earn and recreate for the true Israel of God. The patriarchs knew this and looked right through that small plot of ground on the eastern shore of the Mediterranean to the new world. Abraham "looked for a city which hath foundations, whose builder and maker is God" (Heb. 11:10). All the patriarchs "desire[d] a better country, that is, an heavenly: wherefore God is not ashamed to be called their God: for he hath prepared for them a city" (v. 16).

It is fundamental to the gospel of grace that the prominence of the law in the covenant with Israel not be misunderstood. It was the undoing of the earthly nation of Israel that they inexcusably made this mistake. The law of the old covenant, massive though it is, does not designate that covenant as a renewal of a covenant of works, or as an arrangement by which Israel could have merited Canaan and earthly blessings, or as the fatal conditional contract by which the Israelite could, *and must,* obtain righteousness and salvation by performing the prerequisite conditions. All of these explanations view the covenant with Israel apart from Jesus Christ.

At Sinai God did not forget his decree of Jesus Christ and the covenant of grace in him. He did not install lawgiver Moses as a temporary replacement of the Christ of grace. The prominence of law in the covenant with Israel did not betoken a serious qualification of the covenant established much earlier with Abraham's seed by gracious promise. Had this been the case, Paul declares in Galatians 3:17, the covenant with Israel—the "law"—would have "disannulled" the covenant with Abraham and his seed and would have made "the promise of none effect."

The covenant with Israel, with its burdensome laws, was "added because of transgressions, till the seed should come to whom the promise was made" (v. 19). The purpose of God with the law that was so prominent in the Sinaitic covenant was to drive Israel to Christ, in order to be justified by faith. "Wherefore the law was our schoolmaster to bring us unto Christ, that we might be justified by faith" (v. 24). The covenant with Israel did not present to the Old Testament people another way of salvation and blessing than that of faith alone in the Messiah. This is what many Israelites erroneously made of the law, just as many professing Christians are doing today. The apostle charges against many Israelites that they went about "to establish their own righteousness" by obeying the laws of the old covenant. They were blind to the truth that "Christ is the end [or goal] of the law for righteousness to every one that believeth" (Rom. 10:3–4).

But, as the apostle cries out in Galatians 3:21, the law cannot justify; the law cannot give life. It could not in the Old Testament. It cannot today. Only grace justifies. Only grace gives life. And this grace and life are the gift of God only through faith in Jesus Christ.

The covenant with Israel was an administration of the covenant of grace made by promise to Abraham's seed. In its entirety, the covenant of God with Israel was determined by, and in the service of, Abraham's seed, Jesus Christ, to whom the covenant promise was made, according to Galatians 3:16. It was "not against the promises of God" (v. 21). This means that election determined and governed the covenant with Israel—the election of Christ and, in him, of Israel.

The denial of the relation of covenant and election, specifically, that election governs the covenant, is refuted by Scripture's witness to the close relation between election and the covenant with regard to Old Testament Israel. Moses proclaimed to Israel on the eve of her entrance into Canaan that she was a special people unto Jehovah because "the LORD thy God hath chosen thee" (Deut. 7:6). The election that was the source and cause of the covenant was unconditional; it did not depend upon Israel, which was "the fewest of all people" (v. 7). God chose Israel, because he loved Israel (v. 8).

Again and again, the prophets link covenant and election in the closest union. The covenant has its origin in divine election. Election governs the covenant. Especially does election assure the maintenance of the covenant despite the sins of the people of Israel. And the covenant that has its origin in and depends on election is the covenant of spiritual salvation, accomplishing redemption from sin and bestowing forgiveness.

To Israel in the Babylonian captivity on account of their unfaithfulness in the covenant, Isaiah gave assurance of the maintenance of the covenant by their God. In that covenant, God would redeem Israel, blotting out their transgressions (Isa. 44:22). The explanation of the divine faithfulness to the covenant is God's election of Israel. "Yet now hear, O Jacob my servant; and Israel, whom I have chosen: thus saith the LORD that made thee, and formed thee from the womb, which will help thee; Fear not, O Jacob, my servant; and thou, Jeshurun, whom I have chosen" (vv. 1–2).

Election determined the identity of the covenant people of God in the Old Testament. The true Israel of God was Jesus Christ and the remnant of the nation who, by the grace of election, believed on him and kept the covenant.

Especially Isaiah reveals elect Israel to be the one man who is the head of the covenant and of the covenant people, the Messiah. The Israel who is "my servant" in confirming the covenant is the "man of sorrows," who is "wounded for our transgressions [and] bruised for our iniquities" (Isa. 52:13–53:12).

Israel, "my servant," is the man who will "bring forth judgment to the Gentiles. He shall not cry, nor lift up, nor cause his voice to be heard in the street. A bruised reed shall he not break, and the smoking flax shall he not quench: he shall bring forth judgment unto truth. He shall not fail nor be discouraged, till he have set judgment in the earth: and the isles shall wait for his law" (Isa. 42:1–4). The New Testament identifies this Israel, God's servant, as Jesus (Matt. 12:14–21). His origin is divine election: "my servant . . . mine elect, in whom my soul delighteth" (Isa. 42:1).

But Old Testament Israel was not the promised Messiah by himself alone. Israel was the Messiah and those descendants of Abraham (whether Jews or Gentiles) who belonged to the Messiah according to eternal election and of whom Messiah was the covenant head. Since the covenant of God in the Old Testament was with Israel and since Israel was not all the physical descendants of Abraham, but only the Messiah and those who were his, the covenant of God in the Old Testament was not with all the members of the earthly nation, conditionally. Rather, the old covenant was with Messiah and those who were his by election, unconditionally.

The Old Testament reveals that only some—a very few—of the circumcised Jews were the true Israel. This is the significance of the "remnant" in the book of Isaiah. "Except the LORD of hosts had left unto us a very small remnant, we should have been as Sodom, and we should have been like unto Gomorrah" (Isa. 1:9). Israel is the few that remain faithful to their covenant God, when the majority of the nation has fallen away to idolatry and unrighteousness. The few remain faithful because God "left" them by gracious preservation. This preservation is rooted in election.

Jeremiah 31:7 identifies God's covenant people with the remnant: "O LORD, save thy people, the remnant of Israel." God's covenant people was the remnant of Israel, not all those who were members of the earthly nation by circumcision and physical adherence.

Micah 7:18 restricts the forgiveness of sins to the "remnant of his heritage." In the pardon of the sins of the remnant, God performs the covenant truth to Jacob and the covenant mercy to Abraham that he swore to the fathers by the promise of the covenant (v. 20). The covenant promise and the covenant blessing of justification were for the remnant of Israel, not for all the members of the earthly nation.

God's covenant in the Old Testament was with the remnant, and the remnant only, by virtue of the covenant promise to the remnant, and the remnant only.

And what explains the remnant?

There are two possible answers, and two only.

One is the answer that is given, and must be given, by all those who cut the covenant loose from election. Their answer is that the remnant distinguished themselves from all the others, who were also objects and recipients of the covenant grace of God, by performing the conditions of the covenant. This answer ascribes the salvation of the remnant to the remnant themselves.

The other answer is that given by Scripture. Jehovah God "left," that is, preserved, the remnant by particular, discriminating, sovereign grace. This leaving, or preserving, grace had its source in the election of the remnant. The apostle affirms this answer in Romans 11:5. In both the Old and New Testaments, the explanation of the remnant is election: "Even so then at this present time also there is a remnant according to the election of grace." This answer gives the glory of the salvation of the remnant to God.

Also the New Testament reveals that the Israel of God, with whom in the Old Testament God established his covenant, was some only, not all, of the physical offspring of Abraham. It does so clearly and compellingly.

First, the New Testament denies that the children of Abraham, with whom, of course, the covenant was established, were all Abraham's physical offspring. There were "outward" pseudo-Jews, and there were "inward" real Jews. The pseudo-Jews were attached to the covenant merely outwardly; the genuine Jews were truly members of the covenant. Genuine Jews in the

Old Testament were those, and those only, who were circumcised in the heart, that is, believers. "For he is not a Jew, which is one outwardly; neither is that circumcision, which is outward in the flesh: but he is a Jew, which is one inwardly; and circumcision is that of the heart, in the spirit, and not in the letter; whose praise is not of men, but of God" (Rom. 2:28–29).

The children of Abraham and members of the covenant in the Old Testament were believers, and faith proceeds from election, according to the Reformed creed: "That some receive the gift of faith from God, and others do not receive it, proceeds from God's eternal decree."[3] Election, therefore, determined the children of Abraham, with whom God established his covenant.

Second, the New Testament addresses the issue of the identity of the children of Abraham, to whom the word of God's covenant promise referred, in Romans 9:6–33. To the question who is Israel, the covenant people of God, the answer of the apostle is: not all those connected with Israel by physical birth and outward association. "They are not all Israel, which are of Israel." Many are not Israel. They are merely "*of* Israel" (v. 6). Only some of Abraham's physical offspring are Israel.

The explanation of the distinction between the two kinds of offspring of Abraham and therefore the explanation why some of these offspring, and some only, are the objects of the covenant promise and members of the covenant of grace is God's discriminating, sovereign grace in the decree of predestination. This was God's own explanation in Exodus 33:19, quoted by Paul in Romans 9:15: "[I] will be gracious to whom I will be gracious, and will show mercy on whom I will show mercy." God declared his discriminating grace and mercy, according to his own eternal will, *with regard to members of the earthly nation of Israel, all of whom were physically descended from Abraham and all of whom were circumcised.*

A third, clear, and compelling way that the New Testament reveals that the covenant people of God in the Old Testament were only those who had the faith of father Abraham (as the apostle describes them in Romans 4:12), according to election,

---

3. Canons of Dordt, 1.6, in ibid., 3:582.

is the teaching of Galatians 3:16 and 29 that God made his covenant in the Old Testament with Christ and those who belong to Christ.

It is the teaching of Scripture in both Old and New Testaments that the old covenant was with the Israel of election: the elect Messiah and the remnant according to the election of grace.

With regard to the old covenant, covenant and election were closely, indeed inseparably, related.

New Covenant

Jesus came into our world in the incarnation on behalf of the covenant, particularly the covenant as administered to Abraham by promise to Jesus. So the Holy Spirit described the coming of Jesus in the prophecy of Zacharias:

> To perform the mercy promised to our fathers, and to remember his holy covenant; The oath which he sware to our father Abraham, that he would grant unto us, that we being delivered out of the hand of our enemies might serve him without fear, In holiness and righteousness before him, all the days of our life (Luke 1:72–75).

Zacharias' celebration of the coming of Jesus, at the time in the womb of the virgin, described the realization of the covenant, in its entirety, as the gracious work of Jesus Christ. Our serving God without fear in holiness and righteousness all the days of our life, that is, our covenant faithfulness, is not a condition we must perform. Rather, lifelong service of God, like the redemption that is our deliverance from our enemies, is the gift of God to us by Jesus Christ: "that he would *grant unto us*, that we . . . might serve him . . . in holiness and righteousness before him, all the days of our life" (vv. 74–75; emphasis added).

Jesus came in fulfillment of God's promise of the new covenant in Jeremiah 31:31–34. Christ is the "mediator of the new testament," or covenant (Heb. 9:15). His blood "obtained eternal redemption" for the covenant people of God (v. 12), establishing the covenant on the foundation of the satisfaction of the righteousness of God. Christ is the high priest who enters into the reality of the holy of holies—the presence of God, the most intimate fellowship with God, which is the essence of the covenant—not for himself alone, but for all his people (Heb. 9:11–12, 24; Heb. 10:19–22).

Especially does Jesus Christ realize the covenant in the terms of the promise of the new covenant in Jeremiah 31:33–34: "I will put my law in their inward parts, and write it in their hearts . . . I will forgive their iniquity, and I will remember their sin no more." The writer of Hebrews quotes these words in Hebrews 10:16–17, referring the accomplishment of the covenant salvation they promise to Christ's work of justification and sanctification. Both forgiveness of sins and holiness of life, the two great benefits of the covenant promised in Jeremiah 31:31–34, are the gracious gift and sovereign work of God in Jesus Christ.

Holiness of life, that is, covenant faithfulness, therefore, is not a condition of the covenant that the members of the covenant must perform. It is the covenant itself that God unilaterally, graciously, and sovereignly makes with his people in Jesus Christ. "This is the covenant that I will make with them after those days, saith the Lord, *I will put my laws into their hearts, and in their minds will I write them*" (Heb. 10:16; emphasis added).

This is radically different from the doctrine that teaches that God will make his covenant with you, or maintain his covenant with you, *on the condition that you put his law in your heart and keep it there.*

The incarnation of Jesus Christ, with all of his saving work that the incarnation envisioned and made certain—the substitutionary, lifelong suffering and obedience; the redeeming death; the entering into the highest human life and glory in the bodily resurrection; the lordly sitting at God's right hand; the saving by his word and Spirit of all that the Father gave him; the raising of the elect church from the grave at his second coming; and the eternal life of the new human race in the renewed creation—was the realization of the covenant of grace. Therefore his name is "Emmanuel," that is, God with us—the name of the covenant (Matt. 1:23).

In all his work of establishing and perfecting the covenant, Jesus was, is, and will be the faithful, obedient Son and servant of the triune God. He came into the world in compliance with the sending by the triune God in the decree that elected him (John 6:37–40). From childhood on, his mission was to do his Father's business (Luke 2:49). Especially in the awful matter of the agony of bearing the wrath of God on the cross, Christ was resolved to do not his own will, but the will of God (Matt. 26:39). "Then said I, Lo, I come . . . to do thy will, O God" (Heb. 10:7). This was the entire ministry of the servant of the Lord. Christ obeyed.

Although the description widely passes for orthodoxy, and is usually intended as orthodoxy's defense of grace, it is a mistake to describe the work of Jesus Christ as his fulfilling the conditions of the covenant. So deeply and thoroughly has the alien and dangerous notion of conditionality and conditions infected covenant theology that the notion has invaded the holy relations of God and his Christ. In explanation of Christ's work of salvation, it is commonly said, "The conditions of salvation were lifelong obedience to the law of God and an atoning death, and Christ fulfilled the conditions."

Viewing Christ's work as the fulfilling of conditions subverts his relation to his God and Father. Christ is God's devoted servant, zealous to do God's will. Christ is God's Son, aflame with love to carry out his Father's program. The cross for Christ was not the performance of a condition; it was the doing of his Father's will in love.

In addition, viewing Christ's work as the fulfilling of conditions makes Christ a party alongside God in the establishment of the covenant. Here is the triune God; there are the people who are to be saved in the covenant; in the middle, or coming in from the side, is Christ proposing and agreeing to conditions that will satisfy God and achieve the salvation of the people.

The notion is mischievous, indeed pernicious. Christ is God's man in the world carrying out God's gracious will in God's wise and righteous way. Christ was God himself in the world carrying out his decree of election: "God was in Christ, reconciling the world unto himself, not imputing their trespasses unto them" (2 Cor. 5:19).

It is one thing to proclaim Jesus Christ as the Son sent by his Father to accomplish the work that was necessary for the salvation of the church and the gathering unto himself of all things. It is quite another thing to regard Christ as a relatively independent agent performing conditions stipulated for him by a remote and businesslike deity.

The development of conditional covenant theology into the open denial of justification by faith alone by the contemporary heresy of the federal vision should be the occasion for Reformed churches to purge the notion of conditionality from their doctrine of the covenant of grace.

If this salutary development of the doctrine of the covenant is to take place, the Reformed churches must acknowledge the close relation between the covenant and election.

The view of Christ's work as the fulfilling of conditions has lost sight of the source of Christ and his work in the decree of election. In the decree that chose the Christ, the triune God appointed his Servant-Son a great work. In accordance with the appointment, the Son became incarnate as Messiah. In the love of his heart for his God, the Messiah carried out his mandate. In his Messiah, the triune God established the new covenant, the covenant of grace.

Originating in and governed by the decree of election, this covenant work of Jesus Christ in every aspect was, is, and will be for the elect of the human race. Jesus himself declared that his origin was the electing will of God, that that will set his agenda, that he would stick to that agenda, and that the agenda is the saving of the elect. "For I came down from heaven, not to do mine own will, but the will of him that sent me. And this is the Father's will which hath sent me, that of all which he hath given me, I should lose nothing, but should raise it up again at the last day" (John 6:38–39).

God's heavenly messenger announced that Jesus' conception was the coming of "Jehovah-salvation" to "save his people from their sins" (Matt. 1:21).

For the elect the Savior died to confirm the covenant with them: "I lay down my life for the sheep" (John 10:15).

> It was the will of God, that Christ by the blood of the cross, whereby he confirmed the new covenant, should effectually redeem out of every people, tribe, nation, and language, all those, and those only, who were from eternity chosen to salvation, and given to him by the Father.[4]

Throughout the present gospel-age, the risen, omnipotent Jesus Christ calls God's elect out of spiritual death into spiritual life by the preaching of the gospel, made effectual by his almighty Spirit.

> We are bound to give thanks always to God for you, brethren beloved of the Lord, because God hath from the beginning chosen you to salvation through sanctification of the Spirit and belief of the truth: whereunto he called you by our gospel, to the obtaining of the glory of our Lord Jesus Christ (2 Thess. 2:13–14).

As this passage teaches, the effectual call of the elect is not only unto grace, but also unto glory. Not one recipient of covenant grace will come short of covenant glory. Christ preserves his own in union with himself. Those who abandon the visible church and sphere of the covenant—and many do, as they did already in the apostolic era—go "out from us, but they were not of us; for if they had been of us, they would no doubt have continued with us: but they went out, that they might be made manifest that they were not all of us" (1 John 2:19).

In his day Christ will raise the elect from the dead in the likeness of his immortal, glorious body, justify them publicly, and welcome them into the life and glory of the new world—home of the church and realm of the everlasting Messianic kingdom of God.

> What comfort is it to thee that Christ shall come again to judge the quick and the dead?

---

4. Canons of Dordt, 2.8, in ibid, 3:587.

That in all my sorrows and persecutions, with uplifted head, I look for the self-same One who has before offered himself for me to the judgment of God, and removed from me all curse, to come again as Judge from heaven; who shall cast all his and my enemies into everlasting condemnation, but shall take me, *with all his chosen ones,* to himself, into heavenly joy and glory.[5]

This "heavenly joy and glory" will be the consummation—not the ending—of the covenant of grace. "Behold, the tabernacle of God is with men, and he will dwell with them, and they shall be his people, and God himself shall be with them, and be their God" (Rev. 21:3). Into that perfect fellowship of God with his people in Jesus Christ will enter "they," and they only, "which are written in the Lamb's book of life" (v. 27).

---

5. Heidelberg Catechism, Q&A 52, in ibid., 3:323–24; emphasis added.

EPILOGUE

Very early in their history, the Reformed churches in the Netherlands confessed that the covenant is a covenant of sovereign grace. They confessed that election governs the covenant. They confessed this in two official documents, the Reformed Form for the Administration of Baptism and the Canons of the Synod of Dordt.

In making this confession, guided by God's great servant John Calvin, the Reformed churches in the Netherlands simply applied the Reformation gospel of salvation by grace alone to the truth of the covenant. They based their confession on Scripture, especially Romans 9:6–33.

In relating covenant and election thus closely, therefore, the Reformed tradition has been biblical. To cut the covenant loose from election—these two, dominant, grand themes of the gospel from beginning to end—is to corrupt the revelation of Scripture at its heart.

In relating covenant and election, the Reformed tradition has honored Jesus Christ. To cut the covenant loose from election is to strip Jesus Christ of his status as the covenant head of his people and as the elect of God.

In relating covenant and election, the Reformed tradition has sought the glory of the electing, covenant God. Of him, through him, and unto him—according to the eternal decree—are all things—in the covenant of grace. To him, therefore, is the glory—in, by, and on account of the covenant of grace in Jesus Christ. Amen. To cut the covenant loose from election is to rob God of his covenant glory.

The effect of this early confession of the close relation of covenant and election by the Reformed churches in the Netherlands is to bind all churches and theologians having the Reformed baptism form and the Canons of Dordt as their creeds to the doctrine of a covenant of sovereign grace, that is, the doctrine of a covenant governed by election.

Nevertheless, some Reformed theologians and churches holding these two creeds have embraced a doctrine of the covenant that divorces the covenant from election. This doctrine of the covenant maintains that God's covenant grace extends more widely than the decree of election and that it depends, not upon God's election, but upon human conditions.

For hundreds of years, this doctrine of the covenant has opposed the confessional doctrine in the Reformed tradition. Again and again, the controversy has resulted in schism in the Reformed churches.

Today, the doctrine of a covenant grace that is universal in the sphere of the administration of the covenant, and therefore conditional and resistible, takes fully developed form in Reformed churches in the teaching that calls itself the federal vision. This covenant doctrine openly denies every one of the doctrines of grace, beginning with justification by faith alone. Thus is exposed, finally, by its ripened, bitter fruits the age-old error of a covenant "liberated" from and "not hampered" by election.

By the rank heresy of the federal vision, God sharpens his call to the Reformed churches, especially in the Dutch Reformed tradition, to renounce, once and for all, the doctrine of a covenant of universal, conditional, resistible grace. They must return to their roots in the Reformed baptism form and the Canons of Dordt; in Calvin; and in the Reformation gospel of salvation by sovereign, particular grace alone. They must embrace and confess a doctrine of the covenant in which the covenant is governed by election.

Then all of us must do more.

We must develop this doctrine of the covenant. We must develop it with regard to the demand of the covenant upon the members, with regard to the warnings, with regard to the full, active life of the covenant, with regard to covenant obedience and covenant unfaithfulness on the part of the covenant people, with regard to the important part of the people of God in the covenant, with regard to divine rewards and chastisements, with regard to the genuine mutuality of the covenant.

All of these aspects of the full reality of the covenant, and more, must be developed not in tension with election, certainly not in contradiction of election, but in harmony with election, as the very outworking of the eternal decree.

For election's governing of the covenant is not stifling, restrictive, hampering, and oppressive, as though election will not permit the covenant and its life to be all that they can be, and all that they should be. This is no more true of the will of God regarding the life of his covenant family than it is true of the will of the godly husband and father. The will of the godly husband and father governs his marriage and family. But it does not stifle, rigidly restrict, hamper, and oppress the full, rich, active, lively, exuberant, joyful, delightful fellowship of the marriage and the family.

On the contrary!

The ruling will of the Christian husband and father purposes the full, active life of the family, takes pleasure in such a life, and, under the blessing of God, effects such a life.

No less is this true of the eternal, gracious will of our covenant God.

Election allows for full, rich, active, joyous, fruitful, abundant covenant life.

Election has purposed such a life for the spiritual family of God, and each member of it.

The electing God takes pleasure in such a life.

Election produces and maintains such a life.

And just as children—*genuine* children—bless their godly father and praise his governing will for all they have enjoyed and become by that lordly, beneficent will, so does the church—the *true* church—bless the electing God and praise his election for all she has, all she enjoys, and all she is in the covenant of grace.

Introduction to Appendix

The Declaration of Principles of the Protestant Reformed Churches is a synodical decision taken by the Protestant Reformed Churches in 1951.

The document called The Declaration of Principles, adopted by the Protestant Reformed Synod of 1951, accomplished two perfectly regular and lawful purposes. The first was that it answered the request of the denomination's mission committee for a "form" that could be used in organizing new churches. The Declaration of Principles assured that prospective congregations would know, and agree with, the accepted doctrine of the Protestant Reformed Churches concerning the covenant of grace.

The second purpose was the settling of a doctrinal controversy that was dividing the denomination. The controversy concerned one of the cardinal doctrines of the gospel of Holy Scripture: the covenant of God in Jesus Christ. The issue was the unconditionality, or conditionality, of the covenant, of the covenant promise, of covenant grace, and of covenant salvation.

At stake in the conflict over the covenant was the gospel of (covenant) salvation by sovereign, particular grace as confessed by the Reformed churches in their creeds, especially the Canons of Dordt.

The message of a conditional (resistible) covenant, established by a conditional (resistible) promise, offering a conditional (resistible) covenant salvation, and dependent upon a conditional (resistible) covenant grace, is a form of the false gospel of salvation by man's willing and working that the apostle repudiates in Romans 9:16.

In the form of certain basic truths—"principles"—the Declaration of Principles officially expressed as the Protestant Reformed doctrine of the covenant what, in fact, the denomination had believed, confessed, and preached from the beginning of its existence.

Within a short time, the Declaration of Principles restored peace to the Protestant Reformed Churches by unity of doctrine.

In recent times, with the astounding (but inevitable) appearance and spread of the heresy of the federal (covenant) vision in the Reformed churches in North America, the Declaration of Principles has taken on additional significance, not only for the Protestant Reformed Churches, but also for all the Reformed churches. For it is the doctrine of a conditional covenant condemned by the Declaration of Principles that the federal vision is now developing as a theology of the covenant that denies justification by faith alone and, with this fundamental truth of the gospel, all the doctrines of grace.

The Declaration of Principles is found in the *Acts of Synod [of the] Protestant Reformed Churches of America, 1951*, 201–8.

As published here, as an appendix, it is taken from *The Confessions and the Church Order of the Protestant Reformed Churches* (Grandville, MI: Protestant Reformed Churches in America, 2005), 412–31.

Appendix

Declaration of Principles of the Protestant Reformed Churches

Preamble

DECLARATION OF PRINCIPLES, to be used only by the Mission Committee and the missionaries for the organization of prospective churches on the basis of Scripture and the confessions as these have always been maintained in the Protestant Reformed Churches and as these are now further explained in regard to certain principles.

The Protestant Reformed Churches stand on the basis of Scripture as the infallible Word of God and of the Three Forms of Unity. Moreover, they accept the liturgical forms used in the public worship of our churches, such as: Form for the Administration of Baptism, Form for the Administration of the Lord's Supper, Form of Excommunication, Form of Readmitting Excommunicated Persons, Form of Ordination of the Ministers of God's Word, Form of Ordination of Elders and Deacons, Form for the Installation of Professors of Theology, Form of Ordination of Missionaries, Form for the Confirmation of Marriage Before the Church, and the Formula of Subscription.

On the basis of this Word of God and these confessions:

I. They repudiate the errors of the Three Points adopted by the Synod of the Christian Reformed Church of Kalamazoo, 1924, which maintain:

A. That there is a grace of God to all men, including the reprobate, manifest in the common gifts to all men.

B. That the preaching of the gospel is a gracious offer of salvation on the part of God to all that externally hear the gospel.

C. That the natural man through the influence of common grace can do good in this world.

D. Over against this they maintain:

1. That the grace of God is always particular, i.e., only for the elect, never for the reprobate.

2. That the preaching of the gospel is not a gracious offer of salvation on the part of God to all men, nor a conditional offer to all that are born in the historical dispensation of the covenant, that is, to all that are baptized, but an oath of God that He will infallibly lead all the elect unto salvation and eternal glory through faith.

3. That the unregenerate man is totally incapable of doing any good, wholly depraved, and therefore can only sin.

For proof we refer to
Canons 1, Articles 6–8:

Article 6. That some receive the gift of faith from God and others do not receive it proceeds from God's eternal decree, "For known unto God are all his works from the beginning of the world" (Acts 15:18). "Who worketh all things after the counsel of his will" (Eph. 1:11). According to which decree He graciously softens the hearts of the elect, however obstinate, and inclines them to believe, while He leaves the nonelect in His just judgment to their own wickedness and obduracy. And herein is especially displayed the profound, the merciful, and at the same time the righteous discrimination between men equally involved in ruin; or that decree of election and reprobation, revealed in the Word of God, which, though men of perverse, impure, and unstable minds wrest to their own destruction, yet to holy and pious souls affords unspeakable consolation.

Article 7. Election is the unchangeable purpose of God

whereby, before the foundation of the world, He hath out of mere grace, according to the sovereign good pleasure of His own will, chosen, from the whole human race, which had fallen through their own fault from their primitive state of rectitude into sin and destruction, a certain number of persons to redemption in Christ, whom He from eternity appointed the Mediator and Head of the elect, and the foundation of salvation. This elect number, though by nature neither better nor more deserving than others, but with them involved in one common misery, God hath decreed to give to Christ, to be saved by Him, and effectually to call and draw them to His communion by His Word and Spirit, to bestow upon them true faith, justification, and sanctification; and having powerfully preserved them in the fellowship of His Son, finally to glorify them for the demonstration of His mercy and for the praise of His glorious grace; as it is written: "According as he hath chosen us in him before the foundation of the world, that we should be holy and without blame before him in love; having predestinated us unto the adoption of children by Jesus Christ to himself, according to the good pleasure of his will, to the praise of the glory of his grace, wherein he hath made us accepted in the beloved" (Eph.1:4–6). And elsewhere: "Whom he did predestinate, them he also called, and whom he called, them he also justified, and whom he justified, them he also glorified" (Rom. 8:30).

Article 8. There are not various decrees of election, but one and the same decree respecting all those who shall be saved, both under the Old and New Testament; since the Scripture declares the good pleasure, purpose, and counsel of the divine will to be one, according to which He hath chosen us from eternity, both to grace and glory, to salvation and the way of salvation, which He hath ordained that we should walk therein.

Canons 2, Article 5:

Article 5. Moreover, the promise of the gospel is that whosoever believeth in Christ crucified shall not perish, but have everlasting life. This promise, together with the command to repent and believe, ought to be declared and published to all nations, and to all persons promiscuously and without distinction, to whom God out of His good pleasure sends the gospel.

> The Canons in 2.5 speak of the preaching of the promise. It presents the promise not as general, but as particular, i.e., as for believers, and, therefore, for the elect. This preaching of the particular promise is promiscuous to all that hear the gospel, with the command, not a condition, to repent and believe.

Canons 2, Rejection of Errors 6:

> Article 6. Who use the difference between meriting and appropriating, To the end that they may instill into the minds of the imprudent and inexperienced this teaching, that God, as far as He is concerned, has been minded of applying to all equally the benefits gained by the death of Christ; but that, while some obtain the pardon of sin and eternal life and others do not, this difference depends on their own free will, which joins itself to the grace that is offered without exception, and that it is not dependent on the special gift of mercy, which powerfully works in them, that they rather than others should appropriate unto themselves this grace.

> Rejection: For these, while they feign that they present this distinction in a sound sense, seek to instill into the people the destructive poison of the Pelagian errors.

For further proof we refer to Heidelberg Catechism, Lord's Day 3, Question and Answer 8, and to Lord's Day 33, Question and Answer 91:

> Q. 8. Are we then so corrupt that we are wholly incapable of doing any good, and inclined to all wickedness?

> A. Indeed we are, except we are regenerated by the Spirit of God.

Q. 91. But what are good works?

A. Only those which proceed from a true faith, are performed according to the law of God, and to His glory; and not such as are founded on our imaginations or the institutions of men.

And also to the Belgic Confession, Article 14:

Article 14. We believe that God created man out of the dust of the earth, and made and formed him after His own image and likeness, good, righteous, and holy, capable in all things to will agreeably to the will of God. But being in honor he understood it not, neither knew his excellency, but willfully subjected himself to sin, and consequently to death and the curse, giving ear to the words of the devil. For the commandment of life which he had received he transgressed; and by sin separated himself from God, who was his true life; having corrupted his whole nature; whereby he made himself liable to corporal and spiritual death. And being thus become wicked, perverse, and corrupt in all his ways, he hath lost all his excellent gifts which he had received from God, and retained only a few remains thereof, which, however, are sufficient to leave man without excuse; for all the light which is in us is changed into darkness, as the Scriptures teach us, saying: The light shineth in darkness, and the darkness comprehendeth it not: where St. John calleth men darkness.

Therefore we reject all that is taught repugnant to this concerning the free will of man, since man is but a slave to sin, and has nothing of himself, unless it is given from heaven. For who may presume to boast that he of himself can do any good, since Christ saith, No man can come to Me except the Father, which hath sent Me, draw him? Who will glory in his own will, who understands that to be carnally minded is enmity against God? Who can speak of his knowledge, since the natural man receiveth not the things of the Spirit of God? In short, who dare suggest any thought, since he knows that we are not sufficient of ourselves to think anything as of ourselves, but that our sufficiency is of God? And therefore what the apostle saith ought justly to be held sure and firm, that God worketh in us both to will and to do of His good pleasure. For there is no will nor understanding conformable to the divine will and understanding but what Christ hath wrought in man, which He teaches us when He saith, Without Me ye can do nothing.

Once more we refer to [the] Canons, 3–4, Articles 1–4:

Article 1. Man was originally formed after the image of God. His understanding was adorned with a true and saving knowledge of his Creator and of spiritual things; his heart and will were upright; all his affections pure; and the whole man was holy. But, revolting from God by the instigation of the devil and abusing the freedom of his own will, he forfeited these excellent gifts, and on the contrary entailed on himself blindness of mind, horrible darkness, vanity, and perverseness of judgment, became wicked, rebellious, and obdurate in heart and will, and impure in his affections.

Article 2. Man after the fall begat children in his own likeness. A corrupt stock produced a corrupt offspring. Hence all the posterity of Adam, Christ only excepted, have derived corruption from their original parent, not by imitation, as the Pelagians of old asserted, but by the propagation of a vicious nature.

Article 3. Therefore all men are conceived in sin, and by nature children of wrath, incapable of saving good, prone to evil, dead in sin, and in bondage thereto, and without the regenerating grace of the Holy Spirit they are neither able nor willing to return to God, to reform the depravity of their nature, nor to dispose themselves to reformation.

Article 4. There remain, however, in man since the fall the glimmerings of natural light, whereby he retains some knowledge of God, of natural things, and of the differences between good and evil, and discovers some regard for virtue, good order in society, and for maintaining an orderly external deportment. But so far is this light of nature from being sufficient to bring him to a saving knowledge of God and to true conversion, that he is incapable of using it aright even in things natural and civil. Nay further, this light, such as it is, man in various ways renders wholly polluted, and holds it in unrighteousness, by doing which he becomes inexcusable before God.

II. They teach on the basis of the same confessions:

A. That election, which is the unconditional and unchangeable decree of God to redeem in Christ a certain number of persons, is the sole cause and fountain of all our salvation, whence flow all the gifts of grace, including faith.

This is the plain teaching of our confessions in the Canons of Dordrecht 1, Articles 6–7. See above.

And in the Heidelberg Catechism, Lord's Day 21, Question and Answer 54, we read:

> Q. 54. What believest thou concerning the "holy catholic church" of Christ?

> A. That the Son of God, from the beginning to the end of the world, gathers, defends, and preserves to Himself by His Spirit and Word, out of the whole human race, a church chosen to everlasting life, agreeing in true faith; and that I am, and forever shall remain, a living member thereof.

This is also evident from the doctrinal part of the Form for the Administration of Baptism, where we read:

> For when we are baptized in the name of the Father, God the Father witnesseth and sealeth unto us that He doth make an eternal covenant of grace with us, and adopts us for His children and heirs, and therefore will provide us with every good thing, and avert all evil or turn it to our profit. And when we are baptized in the name of the Son, the Son sealeth unto us that He doth wash us in His blood from all our sins, incorporating us into the fellowship of His death and resurrection, so that we are freed from all our sins and accounted righteous before God. In like manner, when we are baptized in the name of the Holy Ghost, the Holy Ghost assures us, by this holy sacrament, that He will dwell in us and sanctify us to be members of Christ, applying unto us

that which we have in Christ, namely, the washing away of our sins and the daily renewing of our lives, till we shall finally be presented without spot or wrinkle among the assembly of the elect in life eternal.

B. That Christ died only for the elect and that the saving efficacy of the death of Christ extends to them only.

This is evident from the Canons 2, Article 8:

Article 8. For this was the sovereign counsel and most gracious will and purpose of God the Father, that the quickening and saving efficacy of the most precious death of His Son should extend to all the elect, for bestowing upon them alone the gift of justifying faith, thereby to bring them infallibly to salvation; that is, it was the will of God that Christ by the blood of the cross, whereby He confirmed the new covenant, should effectually redeem out of every people, tribe, nation, and language all those, and those only, who were from eternity chosen to salvation and given to Him by the Father; that He should confer upon them faith, which, together with all the other saving gifts of the Holy Spirit, He purchased for them by His death; should purge them from all sin, both original and actual, whether committed before or after believing; and, having faithfully preserved them even to the end, should at last bring them free from every spot and blemish to the enjoyment of glory in His own presence forever.

This article very clearly teaches:
1. That all the covenant blessings are for the elect alone.
2. That God's promise is unconditionally for them only: for God cannot promise what was not objectively merited by Christ.
3. That the promise of God bestows the objective right of salvation not upon all the children that are born under the historical dispensation of the covenant, that is, not upon all that are baptized, but only upon the spiritual seed.

This is also evident from other parts of our confessions, as, for instance: Heidelberg Catechism, Lord's Day 25, Questions and Answers 65–66:

> Q. 65. Since then we are made partakers of Christ and all His benefits by faith only, whence doth this faith proceed?
>
> A. From the Holy Ghost, who works faith in our hearts by the preaching of the gospel, and confirms it by the use of the sacraments.
>
> Q. 66. What are the sacraments?
>
> A. The sacraments are holy, visible signs and seals, appointed of God for this end, that by the use thereof He may the more fully declare and seal to us the promise of the gospel, namely, that He grants us freely the remission of sin and life eternal, for the sake of that one sacrifice of Christ accomplished on the cross.
>
> > If we compare with these statements from the Heidelberger what was taught concerning the saving efficacy of the death of Christ in Canons 2, Article 8, it is evident that the promise of the gospel which is sealed by the sacraments concerns only the believers, that is, the elect.

This is also evident from Heidelberg Catechism, Lord's Day 27, Question and Answer 74:

> Q. 74. Are infants also to be baptized?
>
> A. Yes; for since they, as well as the adult, are included in the covenant and church of God; and since redemption from sin by the blood of Christ, and the Holy Ghost, the author of faith, is promised to them no less than to the adult; they must therefore by baptism, as a sign of the covenant, be also admitted into the Christian church, and be distinguished from the children of unbelievers as was done in the old covenant or testament by circumcision, instead of which baptism is instituted in the new covenant.

That in this question and answer of the Heidelberger not all the children that are baptized, but only the spiritual children, that is, the elect, are meant is evident. For:

a. Little infants surely cannot fulfill any conditions. And if the promise of God is for them, the promise is infallible and unconditional, and therefore only for the elect.

b. According to Canons 2, Article 8, which we quoted

above, the saving efficacy of the death of Christ is for the elect alone.

c. According to this answer of the Heidelberg Catechism, the Holy Ghost, the author of faith, is promised to the little children no less than to the adult. And God surely fulfills His promise. Hence, that promise is surely only for the elect.

The same is taught in the Belgic Confession, Articles 33–35. In Article 33 we read:

Article 33. We believe that our gracious God, on account of our weakness and infirmities, hath ordained the sacraments for us, thereby to seal unto us His promises, and to be pledges of the good will and grace of God toward us, and also to nourish and strengthen our faith, which He hath joined to the Word of the gospel, the better to present to our senses both that which He signifies to us by His Word and that which He works inwardly in our hearts, thereby assuring and confirming in us the salvation which He imparts to us. For they are visible signs and seals of an inward and invisible thing, by means whereof God worketh in us by the power of the Holy Ghost. Therefore the signs are not in vain or insignificant, so as to deceive us. For Jesus Christ is the true object presented by them, without whom they would be of no moment.

And from Article 34, which speaks of holy baptism, we quote:

Article 34. We believe and confess that Jesus Christ, who is the end of the law, hath made an end, by the shedding of His blood, of all other sheddings of blood which men could or would make as a propitiation or satisfaction for sin; and that He, having abolished circumcision, which was done with blood, hath instituted the sacrament of baptism instead thereof, by which we are received into the church of God and separated from all other people and strange religions, that we may wholly belong to Him whose ensign and banner we bear, and which serves as a testimony to us that He will forever be our gracious God and Father.

Therefore He has commanded all those who are His to be baptized with pure water, "in the name of the Father, and of the Son, and of the Holy Ghost," thereby signifying to us that, as water washeth away the filth of the body when poured upon it, and is seen on the body of the baptized when sprinkled upon him, so doth the blood of Christ, by the power of the Holy Ghost, internally sprinkle the soul, cleanse it from its sins, and regenerate us from children of wrath unto children of God. Not that this is effected by the external water, but by the sprinkling of the precious blood of the Son of God, who is our Red Sea, through which we must pass to escape the tyranny of Pharaoh, that is, the devil, and to enter into the spiritual land of Canaan. Therefore the ministers, on their part, administer the sacrament and that which is visible, but our Lord giveth that which is signified by the sacrament, namely, the gifts and invisible grace; washing, cleansing, and purging our souls of all filth and unrighteousness; renewing our hearts and filling them with all comfort; giving unto us a true assurance of His fatherly goodness; putting on us the new man, and putting off the old man with all his deeds.

Article 34 speaks of holy baptism. That all this, washing and cleansing and purging our souls of all filth and unrighteousness, the renewal of our hearts, is only the fruit of the saving efficacy of the death of Christ and therefore is only for the elect is very evident. The same is true of what we read in the same article concerning the baptism of infants:

Article 34. And indeed Christ shed His blood no less for the washing of the children of the faithful than for adult persons; and therefore they ought to receive the sign and sacrament of that which Christ hath done for them; as the Lord commanded in the law that they should be made partakers of the sacrament of Christ's suffering and death shortly after they were born, by offering for them a lamb, which was a sacrament of Jesus Christ. Moreover, what circumcision was to the Jews, that baptism is to our children. And for this reason Paul calls baptism the "circumcision of Christ."

> If, according to Article 8 of Canons 2, the saving efficacy of the death of Christ extends only to the elect, it follows that when in this article of the Belgic Confession it is stated that "Christ shed his blood no less for the washing of the children of the faithful than for the adult persons," also here the reference is only to the elect children.

> Moreover, that the promise of the gospel which God signifies and seals in the sacraments is not for all is also abundantly evident from Article 35 of the same Belgic Confession, which speaks of the holy supper of our Lord Jesus Christ. For there we read:

Article 35. We believe and confess that our Savior Jesus Christ did ordain and institute the sacrament of the holy supper to nourish and support those whom He hath already regenerated and incorporated into His family, which is His church.

In the same article we read:

Further, though the sacraments are connected with the thing signified, nevertheless both are not received by all men. The ungodly indeed receives the sacrament to his condemnation, but he doth not receive the truth of the sacrament—as Judas and Simon the sorcerer both indeed received the sacrament but not Christ who was signified by it, of whom believers only are made partakers.

> It follows from this that both the sacraments, as well as the preaching of the gospel, are a savor of death unto death for the reprobate, as well as a savor of life unto life for the elect. Hence, the promise of God, preached by the gospel, signified and sealed in both the sacraments, is not for all but for the elect only.

And that the election of God, and consequently the efficacy of the death of Christ and the promise of the gospel, is not conditional is abundantly evident from the following articles of the Canons.

Canons 1, Article 10:

> Article 10. The good pleasure of God is the sole cause of this gracious election, which doth not consist herein, that out of all possible qualities and actions of men God has chosen some as a condition of salvation; but that He was pleased out of the common mass of sinners to adopt some certain persons as a peculiar people to Himself, as it is written, "For the children being not yet born, neither having done any good or evil," etc., it was said (namely to Rebecca): "the elder shall serve the younger; as it is written, Jacob have I loved, but Esau have I hated" (Rom. 9:11–13). "And as many as were ordained to eternal life believed" (Acts 13:48).

In Canons 1, Rejections of Errors 2, the errors are repudiated of those who teach:

> Article 2. That there are various kinds of election of God unto eternal life: the one general and indefinite, the other particular and definite; and that the latter in turn is either incomplete, revocable, non-decisive, and conditional, or complete, irrevocable, decisive, and absolute....

And in . . . Canons 1, Rejection of Errors 3, the errors are repudiated of those who teach:

Article 3. That the good pleasure and purpose of God, of which Scripture makes mention in the doctrine of election, does not consist in this, that God chose certain persons rather than others, but in this, that He chose out of all possible conditions (among which are also the works of the law), or out of the whole order of things, the act of faith, which from its very nature is undeserving, as well as its incomplete obedience, as a condition of salvation, and that He would graciously consider this in itself as a complete obedience and count it worthy of the reward of eternal life....

Again, in . . . Canons 1, Rejection of Errors 5, the errors are rejected of those who teach:

Article 5. That . . . faith, the obedience of faith, holiness, godliness, and perseverance are not fruits of the unchangeable election unto glory, but are conditions which, being required beforehand, were foreseen as being met by those who will be fully elected, and are causes without which the unchangeable election to glory does not occur.

Finally, we refer to the statement of the Baptism Form:

And although our young children do not understand these things, we may not therefore exclude them from baptism, for as they are without their knowledge partakers of the condemnation in Adam, so are they again received unto grace in Christ....

That here none other than the elect children of the Covenant are meant and that they are unconditionally, without their knowledge, received unto grace in Christ, in the same way as they are under the condemnation of Adam, is very evident.

C. That faith is not a prerequisite or condition unto salvation, but a gift of God, and a God-given instrument whereby we appropriate the salvation in Christ.

This is plainly taught in the following parts of our confessions:

Heidelberg Catechism, Lord's Day 7, Question and Answer 20:

> Q. 20. Are all men then, as they perished in Adam, saved by Christ?
>
> A. No, only those who are ingrafted into Him, and receive all His benefits, by a true faith.

Belgic Confession, Article 22:

> Article 22. We believe that, to attain the true knowledge of this great mystery, the Holy Ghost kindleth in our hearts an upright faith, which embraces Jesus Christ with all His merits, appropriates Him, and seeks nothing more besides Him. For it must needs follow, either that all things which are requisite to our salvation are not in Jesus Christ, or, if all things are in Him, that then those who possess Jesus Christ through faith have complete salvation in Him. Therefore, for any to assert that Christ is not sufficient, but that something more is required besides Him, would be too gross a blasphemy; for hence it would follow that Christ was but half a Savior. Therefore we justly say with Paul, that we are justified by faith alone, or by faith without works. However, to speak more clearly, we do not mean that faith itself justifies us, for it is only an instrument with which we embrace Christ our righteousness. But Jesus Christ, imputing to us all His merits and so many holy works which He has done for us and in our stead, is our righteousness. And faith is an instrument that keeps us in communion with Him in all His benefits, which, when become ours, are more than sufficient to acquit us of our sins.

Confer also Belgic Confession, Articles 33–35 quoted above. In Canons 3–4, Article 10, we read:

> Article 10. But that others who are called by the gospel obey the call and are converted is not to be ascribed to the proper exercise of free will, whereby one distinguishes himself above others equally furnished with grace sufficient for faith and conversion, as the proud heresy of Pelagius maintains; but it must be wholly ascribed to God, who

as He has chosen His own from eternity in Christ, so He confers upon them faith and repentance, rescues them from the power of darkness, and translates them into the kingdom of His own Son, that they may show forth the praises of Him who hath called them out of darkness into His marvelous light, and may glory, not in themselves, but in the Lord, according to the testimony of the apostles in various places.

Again, in the same chapter of [the] Canons, Article 14, we read:

Article 14. Faith is therefore to be considered as the gift of God, not on account of its being offered by God to man, to be accepted or rejected at his pleasure, but because it is in reality conferred, breathed, and infused into him; or even because God bestows the power or ability to believe, and then expects that man should by the exercise of his own free will consent to the terms of salvation and actually believe in Christ, but because He who works in man both to will and to do, and indeed all things in all, produces both the will to believe and the act of believing also.

III. Seeing then that this is the clear teaching of our confession,
  A. We repudiate:
    1. The teaching:
      a. That the promise of the covenant is conditional and for all that are baptized.
      b. That we may presuppose that all the children that are baptized are regenerated, for we know on the basis of Scripture, as well as in the light of all history and experience, that the contrary is true.

For proof we refer to Canons 1, Articles 6–8; and the doctrinal part of the Baptism Form:

The principal parts of the doctrine of holy baptism are these three:

First. That we with our children are conceived and born in sin, and therefore are children of wrath, in so much that we cannot enter into the kingdom of God except we are born again. This the dipping in or sprinkling with water teaches us, whereby the impurity of our souls is signified, and we admonished to loathe and humble ourselves before God, and seek for our purification and salvation without ourselves.

Secondly. Holy baptism witnesseth and sealeth unto us the washing away of our sins through Jesus Christ. Therefore we are baptized in the name of the Father, and of the Son, and of the Holy Ghost. For when we are baptized in the name of the Father, God the Father witnesseth and sealeth unto us that He doth make an eternal covenant of grace with us, and adopts us for His children and heirs, and therefore will provide us with every good thing, and avert all evil or turn it to our profit. And when we are baptized in the name of the Son, the Son sealeth unto us that He doth wash us in His blood from all our sins, incorporating us into the fellowship of His death and resurrection, so that we are freed from all our sins and accounted righteous before God. In like manner, when we are baptized in the name of the Holy Ghost, the Holy Ghost assures us, by this holy sacrament, that He will dwell in us and sanctify us to be members of Christ, applying unto us that which we have in Christ, namely, the washing away of our sins and the daily renewing of our lives, till we shall finally be presented without spot or wrinkle among the assembly of the elect in life eternal.

Thirdly. Whereas in all covenants there are contained two parts, therefore are we by God, through baptism, admonished of and obliged unto new obedience, namely, that we cleave to this one God, Father, Son, and Holy Ghost; that we trust in Him, and love Him with all our hearts, with all our souls, with all our mind, and with all our strength; that we forsake the world, crucify our old nature, and walk in a new and holy life.

And if we sometimes through weakness fall into sin, we must not therefore despair of God's mercy, nor continue in sin, since baptism is a seal and undoubted testimony that we have an eternal covenant of grace with God.

The Thanksgiving after baptism:

> Almighty God and merciful Father, we thank and praise Thee that Thou hast forgiven us and our children all our sins through the blood of Thy beloved Son Jesus Christ, and received us through Thy Holy Spirit as members of Thine only begotten Son, and adopted us to be Thy children, and sealed and confirmed the same unto us by holy baptism. We beseech Thee, through the same Son of Thy love, that Thou wilt be pleased always to govern these baptized children by Thy Holy Spirit, that they may be piously and religiously educated, increase and grow up in the Lord Jesus Christ, that they then may acknowledge Thy fatherly goodness and mercy, which Thou hast shown to them and us, and live in all righteousness under our only Teacher, King, and High Priest, Jesus Christ; and manfully fight against and overcome sin, the devil, and his whole dominion, to the end that they may eternally praise and magnify Thee, and Thy Son Jesus Christ, together with the Holy Ghost, the one only true God. Amen.

> The prayer refers only to the elect; we cannot presuppose that it is for all.

2. The teaching that the promise of the covenant is an objective bequest on the part of God, giving to every baptized child the right to Christ and all the blessings of salvation.

B. And we maintain:

1. That God surely and infallibly fulfills His promise to the elect.

2. The sure promise of God which He realizes in us as rational and moral creatures not only makes it impossible that we should not bring forth fruits of thankfulness but also confronts us with the obligation of love, to walk in a new and holy life, and constantly to watch unto prayer.

> All those who are not thus disposed, who do not repent but walk in sin, are the objects of His just wrath and excluded from the kingdom of heaven.

> That the preaching comes to all; and that God

seriously commands to faith and repentance; and that to all those who come and believe He promises life and peace.

Grounds:

The Baptism Form, part 3.

The Form for the Lord's Supper, under "thirdly":

> All those, then, who are thus disposed, God will certainly receive in mercy and count them worthy partakers of the table of His Son Jesus Christ. On the contrary, those who do not feel this testimony in their hearts eat and drink judgment to themselves.

> Therefore, we also, according to the command of Christ and the apostle Paul, admonish all those who are defiled with the following sins to keep themselves from the table of the Lord, and declare to them that they have no part in the kingdom of Christ; such as all idolaters, all those who invoke deceased saints, angels, or other creatures; all those who worship images; all enchanters, diviners, charmers, and those who confide in such enchantments; all despisers of God, and of His Word, and of the holy sacraments; all blasphemers; all those who are given to raise discord, sects, and mutiny in church or state; all perjured persons; all those who are disobedient to their parents and superiors; all murderers, contentious persons, and those who live in hatred and envy against their neighbors; all adulterers, whoremongers, drunkards, thieves, usurers, robbers, gamesters, covetous, and all who lead offensive lives.

> All these, while they continue in such sins, shall abstain from this meat (which Christ hath ordained only for the faithful), lest their judgment and condemnation be made the heavier.

The Heidelberg Catechism, Lord's Day 24, Question and Answer 64; Lord's Day 31, Question and Answer 84; Lord's Day 44, Question and Answer 116:

> Q. 64. But doth not this doctrine make men careless and profane?

A. By no means; for it is impossible that those who are implanted into Christ by a true faith should not bring forth fruits of thankfulness.

Q. 84. How is the kingdom of heaven opened and shut by the preaching of the holy gospel?

A. Thus: when according to the command of Christ it is declared and publicly testified to all and every believer, that, whenever they receive the promise of the gospel by a true faith, all their sins are really forgiven them of God, for the sake of Christ's merits; and on the contrary, when it is declared and testified to all unbelievers, and such as do not sincerely repent, that they stand exposed to the wrath of God and eternal condemnation, so long as they are unconverted; according to which testimony of the gospel God will judge them, both in this and in the life to come.

Q. 116. Why is prayer necessary for Christians?

A. Because it is the chief part of thankfulness which God requires of us; and also, because God will give His grace and Holy Spirit to those only who with sincere desires continually ask them of Him, and are thankful for them.

Canons 3–4, Articles 12, 16–17:

Article 12. And this is the regeneration so highly celebrated in Scripture and denominated a new creation: a resurrection from the dead, a making alive, which God works in us without our aid. But this is in no wise effected merely by the external preaching of the gospel, by moral suasion, or such a mode of operation that after God has performed His part it still remains in the power of man to be regenerated or not, to be converted or to continue unconverted; but it is evidently a supernatural work, most powerful, and at the same time most delightful, astonishing, mysterious, and ineffable; not inferior in efficacy to creation or the resurrection from the dead, as the Scripture inspired by the Author of this work declares; so that all in whose heart God works in this marvelous manner are certainly, infallibly, and effectually regenerated and do actually believe. Whereupon the will thus renewed is not only actuated and influenced by God, but in consequence of this influence becomes itself active. Wherefore also, man is himself rightly said to believe and repent by virtue of that grace received.

Article 16. But as man by the fall did not cease to be a creature endowed with understanding and will, nor did sin which pervaded the whole race of mankind deprive him of the human nature, but brought upon him depravity and spiritual death; so also this grace of regeneration does not treat men as senseless stocks and blocks, nor takes away their will and its properties, neither does violence thereto; but spiritually quickens, heals, corrects, and at the same time sweetly and powerfully bends it; that where carnal rebellion and resistance formerly prevailed, a ready and sincere spiritual obedience begins to reign, in which the true and spiritual restoration and freedom of our will consist. Wherefore, unless the admirable Author of every good work wrought in us, man could have no hope of recovering from his fall by his own free will, by the abuse of which, in a state of innocence, he plunged himself into ruin.

Article 17. As the almighty operation of God whereby He prolongs and supports this our natural life does not exclude, but requires, the use of means, by which God of His infinite mercy and goodness hath chosen to exert His influence, so also the before mentioned supernatural operation of God by which we are regenerated in no wise excludes or subverts the use of the gospel, which the most wise God has ordained to be the seed of regeneration and food of the soul. Wherefore, as the apostles and teachers who succeeded them piously instructed the people concerning this grace of God, to His glory, and the abasement of all pride, and in the meantime, however, neglected not to keep them by the sacred precepts of the gospel in the exercise of the Word, sacraments, and discipline; so, even to this day, be it far from either instructors or instructed to presume to tempt God in the church by separating what He of His good pleasure hath most intimately joined together. For grace is conferred by means of admonitions; and the more readily we perform our duty, the more eminent usually is this blessing of God working in us, and the more directly is His work advanced; to whom alone all the glory, both of means and of their saving fruit and efficacy, is forever due. Amen.

Canons 3–4, Rejection of Errors 9:

Article 9. Who teach: that grace and free will are partial causes, which together work the beginning of conversion, and that grace, in order of working, does not precede the working of the will; that is, that God does not efficiently help the will of man unto conversion until the will of man moves and determines to do this.

Rejection: For the ancient church has long ago condemned this doctrine of the Pelagians, according to the words of the apostle: "So then it is not of him that willeth, nor of him that runneth, but of God that hath mercy" (Rom. 9:16). Likewise: "For who maketh thee to differ? and what hast thou that thou didst not receive?" (1 Cor. 4:7). And: "For it is God who worketh in you both to will and to work for his good pleasure" (Phil. 2:13).

Canons 5, Article 14:

Article 14. And as it hath pleased God, by the preaching of the gospel, to begin this work of grace in us, so He preserves, continues, and perfects it by the hearing and reading of His Word, by meditation thereon, and by the exhortations, threatenings, and promises thereof, as well as by the use of the sacraments.

Belgic Confession, Article 24:

Article 24. We believe that this true faith, being wrought in man by the hearing of the Word of God and the operation of the Holy Ghost, doth regenerate and make him a new man, causing him to live a new life, and freeing him from the bondage of sin. Therefore it is so far from being true that this justifying faith makes men remiss in a pious and holy life, that, on the contrary, without it they would never do anything out of love to God, but only out of self-love or fear of damnation. Therefore it is impossible that this holy faith can be unfruitful in man; for we do not speak of a vain faith, but of such a faith which is called in Scripture a faith that worketh by love, which excites man to the practice of those works which God has commanded in His Word.

These works, as they proceed from the good root of faith, are good and acceptable in the sight of God, forasmuch as they are all sanctified by His grace; howbeit they are of no account towards our justification. For it is by faith in Christ that we are justified, even before we do good works; otherwise they could not be good works, any more than the fruit of a tree can be good before the tree itself is good.

Therefore we do good works, but not to merit by them (for what can we merit?), nay, we are beholden to God for the good works we do, and not He to us, since it is He that worketh in us both to will and to do of His good pleasure. Let us therefore attend to what is written: When ye shall have done all those things which are commanded you, say, we are unprofitable servants; we have done that which was our duty to do. In the meantime, we do not deny that God rewards our good works, but it is through His grace that He crowns His gifts.

Moreover, though we do good works, we do not found our salvation upon them; for we do no work but what is polluted by our flesh, and also punishable; and although we could perform such works, still the remembrance of one sin is sufficient to make God reject them. Thus, then, we would always be in doubt, tossed to and fro without any certainty, and our poor consciences continually vexed, if they relied not on the merits of the suffering and death of our Savior.

3. That the ground of infant baptism is the command of God and the fact that according to Scripture He established His covenant in the line of continued generations.

IV. Besides, the Protestant Reformed Churches:
Believe and maintain the autonomy of the local church.
For proof we refer to the Belgic Confession, Article 31:

> Article 31. We believe that the ministers of God's Word, and the elders and deacons, ought to be chosen to their respective offices by a lawful election by the church, with calling upon the name of the Lord, and in that order which the Word of God teacheth. Therefore every one must take heed not to intrude himself by indecent means, but is bound to wait till it shall please God to call him, that he may have testimony of his calling and be certain and assured that it is of the Lord.
>
> As for the ministers of God's Word, they have equally the same power and authority wheresoever they are, as they are all ministers of Christ, the only universal Bishop and the only Head of the church. Moreover, that this holy ordinance of God may not be violated or slighted, we say that every one ought to esteem the ministers of God's Word and the elders of the church very highly for their work's sake, and be at peace with them without murmuring, strife, or contention, as much as possible.

Church Order, Article 36:

> Article 36. The classis has the same jurisdiction over the consistory as the general synod has over the classis.

Only the consistory has authority over the local congregation.
Church Order, Article 84:

> Article 84: No church shall in any way lord it over other churches, no minister over other ministers, no elder or deacon over other elders or deacons.

The Form for the Installation of Elders and Deacons:
"... called of God's church, and consequently of God Himself...."

INDEX OF NAMES

P

Pelagius 29
Perkins, William 95
Pieters, K. J. 11–14, 16–18, 20, 121
Pighius, Albertus 102-4, 145–46,
152–53
Piper, John 90–91

R

Robbins, Carl D. 28–29
Robertson, O. Palmer 30

S

Schilder, Klaas 16, 18, 24–26, 29–30,
52–54, 68, 96–97, 121, 159–60
Schlissel, Steve 2
Shepherd, Norman 2, 28, 31, 68, 131
Smilde, E. 11, 14, 16–18
Snecanus, Gellins 6
Strauss, S. A. 121
Strawbridge, Gregg 44, 46–47

V

Van Limborch, Philippus 6
Van Velzen, Simon 10, 14, 121
Veenhof, Cornelis 16–19, 24, 54–55
Veluanus, Joannes 6
Venema, Cornelis P. 196
Venema, H. 25

W

Wielenga, B. 33, 35
Wiggertsz, Cornelis 6
Wilkins, Steve 2
Wilson, Douglas 2
Witsius, Herman 199
Wright, N. T. 1, 4, 90–91

Z

Zanchius, Jerome 6
Zwingli, Ulrich 111

INDEX OF SCRIPTURE

INDEX OF CREEDS

OTHER WORKS
BY THE AUTHOR

In addition to writing *Covenant and Election*, David J. Engelsma has authored and coauthored numerous other books, written countless articles for the *Standard Bearer* magazine, and penned several pamphlets pertaining to Christian life.

RFPA publications written by David J. Engelsma
Better to Marry: Sex and Marriage in 1 Corinthians 6 and 7
Bound to Join: Letters on Church Membership
Common Grace Revisited: A Response to Richard J. Mouw's
   He Shines in All That's Fair
The Covenant of God and the Children of Believers: Sovereign
   Grace in the Covenant
Hyper-Calvinism and the Call of the Gospel: An Examination of
   the "Well-Meant Offer" of the Gospel
Marriage, the Mystery of Christ and the Church: The Covenant-
   Bond in Scripture and History
Prosperous Wicked and Plagued Saints: An Exposition of Psalm 73
Reformed Education: The Christian School as Demand
   of the Covenant
The Reformed Faith of John Calvin: The Institutes in Summary
Reformed Worship
   (co-author with Barrett Gritters and Charles Terpstra)
Trinity and Covenant: God as Holy Family
Unfolding Covenant History: Judges and Ruth

RFPA publications edited by David J. Engelsma
Always Reforming
Peace for the Troubled Heart: Reformed Spirituality
Righteous by Faith Alone: A Devotional Commentary on Romans
The Sixteenth-Century Reformation of the Church